Heber J.
GRANT

Man of Steel,
Prophet of God

Heber J.
GRANT

Man of Steel,
Prophet of God

Francis M. Gibbons

Deseret Book Company
Salt Lake City, Utah
1979

Library of Congress Cataloging in Publication Data

Gibbons, Francis M   1921-
    Heber J. Grant, man of steel, prophet of God.

    Includes index.
    1.   Grant, Heber Jeddy, 1856-1945.   2.   Mormons
and Mormonism in the United States—Biography.
I.   Title.
BX8695.G7G52   289.3'092'4 [B]   79-11649
ISBN 0-87747-755-8

Contents

Preface

Spanning the period between handcarts and television, the life of Heber J. Grant, if for no other reason than its longevity, presents an object of fascinating study for those interested in the development of the American West and The Church of Jesus Christ of Latter-day Saints. But, when to this impressive accumulation of years is added the fabric of a life, interwoven with conflict and peace, pathos and humor, poverty and wealth, and success and failure; and when all is viewed against the phenomenal growth and expansion of a people, driven into a harsh, inhospitable land by implacable enemies, intent on their destruction, there emerges a story of extraordinary power and appeal. Special ingredients of the story are to be found in the stubborn, unconquerable qualities of President Grant's will, and in the deep and pervasive spirituality that infiltrated and colored all he did, and that ultimately elevated him to the prophetic role that was the crowning achievement of his life.

An important, original source for this biography was President Grant's journals, which he kept faithfully during most of his ministry. While he was an excellent journalist and left a valuable record of what he did and how he felt about persons and events, it is obvious that to him it was a labor of duty, not of love. "I sometimes feel almost like stopping the writing of a journal," he wrote on January 9, 1884, "as my grammar is so poor also my spelling that I dislike to leave any such a record as I have to make under the circumstances; but I am of the opinion that it is almost a matter of duty that I keep a journal and this is the main reason that I am willing to do so." Then providing an important insight into the stimulus which caused him to stay at the task he added: "I would be willing to pay any reasonable amount of money for a record of father's life; but he never recorded any of his acts and there is today nothing worthy of mention on record regarding him." But a more impelling reason for his faithful journal-keeping may be inferred from an experience he had while serving as the president of the Tooele Stake. One day the Tooele Stake Patriarch, John Rowberry, told President Grant he had a blessing of a patriarchal nature for him. "He gave me a most wonderful and marvelous blessing," President Grant wrote, "nearly all of which has been fulfilled to the very letter. He made the remark 'Brother Grant, I saw something I dared not put in your blessing.' I then had the impression . . . that I should live to preside over the church. I have felt that is what he saw. I never spoke of it in my life until I became the president of the Church." Thus, from a time early in his Church career, Heber J. Grant knew by spiritual means that he was destined to preside over the Church; and this knowledge likely helped to fuel the desire, later almost an obsession, to keep an accurate record of his ministry.

In the early years, most of President Grant's journal entries were made in his own classic handwriting. In 1887, however, he altered his method of record-keeping, as explained in this entry made under date of January 14, 1887: "I have made up my mind in the future," he wrote, "to keep my journal in a letter book, as then I will be able to dictate such items as I don't object to his seeing to a short hand reporter I have in my employ and that of H. J. Grant & Co. and when I wish to record a letter that I am willing he should see I can allow him to copy it and make a press copy in my Letter Book Journal. Such items as I may wish to record without his knowledge I can write on a piece of paper and copy it myself into my journal. By doing my journal work in this way, I am confident it will not be so much of a task and I will therefore keep a much more complete record of all of my doings both of a financial and religious character." This change was beneficial as it enlarged the scope and variety of the journal entries, but detrimental as it robbed them of the intimacy and spontaneity that characterized the entries written in his own hand.

The reader will soon detect that the author began his work from the premise that Heber J. Grant was and is a prophet of God. Nothing found during an extensive, minute study of his life altered that assumption. Indeed, it was strengthened, even though, as expected, he was found to be human and fallible, except in matters pertaining to his ecclesiastical and patriarchal callings when he acted or spoke under divine inspiration.

The reader will also note that in some few instances, statements have been made affirmatively, based only upon reasonable inferences drawn from known facts. This has been done merely as a literary device, to avoid encumbering the work unnecessarily with repetitive, qualifying statements, and to make for smoother reading.

The author will consider himself well paid for his efforts if the reader lays down this book with a greater reverence for God and a greater appreciation for the influence he exerts through the lives and works of great men and women.

Acknowledgments

It is both difficult and dangerous to acknowledge the assistance given to an author in producing a literary work: difficult because the author may fail even to recognize the numerous sources from which help has come; and dangerous because the specific mention of some benefactors may wrongly imply a lack of appreciation for the assistance rendered by so many. Despite these difficulties and dangers, and the risks they necessarily entail, I feel impelled to mention a few of those whose contributions have been so significant that, without them, this volume would never have come into existence.

Sincere thanks and acknowledgments are, therefore, extended to the numerous members of President Heber J. Grant's family, who provided essential background information, and especially to Frances Grant Bennett, his youngest and only surviving child, who, in addition to briefing me, read portions of the manuscript; to many surviving friends and associates of President Grant, who carry in their memories, and who shared with me, many experiences that shed important light on his multifaceted personality; to the management and the employees of the Deseret Book Company, and especially to Lowell Durham, Eleanor Knowles, and Emily Bennett Watts, whose friendliness and professionalism have put me deep in their debt; to the managers and employees of the Historical Department of The Church of Jesus Christ of Latter-day Saints, and especially to Donald Schmidt, archivist, whose interest and kindness extended far beyond the call of duty; and to that special friend and mentor whose careful reading of the manuscript, whose helpful suggestions, and whose unfailing encouragement are appreciated beyond my power to express.

Chapter 1

The Prophet Speaks

The tall, straight octogenarian took his place at the pulpit as the last strains of a favorite Mormon hymn, "O My Father," sounded from deep within the throat of the mighty Salt Lake Tabernacle organ. He glanced over the vast audience seated before him on the seemingly endless rows of hard wooden benches (reputed to have been built for discomfort at the direction of Brigham Young to keep the sitters awake at meetings). After adjusting the spectacles that rested on the bridge of his prominent nose, the speaker commenced to read the most significant sermon of his distinguished ministry.

It was not often that Heber J. Grant read a talk in general conference, or anywhere else, for that matter. For over fifty years, since his call as an apostle, he had been noted for extemporaneous speaking and an energetic style. In the days before microphones, he had been able to make his resonant voice heard in the far reaches of the Tabernacle without difficulty. This, along with his flair for the dramatic and his frequent use of apt, entertaining stories, had so conditioned the Latter-day Saints that when he abandoned his accustomed style and read a talk, they knew it was something special. And so, when he commenced by saying that he would read a message from the First Presidency to the Church, the audience gave careful attention.

Actually, many present on this historic occasion in October 1936 had anticipated the subject of President Grant's message. At the previous general conference there had been talk about a "Church Security Plan" to alleviate economic want among Church members that had been brought on by the great depression. It was alarming to the brethren that almost one out of every five Latter-day Saints was dependent upon public help for sustenance. As the dark gloom of want spread over their people, and as more and more of those people had to turn to outside resources to maintain life, the Church leaders began to search for a solution more lasting than friendly cooperation and hand-outs. They knew instinctively that the answer to their dilemma would be found deep within the spiritual roots that had nurtured their pioneer forebears. And they realized too that the solution would not be easily attained, but would require the same singleminded dedication that had enabled their fathers and mothers to make the desert blossom.

The key was found in a revelation given to Joseph Smith in March 1832 as he wrestled with the problem of caring for the throngs of poor people who were flocking to Kirtland, Ohio. At that time this prophet-leader, through whom the Church of Jesus Christ was restored in the latter days, declared that the Lord had revealed that the Church was to "stand independent above all creatures beneath the celestial world." (D&C 78:14.) He stressed the need for an "organization of my people, in regulating and establishing the affairs of the storehouse for the poor of my people." (D&C 78:3.) Thus, the concepts of independence and organization formed the basis of the mechanism the leaders of the Latter-day Saints would create to rescue their people from the morass of the great depression.

In the period between the April and October general conferences of 1936, the first positive steps were taken by President Grant and his associates to implement a vast program of economic self-help among the Latter-day Saints. Production assignments were given to the 117 stakes then in existence, and by the time President Grant read his statement in the October general conference, 98 of them had reported the results. With a tinge of pride and satisfaction the venerable leader reported to the conference what had been accomplished. In that short period 4,000 bushels of wheat, 13,000 pounds of beans, and 23,000 pounds of dried fruit had been raised and stored, along with many other grains and vegetables.

The sisters of the Relief Society had made over 23,000 articles of clothing and more than 2,000 quilts.

Following this recital the speaker assured his people, in a typically positive way, that what he had reported was merely a glowing promise of what they would accomplish when they put their hearts and wills to the work. He elaborated upon the basic aim of the security plan, later to be designated as the welfare program: "Our primary purpose was to set up, in so far as it might be possible, a system under which the curse of idleness would be done away with, the evils of a dole abolished, and independence, industry, thrift and self respect be once more established amongst our people. The aim of the Church is to help the people to help themselves. Work is to be re-enthroned as the ruling principle of the lives of our church membership."

Here was the clarion call for which a dispirited people had been waiting. It awakened them to the ancient truth that security comes from personal initiative and cooperation with others. And it jolted them from a lethargy that had taken hold of many who had looked to the government to cure their economic ills.

The surge of enthusiasm and activity that this announcement unloosed worked a miracle among the Latter-day Saints. Almost overnight, a spirit of dejection and gloom that had hung over them was supplanted by optimism and hope. It was not that the economic picture had changed, for at this early stage it had not. What had changed was their attitude. The miracle was that their fears had been replaced with faith. And the catalyst that had produced such an amazing transformation was this tall, bearded, distinguished-looking leader who, as he concluded his memorable sermon, declared with a vigor that belied his age: "I do not ask any man or child in this Church . . . to work any more hours than I do. . . . I do not think work ever hurts anybody. . . . It seems to me that lazy people die young while those who are ready and willing to labor and who ask the Lord day by day to help them to do more in the future than they have ever done in the past, these are the people whom the Lord loves, and they live to a good old age."

No one who sat in the Tabernacle that day, or who listened to the speech over the radio, doubted the steely determination of the speaker. The legendary stories of his persistence in achieving goals and overcoming obstacles had created a sort of magical aura around President Grant. His lifelong habit of succeeding in spite of difficulties gave his people confidence that once he had set his hand to this work, he would persist in it until the objective had been reached. It was this knowledge, the assurance that the man at the tiller was one who could navigate in the storm, that in large part explained the newfound confidence of the Latter-day Saints.

But there was a deeper, a more subtle and complex reason for this radical change in attitude. While they admired and loved Heber J. Grant as a man, the Saints recognized in him a quality, a special power and aptitude, that set him apart from others. This was not merely another charismatic leader who had demonstrated a special knack or skill. This was a man on whom a distinctive mantle had descended; a man who had been invested with heavenly authority, and who was empowered to speak and to act in the name of Deity. In short, this man was a prophet of God, cast in the mold of those biblical patriarchs who had "subdued kingdoms, wrought righteousness, obtained promises, stopped the mouths of lions, Quenched the violence of fire, escaped the edge of the sword, out of weakness were made strong, waxed valiant in fight, turned to flight the armies of the aliens." (Hebrews 11:33-34.)

It was this prophetic quality, almost ethereal in its substance, that dominated President Grant's character in the later years of his life. It was not possible to go into his presence or to hear him speak without feeling and being influenced by it. The essence of this quality was captured by a newspaperman who composed a discerning obituary upon President Grant's death. Wrote he: "Tall, slender, bearded, gray and grave, of striking appearance and patriarchal bearing, President Grant might have stepped forth from an illustrated page of the Old Testament. Had he lived in those far-distant days he would have seemed, and no doubt felt, at ease and at home in

the tents of Abraham, Isaac, and Jacob. He would have
taken high rank among the potentates and prophets of
olden times as a shrewd and sagacious director of temporal affairs, a rigid disciplinarian in spiritual matters.
. . . It would have required no great stretch of imagination to picture him leading the children of Israel through
the wilderness, counselling with tribesmen of Canaan
about their flocks and herds, hurling anathemas at idola-
tors from the foot of Sinai, driving the chariot of Jehu
toward Jezreel, swinging the sword of Gideon against the
Midianites, smiting the walls of Jericho in righteous
wrath, or marching at the head of triumphant legions
singing 'Hosanna to the Highest.' " (Salt Lake *Tribune*,
May 16, 1945.)

President Heber J. Grant was the seventh prophet-
leader in an unbroken line that commenced in 1830, the
year in which The Church of Jesus Christ of Latter-day
Saints was organized. The first in this distinguished line
was Joseph Smith, the young seer and revelator who had
solidly laid the foundation of the Church and completed
his ministry before age thirty-nine. Serving as the head
of the Church for fourteen turbulent years, during which
his people were driven from New York to Ohio, from
Ohio to Missouri, and from Missouri to Illinois, he
suffered a martyr's death in 1844 at the hands of a mob.

Brigham Young, on whom Joseph's mantle fell after
the martyrdom, an intrepid and resolute pioneer and
modern Moses who led the Latter-day Saints on the
exodus into the Rocky Mountain wilderness, was the
second in the line of prophets. He was followed by the
aristocratic John Taylor, who presided during the
dismal years of the Underground, and who carried to his
grave the scars of the gunshot wounds he suffered in
1844 in the martyr's cell. Wilford Woodruff, the tireless
missionary and diarist, was next in line, followed by the
aged Lorenzo Snow. The last of President Grant's
predecessors in this modern prophetic line was Joseph F.
Smith, whose father, Hyrum Smith, shared a martyr's
crown with his famous brother, the Prophet Joseph.

While a comparison reveals many similarities, the
most significant character trait President Grant shared

with his predecessors was a simple, childlike faith. The unfaltering way in which he pushed the welfare plan forward, without being intimidated by the pitfalls that lay ahead, was reminiscent of the way each of his predecessors overcame difficulties. Their conduct was anchored in a great truth. They undertook a task with an assurance, an unwavering assumption that they would succeed in it. Any hindrance was viewed not as an impediment, but as a problem to be solved, and out of each solution came an increased ability to unravel even more complex problems. So instead of being cowed by adversity, these men thrived on it, even welcomed it, as a means of sharpening their skills. They had been schooled in the law of opposites, which taught that happiness, joy, pleasure, or health have no real meaning to one who has not experienced unhappiness, sadness, pain, or illness.

These attitudes formed the foundation of the unusual system of religion these men practiced, a foundation constructed with the underlying principle of faith. These leaders believed that the worlds are and were created by faith; and bringing the application down to the level of daily living, they believed that any objective could be attained by faith—through the exercise of initiative, will, and hard work. But this belief had a by-product that transcended anything achieved by their own efforts, typified by the farmer who ploughs, plants, cultivates, and harvests, but who really plays little part in the miraculous transformation from seed to seedling to plant to fruit. Similarly, these men were confident that when they had stretched their capabilities to the limit, a power beyond the scope of their own competence would take over and produce a result that, like the parting of the Red Sea or the collapse of the walls of Jericho, might appear miraculous in its proportions.

Heber J. Grant had imbibed deeply of this spirit, so much so that it was second nature for him to commence an undertaking like the welfare plan without fully comprehending the means by which it would be carried out. It was sufficient that he could see clearly enough to take the first step and that he had a spiritual confirmation that he was going in the right direction.

The need for such great faith soon became evident as the welfare plan unfolded. Its course was not smooth and constant; there were many stops and starts, critics and gainsayers. There was a great inertia among some of the people that had to be overcome by constant instruction and motivation. Slowly but surely as the vast outline of the plan began to take form, even the most myopic among the people began to see what the prophet had instinctively known all along. They saw a mechanism that would provide the best possible protection against economic want while safeguarding the dignity and self-esteem of the individual. They saw the chance to institutionalize the idea that man is his brother's keeper. They saw an opportunity to develop their character through service to others. And many saw in the plan a forward step toward the perfect society in which all will share willingly.

What was dimly seen in that day is now seen with clarity. The hundreds of welfare projects now operated by the Church—farms, ranches, dairies, orchards, canneries, mills, hatcheries, and storehouses—attest to the fact that the Latter-day Saints can care for their own in time of want while providing them with gainful, dignified employment. The projects also testify of the character and the achievements of the leader whose prophetic insight and electrifying words set in motion the chain of events that produced them.

Chapter 2

Ancestral Roots

Heber J. Grant's roots were planted deep in the soil of the American frontier and in Great Britain. His paternal ancestors were of Scottish and English descent; his mother's people came chiefly from England. These forebears were tenacious, frugal, and adventuresome, qualities that appeared in their famous offspring in rich abundance.

President Grant's father, Jedediah Morgan Grant, called Jeddy by his friends, was born February 21, 1816, in Windsor, Broome County, New York. Jedediah's parents, Joshua and Athalia Howard Grant, were from Connecticut. A lumberman, Joshua moved westward to New York, following the mobile population into new areas where there were ample forests to be made into houses and barns.

In his childhood and adolescence, Jedediah was exposed to the religious fervor that gripped the area around Windsor, where he was born. The numerous Protestant sects established there often held revivals and camp meetings to awaken people to their sins and to ignite a dormant spirituality. There can be little doubt that the unusual skill in extemporaneous speaking Jedediah showed in later years traced in large part to an early exposure to the fiery eloquence of revivalist and camp meeting speakers. It is also likely that the awareness of things spiritual induced by this exposure helped to ripen him for conversion to The Church of Jesus Christ of Latter-day Saints in 1833, when he was seventeen years old.

The depth of the commitment that produced this conversion can be gauged by the fact that the next year found Jedediah a member of Zion's Camp, a famed paramilitary group organized in Ohio by Joseph Smith to bring relief to the Saints who were suffering intense persecution on the Missouri frontier. Though only eighteen, Jedediah showed unusual qualities of manliness and dependability during this perilous undertaking. He was marked at that time by his leaders as a young man who would bear watching, a prediction that later saw fulfillment in his call at age thirty-eight as a member of the First Presidency, the chief governing body of the Church.

In the meantime, Jedediah underwent a thorough apprenticeship typical of those holding positions of principal authority in the Church. After being ordained a seventy in February 1835, he filled successive proselyting missions in Ohio, New York, Pennsylvania, and North Carolina. He devoted ten years to this itinerant ministry, being almost constantly on the move, tracting, preaching, counseling, debating. Often he traveled without purse or scrip, relying on the generosity of the people for his sustenance. This nomadic kind of life, with its attendant hazards, tempered a character that was inherently strong. It developed a resiliency, a buoyant self-confidence, that was to make Jedediah even more trusted by those both above and below him in the hierarchy of the Church.

Given these qualities, and set in an environment where they showed to the best advantage, Jedediah naturally gravitated to positions of leadership. At age twenty-nine, prior to the exodus from Nauvoo to the Salt Lake Valley, he was called to the First Council of the Seventy. In 1851, he was elected the first mayor of Salt Lake City, retaining that position until his death in 1856. In 1852, he was chosen as speaker of the Territorial House of Representatives.

By 1854 Jedediah, then only thirty-eight years old, was a man of proven ability, seasoned and ready for major service in the Church. It was in that year, upon the death of Willard Richards, that he was elevated to the First Presidency from the First Council of the Seventy. The significance of this call comes into sharper focus when one realizes that the Council of the Twelve was comprised of men of unusual ability and achievement, including three future presidents of the Church—John Taylor, Wilford Woodruff, and Lorenzo Snow—all of whom were older and more experienced than the new counselor. For many years they had been members of the quorum that had exercised leadership authority over Jedediah and his brethren of the First Council of the Seventy. The Twelve accepted Jedediah's call without rancor and gave their new leader unqualified support, but it was awkward for him to be a presiding officer over men he had followed for so many years and to whom he had given obedient service. To compensate for his sense of inadequacy Jedediah launched into his new duties with a selfless zeal that probably contributed to his death less than three years later.

In selecting this articulate young man as a counselor, Brigham Young had a specific role in mind for him to play. At this time the Saints had been in their wilderness home for seven years, preoccupied with founding a new civilization in a wasteland no one else wanted. There were raw lands to be cultivated, streams to be harnessed, forests to be cut, roads to be built, and whole villages to be raised on the desert floor. So pervasive and demanding were the Saints' physical wants that in time these came to dominate their thoughts, often to the exclusion of spiritual things. Over a period of several years, this change in focus radically altered the general climate of the Mormon communities. Instead of aiming toward moral perfection, too many of the Saints fixed their sights on temporal goals, and with these changes came a consequent relaxation of church standards. Profanity, stealing, sabbath-breaking, and sexual sins occurred with increasing frequency. A divisive spirit of fault-finding and destructive criticism crept in, replacing the attitude of love and cooperation that had existed before. Concerned over this spiritual retrogression in the Saints, Brigham Young was determined to alter their attitudes and conduct. Thus was introduced among the Latter-day Saints what was later styled the "reformation." In effect, it was a call to repentance, an insistence by the Church authorities that the Saints return to the basics of their religion. And Jedediah M. Grant, with his practical eloquence and his fierce loyalty to the cause, was the perfect vehicle for this message.

Propelled by a desire to please his leader, a zeal for reform, and the goad of his sense of inadequacy, Jedediah was tireless in discharging his duties. There were few communities in Zion that did not feel the lash of his tongue. He was explicit in defining the sins of the people and unyielding in his demands that they be forsaken. He continued in this arduous work until almost the end of his days. His last recorded sermon, given in the Salt Lake Tabernacle on November 9, 1856, stands representative of his character and the nature of his last ministry. Said he: "The result of the teachings we are receiving, if practised, will reform the whole community. When you are right we will cease to chastise, we will cease to rebuke; we will cease throwing the arrows of the Almighty through you, we will cease telling you to surrender, to repent of all your sins. But until you do this, we will continue to throw the arrows of God through you, to hurl the darts of heaven upon you and the power of God in your midst; and we will storm the bulwarks of hell, and we will march against you in the strength of the God of Israel. And by the power of the Priesthood restored by the Prophet Joseph, by the light of heaven shed forth by brother Brigham and his associates, we expect to triumph; and in the name of Jesus Christ, we do not mean to surrender to evil."

Less than a month after delivering this provocative sermon, Jedediah M. Grant was dead. The constant exertions required in pushing the reformation had weakened his body and hastened his passing. At the funeral, Brigham Young dwelled on the accomplishments Jedediah had achieved in the short span of forty years. "He has been in the Church upwards of twenty-four years," said President Young, "and was a man that would live, comparatively speaking, a hundred years in that time. The storehouse that was prepared in him to receive the truth, was capable of receiving as much in twenty-five years as most of men can in one hundred." (*Journal of Discourses* 4:130.)

Seated in the audience at Jedediah's funeral was his wife Rachel, who, only nine days earlier, had given birth to her first son, Heber Jeddy. The words spoken by Brigham Young on that occasion may have aroused in Rachel the first vague impressions about the future of her baby. "Brother Grant we call a great man," President Young continued, "a giant, a lion; but let me tell you that the young whelps are growing up here who will roar louder than ever he dare, and . . . the very sons of these women that sit here will rise up and be as great as any man that ever lived, and as far beyond Jedediah, or myself, and Brother Heber, as we are in the Gospel beyond our little children."

Whether or not this funeral speech sparked it off, at some point in the infancy of Heber J. Grant his mother became convinced that her child was destined for greatness in the Church. Out of the grief she experienced in laying her brilliant young husband to rest grew the determination to nurture her baby to physical and spiritual maturity so he could take his place alongside the greatest leaders of her adopted church.

This young widow, left alone with her baby in a wilderness community and separated by a continent from her family, which had looked with disdain upon her affiliation with the Latter-day Saints, faced the future without noticeable concern. She had already safely passed through her Gethsemane years before, when she had struggled against forces that were pulling her into the Mormon church. The product of a strict Quaker upbringing, and a later convert to the Baptist faith, Rachel was a religious girl with high moral principles and a keen sense of duty. This last quality, intermixed with a large dose of falsehoods then circulating about the Latter-day Saints, once caused her to pray earnestly for forgiveness for having attended a meeting conducted by Mormon elders. But her prejudices melted away as she commenced to read the literature constantly fed to her by her converted sister, Anna, and the missionaries. As understanding and conviction came, Rachel was inclined to cast her lot with the Saints, but she was deterred in doing so by a lingering sense of loyalty to her then current religious affiliation. This obstacle was suddenly removed when her Baptist minister threatened disfellowshipment if she did not stop attending Mormon services. Instead of anchoring her to the Baptist faith as the minister had expected, this bald attempt at coercion severed old religious moorings and propelled Rachel into Mormonism, where she was to be harbored for the remainder of her life.

Shortly after her baptism, Rachel felt the spirit of gathering that touched the lives of so many early converts to the Church. In company with her sister Anna and her brother-in-law, she joined the Saints in the beautiful city of Nauvoo on the banks of the Mississippi.

The energetic spirit of self-improvement that had enabled the Mormons to redeem the swampland and build a city there was still prevalent in Nauvoo when Rachel arrived in 1842. Literary and debating societies, lectures and lyceums, fairs and bazaars abounded, offering numerous opportunities for the Saints to display and improve upon their talents. More important to Rachel than any of these attractions, however, was the presence in Nauvoo of Joseph Smith, the young seer and revelator. Rachel came to know the Prophet well in the two years before his death, and there appears to have been an understanding between them, since, years later, in Salt Lake City, Brigham Young sealed Rachel to Joseph Smith for eternity when she married Jedediah M. Grant for time.

Heber J. Grant was thus deemed to have been born in the covenant of Rachel's sealing to the Prophet Joseph Smith. It was on this account that President Grant was occasionally heard to say that he was "the son" of the Prophet Joseph Smith, who was killed over twelve years before he was born. Though it is impossible now to measure it accurately, the psychological effect upon Heber of this relationship with the prophet of the restoration was most probably profound.

Chapter 3

The Boy—Ancestor to the Man

The Jedediah M. Grant residence in Salt Lake City stood on the east side of Main Street, the second lot from South Temple, sandwiched in between the home of Daniel H. Wells on the north and the home of Bishop Edward Hunter on the south. At the time of Jedediah's death, the home was occupied by his six living wives and nine living children: six boys, including Heber, and three girls.

Typical of such households, the wives of Jedediah M. Grant entertained feelings of sisterly love toward each other, and the children made little differentiation in their minds between their natural mothers and the other mothers in the home, who were affectionately referred to as "Aunt."

Heber and his mother were to remain in these circumstances for seven years, during which they lived on the resources Jedediah had accumulated and on the income the wives were able to generate from their stitchery and other domestic skills. Surrounded by those who loved them, and being accorded special privileges and prestige as the family of one of the high leaders of the Church, the Grants lived as comfortably and securely as conditions in a frontier community would permit. The presence in the immediate household of others who shared their sorrow and sense of deprivation cushioned the blow of losing a husband and father.

While Heber undoubtedly missed the personal, intimate relationship of a natural father, his environment was filled with men whose influence helped to fill that great void and set before him an inspiring and tangible pattern of conduct. In this child's life, a prophet was not some vague, amorphous personage whose distant exploits were recorded in ancient writ. He was, instead, the youth's kindly neighbor, Brigham Young, who one day would retrieve him from behind the president's sleigh, where he was hitching a ride, and invite him to share the comfort of the upholstered sleigh seat and a warm lap robe. Or he was the dynamic Heber C. Kimball, for whom the boy had been named, who, during one of his frequent prophetic moods, gazed intently at young Heber and predicted that he would become an apostle of the Lord Jesus Christ and would be a greater man in the Church than his natural father, Jedediah M. Grant. A prophet to young Heber was John Taylor, Orson Pratt, Wilford Woodruff, Lorenzo Snow, each of whom was a man of deep spirituality, grave, dignified, self-assured, and energetic. These were the life models that were daily held up to the view of the impressionable young prophet-to-be.

Then there were the numerous brothers and sisters, all vying for the attention and recognition children naturally seek, from whom Heber learned early to share and to follow the rules of the house. In this kind of setting the separate identity, the special characteristics and qualities of a child, are often hidden by a conformity that descends like a mantle upon all. In Heber's case, however, there was no regimen, no family stricture, no maternal prohibition that could obscure the main character trait for which he was to be noted throughout life. That trait can best be described as a resolute and untiring determination to achieve any goal, to surmount any obstacle that seemed to him deserving of his efforts.

It is not uncommon for one to vow to do or to refrain from doing some act that at the moment seems important or has special appeal. What is uncommon is for one to take it in his mind to do something and then to go forward to do it unrelentingly, without deviation or hesitance. Gauged by this standard, Heber J. Grant was an uncommon man of the first rank. This quality of unwavering perseverance, of dogged determination, was evident in him at a very early age. One of the most unusual manifestations of it occurred when Jedediah's estate was finally settled seven years after his death, in

connection with which the family home was sold and the
wives and children went their separate ways, with
Rachel and Heber moving to a much smaller home on
Second East. On the day of the move Heber returned
home from school to find the family home on Main
Street deserted. Saddened at the thought of leaving such
a large, attractive home to live in a cramped, one-story
adobe house, and of being separated from his brothers
and sisters, Heber later recalled that he sat down on the
ground at the step by the front gate and wept. To this
point, the boy's conduct seems natural for any youngster
overcome with emotion at the thought of leaving his
childhood home. The scene that follows, however, is so
unusual in its aspect as to arouse high interest in the
character and destiny of the boy who acted it out. "I got
up," he reported, "and shook my fist at the old house
and said, 'When I'm a man, I'll buy you back.' " The
culmination of the story came over twenty-five years
later when the U.S. government was threatening to
confiscate the properties of the Church. President Grant,
who was then a member of the Council of the Twelve,
formed syndicates to acquire ZCMI, which stood on the
site of the old Grant homestead. Recounting the incident
and reflecting upon his boyhood resolve, President Grant
wrote: "For some five years I held proxies from these
syndicates, which gave me a majority of the votes at the
annual election so that was about as near as I came to
making my childhood promise to [buy] the old place
back come true."

One is struck by the fact that President Grant remembered the pledge he had made so many years
before, that he took satisfaction in knowing he had seen
at least a partial fulfillment of it, and that he seemed to
feel some sense of disappointment at not having owned
the old home outright.

The unusual quality of his character suggested by
this incident is perhaps best illustrated by two other
experiences from his early life. The setting of the first
was again Main Street, where Heber and several of his
boyhood friends were playing marbles. Heber's
concentration on the game was interrupted when one of

his playmates, pointing to a prosperous-looking man on the other side of the street, said, "Hebe, you see that long fellow across the road? He is working in Wells Fargo Bank, and gets $150 a month." Heber was duly impressed by this bit of knowledge, and it immediately set his analytical mind to work. At that time his main source of income came from shining the shoes of his mother's boarders for five cents a pair. He quickly calculated that this man made six dollars a day, which would be the equivalent of 240 shoes. "As I saw in my mind's eye 240 shoes to be shined to get six dollars," Heber later mused, "I decided that I would learn penmanship and bookkeeping, and some day, keep books in the Wells Fargo Bank." He later rejoiced to have this prophecy come true when he obtained employment with the bank.

What is perhaps the most interesting aspect of this affair, however, is the way in which Heber became proficient in penmanship, a skill that in that day was essential to success as a bookkeeper. Realizing this, he enrolled in a penmanship and bookkeeping class. Once during a class period several friends gathered around his desk and, in jest, made slighting remarks about his handwriting. One asked the taunting question, "What is it?" Another said, "It's too much for me," while still another said derisively, "It's hentracks." The final insult came from a boy who declared, "I know what it is— lightning has struck an ink bottle." Into the general hilarity that followed was injected a startling, wholly unexpected note that none of those present would ever forget. "I jumped up," Heber recorded, "and struck the table with my fist and declared that I would live to set copies for every last one of them, that I would live to write as well and better than the professor of penmanship, that I would live to some day be the professor of penmanship in the Deseret University!"

One can well imagine the look of startled surprise that this unexpected outburst produced and the incredulity with which his companions looked upon Heber's self-prophecies. But there was about this boy a latent force that was evident to all who knew him and that foreshadowed some eminence, some high achieve-

ment he would attain in life. Thus, while Heber's friends
may have openly scoffed at the seemingly rash predictions he had just uttered, it is likely that there stirred
within them, or at least within some of them, secret, un-
spoken prophecies about the future heights this thin,
voluble, intense boy would eventually scale.

The fact is that Heber J. Grant achieved each of the
penmanship goals he had set for himself that day. This
skill, in fact, became the means by which he was able to
earn extra money in his struggling years; during this period he spent much of his spare time, especially near
holidays, inscribing greeting and calling cards, for which
he occasionally received more compensation than from
his regular employment.

The second episode dramatizing Heber J. Grant's
penchant for tenacity and concentration occurred a few
years after he and his mother moved to the small cottage
on Second East Street. As Heber was Rachel's only
child, she was inclined to be overprotective of him, so
much so that he later remarked that he "was raised like
a hothouse plant." Because of this, he was less inclined
than most boys to participate in the active sports of the
day. When he finally did begin to play baseball with his
friends, he discovered to his embarrassment that he was
so devoid of skill, due to a lack of practice and competi-
tion, that he was assigned to the third team, comprised
mostly of boys much smaller and younger than he. One
can visualize this tall, slender boy, towering above his
teammates, trying mightily to conceal the ineptness that
his lack of experience had produced. In his overanxiety
to do well, to be accepted and admired by his friends, he
became a laughingstock, the object of many practical
jokes and unkind remarks that too often characterize ju-
venile relationships. "Throw it here, Sissy," his friends
would taunt when the ball came his way.

It would be difficult to imagine a nickname more
loathsome to a young boy than "sissy," especially to one
who had managed at last to emerge from his mother's
protective care, and who was trying to find a niche in a
boy's world. However, instead of being intimidated or
crushed by this treatment, as a less resilient boy might

have been, Heber was driven and motivated by it. Unlike the instance when he was taunted for his poor writing, he did not react openly to his playmates, perhaps because he suffered feelings of embarrassment over his clumsy play. But out of the hearing of his tormentors, he declared to his mother that he would play on the team that would win the championship of the Territory of Utah. Having made that prediction, he took immediate steps to put a foundation under it. "I shined forty shoes and I got a baseball," he reported. Then, with a tenacity almost frightening in its proportions, he commenced the laborious process of acquiring the skill necessary to fulfill his prediction. Reflecting on that process, he recorded: "I stood up behind my mother's home and threw a ball night after night, week after week, and month after month at Bishop Woolley's barn!"

The neighbors became well acquainted with the rhythmic thumps reverberating daily from Widow Grant's backyard. Their first impression must have been that the noise would soon end and that the neighborhood would be restored to its usual calm. It was not to be so. Instead of abating, the noise increased as the boy's arm strengthened through constant exercise and as the tempo of the thumping quickened.

It is not difficult to understand why the neighbors would have misinterpreted Heber's conduct and attributed to him qualities of character quite the opposite of those he actually possessed. Hearing the incessant noise and, perhaps, being a little irked at the merciless beating his barn absorbed day after day, Bishop Woolley branded Heber as "the laziest boy in the Thirteenth Ward." This characterization was not the mere reflection of a momentary pique, brought on by the bishop's annoyance at the neighbor boy who seemed intent on destroying his barn. Rather, it represented a long-held judgment that he often expressed, occasionally with some feeling. Such an occasion arose when the bishop discovered that Widow Grant's roof leaked badly and needed extensive repairs. Knowing of the family's pinched finances, he offered to pay for the roofing out of fast-offering funds, an offer that the independent widow declined. In doing so, she advised the bishop with an air of motherly confidence and pride that when her Heber grew to manhood, he would build her a new house. This idea seemed so ludicrous to the bishop, who had written Heber off as a ne'er-do-well, that he was later heard to say that if Widow Grant were to wait for a sound roof until *that* boy built her a new home, she would wait forever.

As one acquainted with Heber's character would surmise, he did ultimately play on the baseball team that won the territorial championship, and he did ultimately build his mother a new home. And when the home was completed, Heber, remembering the uncomplimentary remarks Bishop Woolley had made, invited him to pronounce a dedicatory prayer upon it. In doing so, he advised the bishop that the fine compliment he had paid him helped him build it quicker than he otherwise would have done, and he was much obliged. At that the good bishop, who was a great man in his own right, apologized to Heber and declared him to be "the hardest worker and the most industrious boy in the Thirteenth Ward." To demonstrate the genuine love he felt for the widow's son, Bishop Woolley later attended the conference where Heber was sustained as the president of the Tooele Stake and remarked to the congregation: "Maybe you think you have a boy coming out here to preside over Tooele Stake, but I want to tell you you have a full-grown man, although he is not very old."

Alongside the quality of stubborn perseverance here demonstrated, a second, perhaps more important character trait, appeared. This quality as applied to Heber J. Grant is best described as forthright and independent integrity—the complete absence of any sham or pretense and a rocklike insistence upon truthfulness and fairness in all his dealings. The record of his life will be searched in vain for any evidence suggesting that he was ever devious or unreliable. On the contrary, his actions were typified from beginning to end by a candor that was at once both refreshing and blunt.

In his youth, Heber attended a school directed by

Abraham Doremus and his wife. Later he was to attend the private school that was conducted for the numerous children of President Brigham Young and for others who, like Heber, attended on special invitation. Like most frontier schools, these were marked by a loose informality, the lack of a solid curriculum, and a faculty more inclined to win attention by punishment, or the threat of it, than by professorial skill. Years later Heber was to recall "a very great and important willow" that Brother Doremus kept as a symbol of his authority and that was used with some frequency to promote obedience and scholarship.

On only one occasion did the schoolmaster discipline Heber with the willow: when the boy refused to apologize for conduct that he considered appropriate but that Mr. Doremus thought was deserving of censure. Unable to obtain an apology voluntarily, the schoolmaster sought to extract one by force. Of the incident, Heber commented that the teacher "whipped me until he finally, I believe, must have been ashamed of himself and stopped. He could not get me to say I was sorry. It was something I had done that I felt was alright, and I would not announce that I was sorry for it."

Here, then, emerges the image of a boy who was unwilling to deviate from the course he considered to be right, who would adhere to the truth regardless of the consequences. These characteristics once prompted Mr. Doremus to award Heber the prize of a small slip of paper on which had been printed in block letters the word "TRUTHFUL." In his mature years, President Grant noted that he valued this award highly, "because it was given to me to emphasize the fact by Mr. Doremus that I always told the truth no matter what the consequences might be." We gain some insight into the importance he attached to this simple yet meaningful award from the following entry in his reminiscences: "I have always regretted that I did not save this little slip of paper; I had it for many years, and I do not know at this writing what has become of it."

The traits of character demonstrated by these incidents from the childhood and youth of President

Heber J. Grant were to appear again and again during his long career, like brilliant threads in a tapestry. They explain in large measure why he succeeded where others would have failed, why the projects he undertook generally reached fruition, why he was selected for high leadership at an early age, and why associates in business and church circles always deferred to him and looked to him for leadership.

Chapter 4

Emergence

Some people have a certain propensity, a skill, or an aptitude whose origin does not seem to trace to any human experience or discipline. There are, for instance, numerous examples of child prodigies whose mathematical or musical abilities emerge full-blown at an age when most children are struggling with the most rudimentary learning. While training and practice are necessary to bring such inherent talent to its highest degree of perfection, one recognizes in this a process similar to that of bringing out the lustrous beauty of a precious gem by constant polishing and burnishing. Philosophers and sages have been at a loss to explain this interesting phenomenon, but it manifests itself to a lesser extent in numerous people through a special knack or tendency that gives direction and impetus to their lives. Perhaps the most satisfactory explanation of Heber J. Grant's achievements is to be found in the theology he was taught in his youth, from which we learn that there is no beginning nor end to one's existence. Thus, the infant born to Rachel Grant on November 22, 1856, consisted not only of a weak, untrained physical body, visible to the human eye, but also of an ethereal, invisible spirit, the offspring of deity. This spirit was ageless, intelligent, and experienced, had been trained through eons of time by an omniscient, loving parent, and had agreed to assume bodily form and to be alienated from God by a curtain of forgetfulness in order to demonstrate his capacity to live by faith. Through obedience, he could become entitled to the status of exaltation enjoyed by his heavenly parent.

Judging from the self-confident way in which Heber J. Grant launched his business career, and the manner in which his enterprises prospered and flourished under his sure hand, one is led to speculate whether in pre-earth life he was distinguished for a special capacity to organize individuals and things and to calculate the outcome of events so as to bring about a desired result at a predetermined time and place. If not, then this unusual man must have possessed a treasure of intuitive knowledge, locked away from most others, or had access to a divine monitor that enabled him to move forward unerringly toward his business and financial goals.

We have already noted how he saw the need to achieve proficiency as a penman in order to become an accountant, and how he acted promptly and successfully to fill that need. Before he reached the age of sixteen, Heber had accumulated the credentials necessary to serve efficiently as an accounting assistant in a business office. At this stage in his career, he fortunately became associated with an able, considerate insurance agent named H. R. Mann, who took his place as one of the many surrogate fathers this fatherless boy had during his growing-up years.

This was an exciting time for a young man to enter upon a business career in Salt Lake City. Only three short years before, the transcontinental railroad had been linked up at Promontory Point, just a few miles northwest of Salt Lake. This historic event had signaled the end of the pioneer era for Utah and the beginning of a period of vigorous business and industrial growth. Businesses such as Zions Co-operative Mercantile Institution, Zions Savings Bank & Trust Company, and the Salt Lake City streetcar and gas companies had been organized, all of which served to attract capital and encourage the establishment of support businesses and industries. This in turn accelerated the construction of private homes and brought activity and prosperity to the building trades. All this augered well for the insurance business and, more to the point, for Heber's employer, H. R. Mann.

That the relationship between this pair took on more of a father-son flavor than the usual business arrangement is shown by the mutual affection they always

manifested toward each other. Heber characterized Mr.
Mann as "one of the most generous men with whom I
have ever been acquainted." This was demonstrated by
an unusual custom that developed between them: knowing of the boy's interest in baseball, Mr. Mann often directed Heber to attend a baseball game in the afternoon
and to report on the outcome at supper. So grateful was
the boy for this show of affection and interest that many
years later he could still recall with pleasure how this
exciting process was once repeated five times in a single
month.

Some time after Heber went to work for him, Mr.
Mann formed a partnership with Henry Wadsworth, the
Salt Lake manager of the Wells Fargo Bank and Express
Company. Heber then commenced to do some part-time
bookkeeping for the bank. In addition, he did part-time
bookkeeping at night for the Sandy Smelting Company
and for several mining companies. It was at this point in
his career that he began to supplement his growing income by writing calling cards, greeting cards, and wedding invitations in his spare time. This was ordinarily
done at his office after working hours so he would have
ample desk space on which to spread out the cards to
dry. One New Year's Eve his employer, Mr. Wadsworth,
entered the office late to find Heber busily engaged writing greeting cards. "What on earth are you doing?" he
asked in surprise. "Getting ready for a harvest tomorrow," Heber answered in his jocular, self-confident way,
going on to explain how he supplemented his income.
Then followed a comment by Mr. Wadsworth that
Heber treasured throughout life and often repeated as a
means of encouraging young men to be diligent and to
go the extra mile in serving their employers. Said Mr.
Wadsworth, "Well, my boy, it never rains but what it
pours. You are the only one in this bank that I am going
to make a New Year's present to. Here is a check I
intended to give you tomorrow." Handing Heber a
check for a hundred dollars, he continued, "You never
watch the clock but seem to enjoy work and are willing
to stay after office hours while most of the boys watch
the clock to see how quick they can get out after three

o'clock in the afternoon. I want you to know that this hundred dollars, in my judgment, is not a present, but that you have actually done a hundred or more dollars of work that you were not paid to do, on personal matters for me, and I appreciate your willingness to work."

While the money was welcome and needed, the knowledge that he enjoyed the respect and goodwill of his employer was of far greater significance to Heber. He alluded to this incident again and again over the years, and it served as a spur to his determination to succeed as a businessman and to achieve a position of importance and trust in the community.

After about four years under the expert tutelage of Mr. Mann and Mr. Wadsworth, Heber was prepared and anxious to strike out on his own. The opportunity to do so came when Mr. Wadsworth was transferred to California as cashier of the Wells Fargo Bank, Mr. Mann having previously left the state. At Mr. Wadsworth's departure, Heber purchased the goodwill of the insurance business and carried it on successfully, although he was only twenty years of age. It was later that he learned to his chagrin that, not yet having attained his majority, neither the contract to purchase nor the contracts entered into in carrying on the business prior to his twenty-first birthday were legally enforceable.

That Heber was a minor had never even occurred to his business associates. By this time he had reached physical maturity, having topped out at about 6 feet 2 inches. Although he was of a cheerful temperament, he was deadly serious in his business dealings and mature in his judgments, and naturally inspired feelings of confidence in those with whom he came in contact. Furthermore, he had been active in business circles for over five years, and it simply did not occur to his associates that he had made such an early start on his career. Beyond these considerations, Heber had been the principal support of his mother during a time when most young men are still dependent, and this had invested him with a gravity and a sense of responsibility that belied his years.

Shortly before reaching age 21, Heber was employed

temporarily as the assistant cashier of Zion's Savings Bank, replacing Bernard Schettler, who had been called on a mission to Holland. His duties there were light enough to enable him to carry on his expanding insurance and brokerage business. He was permitted to use his office in the bank to handle his personal affairs, greatly reducing the overhead and adding to his growing wealth. He took pride in the fact that President Brigham Young, who was the president of the bank, agreed to endorse the $25,000 bond Heber had to post in order to serve as assistant cashier. This was the final kindness the great Mormon colonizer was able to extend to his young friend before his death a few months later. "When he passed away," Heber noted afterward, "I wondered where in the world I could get anybody to sign a bond for me for twenty-five thousand dollars, and inasmuch as the directors never called my attention to the failure to give a bond, none was ever issued."

When Brother Schettler returned from his mission, Heber left the bank to pursue his own business interests, which now commenced to burgeon. He formed an insurance and brokerage partnership with Nephi Clayton that proved to be very lucrative. Heber's thorough grounding in business principles under the supervision of able, experienced men, his aggressive and outgoing personality, and his wide acquaintance in the community with business and ecclesiastical leaders acted as a magnet in attracting substantial clients to his firm. In addition to extensive insurance dealings, the firm sold territorial warrants, railroad company bonds, and ZCMI and other securities. Later, while in the brokerage business with D. W. Jennings, Heber and his partner represented Dupont Powder Company and many other prominent institutions.

Once his business career was underway, Heber began to focus his attention on more distant career goals as well as on other intimate, personal goals that had been simmering in his consciousness for years. In his reminiscenses he provides us with this insight into the process and scope of his goal setting: "I promised myself when I was a young man that I would be married before

I was twenty-one if I could persuade some good girl to marry me, so that I would start out as a full-fledged man when I reached my majority. . . . At the same time that I made this promise, I mapped out my life until I was thirty-odd years of age, and made up my mind as to the things that I was going to try to accomplish. . . . One was to make several hundred dollars a month before I was twenty-five, in which I was successful; another was to make something over ten thousand dollars immediately after I was thirty."

He also recorded another of his youthful goals—one that he failed to achieve. "Another ambition of mine," he wrote, "was to be elected mayor of Salt Lake City and subsequently to go to Congress." While he was prevented from seeking this goal because of intervening ecclesiastical responsibilities, little doubt exists that he would have attained it ultimately had he pursued it. One is impressed by the steps he actually took toward this goal before he was summoned to other duties by the leaders of the Church. "I used to read the reports, every day, of the proceedings in Congress," he recorded, "about as faithfully as I would say my prayers." Then, noting that his call to go to Tooele had interrupted these plans, he concluded: "Goodbye Mr. Mayor, goodbye Congress, goodbye political ambitions of every kind. If I behave myself, I'll be buried alive down in Tooele. No hope for any political preferment, or any political ambition. It will keep me busy to make a bare living out in a country town, attending to my ecclesiastical duties with little opportunity to study politics, and no hope of ever being the mayor of Salt Lake. And unless I become the mayor of Salt Lake, I doubt whether it would be worth while to try to go to Congress."

Although his business career and political ambitions seemingly dominated Heber's thoughts during these formative years, these were actually subordinate to his more enduring goals of marriage and service to the Church. We have already noted how, in his youthful goal setting, Heber had fixed twenty-one as the target age for his marriage. Looking toward that goal, he commenced during his teens to develop the social graces and contacts essential for its attainment. As a youth in the Thirteenth Ward, he regularly attended the parties and dances that were the customary fare for the young people of the day. He was to remember an embarrassing instance when he called to escort a young lady to a dance at a time when his persistence in throwing at Bishop Woolley's barn had earned him an ill-deserved reputation for laziness. Through an open transom he heard the girl's father declare that his daughter could not go "with any such a worthless, shiftless, lazy, good-for-nothing boy as he is." Heber observed dryly that he quit taking this young lady out, "seeing the father had such an exalted opinion of me."

Undeterred by this unjust criticism, or by the fact that his tone deafness handicapped him in learning to dance with grace, he persisted in dancing and taking dancing lessons until he had attained a desired proficiency. "I determined to learn to dance," he wrote, "so I joined a dancing school, and paid lessons to a dancing master by the name of Sheldon. . . . I had about as hard work learning to dance as I did learning to play marbles and write, but I finally mastered it and became a pretty good dancer." In the process he acquired a great liking for this diversion, and was later to say that he "would sooner waltz than eat."

In time, so-called round dancing became the favorite diversion of Heber's social group; it was such a rage that President Young decreed that there were to be only two or three round dances in an evening, with the balance of the program being taken up with the more conventional and less daring square dances. During intermissions, the young people often frequented an oyster parlor in downtown Salt Lake to partake of the current refreshment craze. On these occasions Heber would invariably order a beefsteak, since he "tried in vain to learn to like fresh oysters."

Too often these dances, with their lengthy intermissions and extended programming, carried on into the early hours of the morning. This was especially hard on active young men like Heber who had to be at the top of their form at the office or in the classroom the next morning. To avoid this, while preserving the delightful aspects of the dance, Heber and his friends organized what was later to be known as the Wasatch Literary Association, which, among other things, sponsored its own dances. Operated on the Cinderella principle, these dances always ended at five minutes before midnight to enable the dancers to get home at a reasonable hour.

It was during this period of active dating that Heber commenced searching in earnest for a wife. While he had resolved in advance to be married by age twenty-one, he did not intend that this would precipitate him into an unwise or premature relationship. The method he used in selecting his wife is a sure index to his character, and it foreshadowed the procedure he was to use again and again to solve difficult personal, business, and ecclesiastical problems.

As he progressed in his courtship and dating cycle, he narrowed his interests to Emily Wells, the vivacious and beautiful daughter of Daniel H. Wells, one of the prominent leaders of the Church. Aside from the customary physical, intellectual, and social attractions he felt toward Emily, he was drawn to her also because of the common heritage they shared. Both of their fathers had served as mayors of Salt Lake City and as counselors to President Brigham Young. Furthermore, both fathers had been successful businessmen and dedicated, practicing churchmen. With these common roots Heber, who was then imbued with the dual ambitions of business and politics, felt that Emily would be the ideal wife for him, providing not only love and companionship, but also the motivation and understanding counsel necessary for the attainment of his secular goals.

Suddenly, however, there was injected into a relationship that seemed so secure, so right for both parties, a schism that appeared irreconcilable: a clash of opinion about plural marriage. Heber, the son of a polygamist relationship, had been taught the principle not only by the example of his parents, but by the precepts of his mother, and had determined at an early age that he would be a polygamist. He had assumed that Emily shared his views regarding this principle and would willingly consent to being a polygamous wife. It came as a jolting surprise, therefore, to learn that she not only rejected the principle, but also seemed to hold it in derision. Because of "some very sarcastic remarks" she made about plural marriage, Heber commenced a painful reappraisal of his relationship with her. What followed turned out to be one of the most traumatic and sorrowful episodes of his entire life. Always prayerful by nature, Heber had sought for inspiration in the selection of a mate, so when Emily's negative attitude about plural marriage finally surfaced, he resorted again to that source of help. "I supplicated the Lord with all the power of my being," he wrote, "to direct me whether I should continue to try and win the affection of this young lady." The negative answer he received was wholly unexpected, and brought on one of the few seasons of melancholy he was to experience during his eighty-eight years of life. "It was a very great shock to me at the time," he recorded, "and caused me to shed some very bitter tears at the thought of not winning this young lady, as I admired her very much."

This shock to Heber's system seemed to derive not only from the genuine regret of severing a relationship with one he loved, but also from the inner doubts he suffered as to whether earlier favorable impressions he had received about his relationship with Emily had not been founded in truth. The passage of time entirely healed the deep wound that this terrible experience inflicted. In 1884, a little less than seven years after Heber J. Grant first married, a mature and much wiser Emily Wells became his third plural wife, and thereafter she bore him four attractive and accomplished daughters, all of whom grew to maturity, and one cherished son, Daniel Wells Grant, who died in childhood.

But for the young suitor, these events were shrouded in uncertainty and were to be unfolded to him only in the distant future. For the moment, therefore, it became necessary to try to introduce some order and meaning into the chaos created by the breakup of his relationship with Emily Wells. To this task he brought the only tool

that, at this unsettled and turbulent moment, he felt any
confidence in using: "I then prayed for the Lord to direct me in the right direction to secure a wife."

The direction he sought was not long in coming.
Shortly after terminating his courtship of Emily Wells,
Heber began to socialize with Lucy Stringham, the attractive and highly intelligent daughter of Briant Stringham, one of the Mormon pioneers of 1847. Heber had
known the Stringham family and daughter Lucy all his
life; they lived just through the block from Rachel
Grant's little adobe home. Lucy's brothers Phil and Jim
were close friends of Heber, and they frequently visited
in each others' homes. Moreover, Heber and Lucy had
attended Miss Mary Cook's school together and had
enjoyed frequent contact with each other through
church socials. Notwithstanding this, their relationship
had barely progressed beyond the nodding stage, due to
Heber's preoccupation with Emily Wells and the wide
gulf of two years separating them in age.

Heber's first overtures to Lucy were met with a
response that could hardly be called enthusiastic. He
started by walking her home from Sunday evening meetings, a frequently used courting device of the day. It was
customary, however, for the young lady to invite her escort to join her in the family sitting room, where they
could engage in serious or flirtatious talk and perhaps
enjoy some refreshments, all under the careful scrutiny
of the girl's parents. Sunday after Sunday, however,
instead of receiving a hoped-for invitation into the
Stringham sitting room, Heber received a somewhat
indifferent, even chilly, "good night" at Stringham's
gate. That he was not deterred by this unencouraging
treatment is still another evidence of Heber J. Grant's
characteristic perseverance.

The turning point in this tepid courtship occurred
one Sunday evening when Rodney C. Badger walked
past the Stringham's gate just as Heber received his customary "good night" from Lucy. As these two friends
walked together to the corner, Heber, instead of turning
south toward his home, told Rodney, "I'm going down
to Wells corner and visit with some of the girls there."

Shocked at what he interpreted as fickleness, Rodney chided Heber for leaving one girl only to go in search of other female companionship. Rodney appeared satisfied, however, when Heber explained Lucy's distant attitude toward him.

Whether Rodney planted a seed in Lucy's mind or mere chance intervened, the very next Sunday Heber received an invitation into the Stringham sitting room, where he became almost a fixture until the time of his marriage to Lucy a few months later. It turned out that Lucy's initial reluctance came not from a lack of feeling for the great man she was later to marry, but from the false notion that she was merely a temporary substitute for Emily Wells.

Once the ice was broken and Lucy realized that Heber had matrimony in view, their courtship sped toward its inevitable culmination. They were married in the St. George Temple on November 1, 1877, three weeks prior to Heber's twenty-first birthday. It was a source of satisfaction to Heber to know that another of his cherished goals had been realized. And he was always to congratulate himself on his good fortune at having found a wife who was so loving and supportive as well as gifted with a sound business sense and a penchant for orderliness. Time and again, he was to rely on her wise counsel as he wrestled with difficult problems of finance.

Little did Heber realize at the time of their marriage that he was to be blessed with Lucy's companionship for only sixteen years. During that brief period she lived a full life, bearing President Grant six children: five daughters and a son. All of the daughters lived to maturity, marrying men of calibre and achievement, two of whom, John H. Taylor and Clifford E. Young, became General Authorities of the Church. The son, Heber Stringham Grant, died at age seven, bringing deep remorse to his father and foreshadowing one of the few disappointments of President Grant's life—that he never had a son who lived to maturity, although the ten daughters who ultimately blessed his home made up in large part for this lack.

Chapter 5

Spiritual Awakening

Once married, and with his business career developing satisfactorily, Heber began to focus his attention more and more upon spiritual matters and his role in the Church. Though other things had taken momentary precedence, the Church had never been far from his mind. Indeed, it would not have been possible for him to forget his future in the Church in view of his mother's frequent reminders that he was destined to play a leading role in it.

Rachel's knowledge about the future eminence of her son came, in part, from an unusual spiritual experience she had had in a Relief Society meeting when Heber was a baby. In bearing testimony, poet-prophetess Eliza R. Snow pointed at young Heber, who was crawling on the floor, and, speaking in tongues, predicted that this infant would in his maturity stand as one of the high leaders of the Church, providing motivation and direction for thousands of Latter-day Saints. The interpretation of this prophetic utterance was made by Zina D. Young, another wife of Brigham Young. In retrospect, there seems to be special significance in the fact that all three of the women involved in this unusual incident were sealed to Joseph Smith, the first president of the Church, and all had been married for time to men who had been or who were then in the First Presidency. Thus there was among them a sort of communal, proprietary interest in the baby, both because of the relationship they bore to him and because of their participation in the spiritual manifestation that had identified him as a man of destiny. Throughout the childhood and adolescence of her son, Rachel never missed an opportunity to remind him of the role that had been marked out for him and of his need to live in a manner that would entitle him to fill it.

There were times when Heber, in a half-joking way, would insist that Rachel's ideas about his future were dictated by maternal prejudice and that, anyway, he was interested in a business or political career, not an ecclesiastical one. But deep down he knew that his mother spoke the truth and that his course in life would lead him inevitably to the high echelons of church leadership. Thus, he was inspired when, as a child, he received a patriarchal blessing promising that he would be called to the ministry in his youth. Taking as examples Joseph F. Smith and Erastus Snow, both of whom were called on missions in their mid-teens, Heber interpreted this statement in his patriarchal blessing to mean that he too would be called as a very young man to fill a mission. In this he was mistaken, as at the age of twenty-three he had not yet been called, not because of a lack of ability or personal unworthiness, but apparently because of the dependence of his mother. Whatever the reason, this failure created in him moments of self-doubt and anguish, stirring up questions about his status, about whether the patriarch had been inspired in conferring the blessing, and, worse still, about whether or not the whole Church system was reliably founded upon principles of truth. During moments of deep reflection he realized that there could be no doubt about the reality of God and the truthfulness of the revelations given to the Prophet Joseph Smith. There was too much evidence; he had received too many personal confirmations to doubt. And because of the innate self-confidence he had always possessed, this conclusion led him to believe that the patriarch had made a mistake. However, the implications of this belief continued to bring occasional doubts and uncertainties until an event took place that stands as one of the most significant turning points in his life.

While walking down Main Street one day, "I had stopped and spoken out loud," he wrote, "though there was nobody to hear me. For a number of years there had been a spirit telling me that the patriarch had lied to me, that he had promised me a mission in my youth, that I had never been on a mission, that I was now nearly twenty-four years of age, and yet I had not been upon a mission." He had never told anyone, not even his mother, that this had troubled him, that it had sorely tried his faith. At this point, he recalled, he "stopped, turned around and said aloud, 'Mr. Devil, shut up. I don't care if every patriarch in the Church has made a mistake in a blessing, and told a lie, I believe with all my heart and soul that the gospel is true and I will not allow my faith to be upset because of a mistake of a patriarch.' "

Never again was Heber J. Grant to be bothered by this negative, questioning spirit. And within a few weeks he was called to serve as the president of the Tooele Stake. It was then he realized that his blessing had promised that he would be called to the *ministry* in his youth, not that he would be called on a mission. The fulfillment of this unusual prediction was made even more dramatic when it became known that Heber was the youngest stake president in the entire church.

It seems very simple and is entirely correct merely to say that Heber J. Grant was sustained as the stake president in Tooele on October 30, 1880, and served in that position until he was called as a member of the Council of the Twelve Apostles less than two years later. What such a sterile account fails to reveal, however, is the excitement and trauma of the call and subsequent service, the physical discomforts or disabilities involved, and the problem of changing the attitudes of some of the members in Tooele who were a little less than enthusiastic about having a twenty-three-year-old city dweller serve as president of their rural stake.

A change in the Tooele Stake presidency was signaled at general conference in October 1880 when the stake president, Francis M. Lyman, was called as one of the Twelve. The First Presidency—John Taylor, George Q. Cannon, and Joseph F. Smith—had watched with interest the steady rise in prominence of Elder Heber J. Grant. So, when the time came to call a replacement in Tooele, they took an intense look at him as a potential choice. He seemed to possess all the necessary creden-

tials. He was happily married to a charming and supportive wife, who had borne him one child and was expecting a second one soon. He was a man of affairs with
adequate means and a growing business. He enjoyed an
impeccable reputation for honesty, was aggressive and
outgoing, and inspired feelings of confidence and loyalty
in his associates. More important than all these,
however, he was a man of faith and spirituality who had
always demonstrated the principles of his religion
through his conduct. The only possible question about
his suitability as a replacement for Elder Lyman was his
age. Even by frontier standards, which traditionally lean
toward youth, twenty-three was quite young for a stake
president, especially considering the maturity and the
pioneering experience of the people over whom he would
preside. But Heber had more than held his own in the
rough-and-tumble of the Salt Lake business world, and
the brethren apparently felt that with this capability he
could in time win the complete confidence of the people
and overcome their initial resistance to his call.

Under normal circumstances, the new stake president would have had an interval of relative peace,
between the time of his call and the time of his installation, in which he could give unhurried consideration to
the work that lay ahead. This was not to be so with
President Grant.

On October 5 and 6, 1880, the Grants went to Park
City for a little outing to see the beautiful colors as the
foliage turned. While there, Heber picked some autumn
leaves for Lucy to use in decorating their home. On the
following day Heber broke out in an ugly, painful rash.
Investigation showed poison ivy to be the source, and the
seemingly harmless and beautiful autumn leaves proved
to be the carrier. From then until the eighteenth, he
suffered such intense pain and discomfort that he was
able to do little if any work. For one so active, this period
of enforced idleness was galling, especially because of the
many things that he needed to be doing. But what he
had suffered to this point proved to be only a mild
prelude to the woe that lay ahead.

Starting on October 18, Heber spent ten days in bed,

covered with boils caused by the poison ivy. By the twenty-ninth he was able to return to his office for a while, and on the next day he accompanied the First Presidency to Tooele, where he was presented and sustained as the new stake president.

On October 22 while Heber had been in bed fighting off the effects of his encounter with the poison ivy, his wife had given birth to their second daughter, Lucy. Since she was nursing this child at the time, and in addition had two-year-old Susan Rachel to tend, she was unable to go to Tooele to witness her husband's installation as stake president. The Salt Lake party that did attend included all of the First Presidency; their secretary, George F. Gibbs; John W. Taylor, and Heber J. Grant. They were met by Francis M. Lyman, Heber's predecessor.

There was a feeling of excitement and anticipation among the members of the stake who had come to the conference from the outlying communities. From the time of Elder Lyman's call to the Twelve, they had been engaged in speculating on who the new president would be. Each seemed to have his own candidate in mind. There were many able, dedicated men in the stake, some of whom had been in the area from the time Tooele Valley was first settled more than thirty years before. It was difficult to select one from among these. There were hardy and tough ranchers and farmers; frontier merchants and businessmen; artisans and tradesmen; and a few professionals—doctors, lawyers, and newsmen. The fact that the area had been organized as a separate stake three years before was indicative of the number and capabilities of the members who inhabited it. So the real problem facing the speculator, or the predictor, was to come up with the best, the most able and qualified man out of a large selection of potential candidates.

It is probably safe to say that, with the possible exception of Francis M. Lyman, not one member of the Tooele Stake was correct in predicting who the new president would be. In fact, it is unlikely that more than a small handful of members there had even heard of Heber J. Grant. Those who may have seen the official party arrive would not have attached much significance to the presence of the tall, bearded, well-groomed young man with the remarkably clear complexion. Anyone interested enough to inquire would have learned that he was one of the sons of President Jedediah M. Grant, whose eloquence and dynamic personality would have been remembered well by some of the old-timers. Anyone seeing Heber with the First Presidency might logically have speculated that he was an understudy for their faithful secretary, George F. Gibbs. But who, in the most uncontrolled flight of imagination, would ever have assumed that this young man, attired in the most stylish clothes of the day and carrying about him the cultural aura of the Salt Lake metropolis, was to be the new president of this rural, unsophisticated stake?

Under these circumstances, it came as no great surprise that when this pleasant, young stranger was presented to the conference for sustaining vote, many of them did not vote for the new president. On the following day, October 31, when the entire slate of general and stake officers was presented to the conference for a vote, President Grant noted with evident satisfaction, "I did not notice that there was any falling off in the vote when my name was presented as there had been the day before." Later, he was to record the reaction of some of the Tooele Saints to his call as reported to him by a friend: "I learned from him that some of the people in Tooele Stake considered it an insult to have a young man like myself—and one residing out of the county called to preside."

But it was not possible for any but his most obdurate critics to harbor resentment or animosity toward Heber J. Grant. He was too open and forthright, too friendly and outgoing, for anyone to reject him for long. The Tooele Saints discovered this when he delivered his maiden speech. It was probably the impact of this speech as much as anything else that moderated their feelings between the two meetings where he was presented for sustaining vote. Of this speech, he wrote: "I told everything I could think of in seven minutes and a half, and part of that over twice . . . announced to the good people that I had little or no knowledge whatever of the duties or responsibilities of the president of a stake, but I pledged to them my very best efforts; I pledged that I would be as faithful a tithepayer as any man in the stake, that I would observe the Word of Wisdom as faithfully as any man, that I would be as liberal with my means in proportion to the amount that I had for any public enterprise as the others, and would do my best."

The spirit of this talk was one of humility and self-deprecation intertwined with humor and self-confidence. It seemed to set well with these down-to-earth Saints, who were quick to detect any sign of insincerity or posturing in their leaders.

Following the session where Heber was first sustained, the official party adjourned for dinner at Elder Lyman's home. During the conversation accompanying the meal, President Joseph F. Smith turned to the new stake president. "Heber," he said, "you did not bear your testimony that you knew that the gospel was true." President Smith hardly expected the answer: "I did not bear it because I do not know it. I believe it with all my heart, but I do not know it." After a contemplative pause President Smith turned slowly to President Taylor and said, "I believe that this afternoon, President Taylor, we ought to undo the work that we have done this morning. I don't think any man should be permitted to be the president of a stake who does not know that the gospel is true!" "Well, I do not, Brother Smith," Heber answered, "and I did not seek this office and I will be only too willing to be relieved of it."

The tension of this interchange was broken when President Taylor interrupted in a jovial way to observe, "Brother Joseph, that young man knows the gospel is true just as well as you and I. The only thing that he does not know is that he does know it, and it will be a very short time till he will know the gospel is true and bear his testimony." This statement proved to be prophetic: within a few weeks, through prayer and reflection, the promising young leader was able to testify with honesty and conviction that he knew the work in which he was engaged was of divine origin. That testimony, which he would bear again and again throughout his life, was later confirmed by many spiritual promptings and insights and was the means of bringing strength and stability to thousands of people.

The new stake president found a well-ordered and disciplined constituency in the pioneer communities over which he presided. In addition to the ward in Tooele, there were wards in Grantsville, Lake Point, Lakeview, St. John, and Clover. There were also many members living in isolated areas in Rush and Skull valleys to the south and west who were attached to the organized wards. Curiously enough, the area around Oakley, Idaho, comprised a branch of the Grantsville ward. President Grant could never understand the logic of this; the first motion he made as a member of the Council of the Twelve was that Oakley and its environs be transferred from the Tooele Stake to the Box Elder Stake.

A trip by the stake president into Rush or Skull valleys was ordinarily a three- or four-day affair. When going to Skull Valley, for example, he would travel from Tooele to Grantsville in one afternoon, spend the night with Samuel Woolley, and complete the four- or five-hour wagon trip the next day, returning a day or two later. However, a trip to Oakley was quite another matter, requiring two weeks or more and involving logistical problems of the greatest magnitude.

Generally, a traveling party to Oakley consisted of President Grant, members of his administrative staff, and some General Authorities who would transact Church business in several stakes along the way. About six white-top buggies with teams would be loaded with hay for the animals, food, and camping gear. Ahead lay a well-traveled but rough wagon road that wended its tortuous way northward from Tooele along the western slope of the Oquirrh mountains, past Lake Point near the southern shore of the Great Salt Lake, thence almost due east to Salt Lake City. From there, the road turned northward through Bountiful and Ogden and to a point some distance beyond Brigham City, where it angled in a northwesterly direction toward Oakley, located on the north side of the lake, opposite Tooele and Grantsville. The party could stay with hospitable Saints in Salt Lake City and the settled communities to the north, but on the last leg of the journey, which traversed an area singularly barren and lonely in its appearance, they had to camp out under the stars.

These lengthy trips through open, unsettled country with broad vistas and quiet solitudes were conducive to the development of lasting friendships. The easy pace of travel promoted conversation or silent reverie, depending on the moods of the travelers. At rest stops, they would test their athletic skills in throwing or shooting competitions. And, not infrequently, the travelers added variety to their journey by singing.

It was on one of his trips to Oakley from Tooele that Heber was first imbued with the desire to learn to sing. On this particular trip, Elder Francis M. Lyman's son relinquished his seat in his father's white-top to Heber. In the course of the day Elder Lyman sang a number of songs for his guest, including the old favorite, "Let Each Man Learn to Know Himself," whose chief message is condensed at the end of the last stanza: "So first improve yourself today and then improve your friends tomorrow."

So impressed was Heber by this song that he persuaded Elder Lyman to sing it again as they gathered around the campfire that evening. As he did so, Heber wrote down the words and committed them to memory. When he later learned to sing, persevering in spite of his tone deafness, this song became one of the mainstays of his repertoire. Of it he was to write: "I have repeated this song from one end of the church to the other—from Canada on the north to Mexico on the south, in the Hawaiian Islands, and over in Japan and in different parts of Europe and have asked missionaries at home and abroad to learn it off by heart."

The Tooele interlude, brief though it was, was essential in training Heber for the important leadership roles he was to play in later years. It gave him a clear insight into the problems of administering the Church at the grass-roots level. It made him conscious of the aspirations of the stalwart people who formed the backbone of the Church. It taught him humility and reliance on the divine power. It demonstrated the necessity of being disciplined and consistent in the budgeting and use of time. And it revealed his own limitations while magnifying his potential for achievement.

Chapter 6

The Youngest Apostle

The Council of the Twelve Apostles in The Church of Jesus Christ of Latter-day Saints is one of the most unusual and prestigious bodies known to either ecclesiastical or civil government. It is subordinate in authority and influence only to the First Presidency, which wields dominant power in directing the worldwide affairs of the Church. Yet, in a sense, it is mother to the First Presidency, for out of its number comes the man who ascends to the pinnacle of earthly responsibility after the death of a Church president. And unlike the First Presidency, which ceases to exist temporarily when a president dies, the Council of the Twelve has had unbroken continuity since it was first organized in modern times in 1835.

The act of selecting a new member of the Twelve is fraught with great significance and produces feelings of high excitement among the general Church membership. These feelings were greatly magnified as the general conference of October 1882 approached, for there were two vacancies in the Council of the Twelve. While there was no assurance that either or both of the vacancies would be filled at the time, the Saints were not deterred from engaging in the kind of speculation that had preceded Heber J. Grant's call as president of the Tooele Stake. In this case, however, the extent and intensity of these speculations were multiplied many times over, since the vacant positions were much nearer to the top rung of the hierarchal ladder and affected the members in every stake.

This enthusiasm helped somewhat to counteract a cloud of discouragement brought upon the Saints by national affairs. A few months earlier, in March 1882, the president of the United States had approved the Edmunds Act, making it unlawful for persons to practice plural marriage, under threat of criminal penalties.

While Heber was infected to a degree with the sense of foreboding this act brought on, he was perhaps less influenced by it than were most others because of the many things that competed for his attention. His wife and children, his mother, the stake, his growing business interests and political involvements, all cried out for their share of his time. The past two years had been growing years for the young stake president, and chief among his satisfactions as he prepared for general conference that October was the knowledge that he had earned the support, even the admiration, of the members of his stake.

The customary feeling of anticipation had settled upon the Latter-day Saints as they thronged to Temple Square for the last session of the conference Sunday afternoon. Ahead of them lay the exciting drama of sustaining the General Authorities. As Heber made his way toward the oval-domed Tabernacle, there was nothing in his consciousness that portended the shocking revelation that was to come to him in a few moments, nor the sense of empty disappointment that was to follow within the hour. Greeting acquaintances as he moved along, he did not see his friend and fellow stake president, George Teasdale, until he had reached the entrance to the Tabernacle. Other than the fact that these two men shared a conviction of the truth and importance of the work in which they were engaged and were leaders of adjoining stakes, they had little in common. A generation separated them in age. The older man, with his clipped British accent and professorial ways, was more introspective, more disposed toward a clerical, literary style, while Heber was outgoing, almost flambuoyant in his leadership. The personalities of these two men presented an almost classic example of the contrasts between a middle-aged introvert and a young, aggressive extrovert. But these and other differences evaporated when they met on the common ground of devotion to the Church. As they saw each other while en-

tering the Tabernacle, Brother Teasdale's face lit up
in recognition and, extending a hand toward his
young friend, he said, "Brother Grant, you and I are
going to—" At that, he commenced to cough and was
unable to complete the sentence. No other words passed
between them, and they were soon separated by the mill-
ing crowd moving toward the vacant seats in the
Tabernacle. But while Brother Teasdale failed to complete his statement, his meaning was not lost. "It came to
me as plain as if he had continued the sentence," Heber
said, " 'going to fill the vacancies in the quorum of the
twelve Apostles.' " Heber later recorded that he went to
the meeting "swelled up with importance and was
willing to vote for myself, but the meeting adjourned
without filling the vacancies."

In this incident, we see a repetition of what occurred
in respect to Heber's patriarchal blessing. The spiritual
message transmitted on this occasion was accurate in its
meaning but was misinterpreted by the recipient. Knowing that the General Authorities were to be presented at
the last session of conference and that two vacancies
existed in the Council of the Twelve, he erroneously
assumed from the impression he had received that a call
to the apostleship would be extended to him at that
session. Later events proved the impression to be correct;
the error lay in the interpretation as to when it would
take place, for no names were presented at the
conference for sustaining to the Council of the Twelve.

Heber was not to discover his error for eight days.
During the week following the conference he busied
himself with the usual business and church affairs. Leaving Salt Lake City for Tooele on the 8:10 train Saturday
morning, he faced another busy weekend, including a
thorny church court trial scheduled that afternoon. On
Sunday he attended meetings in Tooele, where he addressed the Saints and counseled with ward and stake
leaders. That evening at the home of his counselor,
Hugh S. Gowans, he received a telegram from Francis
M. Lyman of the Council of the Twelve, instructing him
to report at the Council House in Salt Lake City at 3:30
the next afternoon. This was not unusual, as Heber

frequently attended meetings there. But he did wonder
what may have prompted the telegram, as he had
known of nothing prior to his departure from Salt Lake
City that would require such a precipitate, unscheduled
return.

Heber's curiosity was aroused even further when he
was met at the Salt Lake depot by William Clayton, the
long-time confidant of the First Presidency, who had
served since the days of Joseph Smith, and who now
drove Heber directly to President John Taylor's office.
Waiting for him there were all of the First Presidency:
John Taylor, George Q. Cannon, and Joseph F. Smith.
Also present, seated in order of their seniority, were the
apostles: Wilford Woodruff, Lorenzo Snow, Erastus
Snow, Franklin D. Richards, Brigham Young, Jr.,
Francis M. Lyman, and John Henry Smith. In addition,
four presidents of the First Council of the Seventy—
Horace S. Eldredge, John Van Cott, W. W. Taylor, and
Abraham H. Cannon—were there, along with the secre-
tarial staff of the First Presidency: John Nuttall, George
Reynolds, and George F. Gibbs. But despite the
awesome presence of all these General Authorities, the
person who caught Heber's eye more than anyone else in
the crowded room was his friend George Teasdale, who
sat apart from the others, along with Seymour B. Young.
Heber may not have guessed why Brother Young was
there, but with an electric thrill he knew instantly why
George Teasdale was there and why he himself was
there. The spirit that had borne witness to him eight
days before again affirmed that he and Brother Teasdale
were to be ordained to fill the vacancies in the Council of
the Twelve.

The exact sequence of the events of that meeting
were forever to remain jumbled in Heber's mind. So
many extraneous thoughts kept drifting in and out,
thoughts about the path that had led him here, about
the uncertain but exciting future that lay ahead and,
perhaps above all, about his qualifications to fill the role
that had been thrust upon him so suddenly in his youth
and that now seemed almost overwhelming in its complexity and magnitude. President Taylor announced

that the word of the Lord had come to him; and never could Heber erase the combined feelings of excitement, joy, and apprehension that were aroused in his mind as George Reynolds commenced to read the revelation. "Thus saith the Lord," it began, "to the Twelve and to the Priesthood and people of my church: Let my servants George Teasdale and Heber J. Grant be appointed to fill the vacancies in the Twelve, that you may be fully organized and prepared for the labors devolving upon you, for you have a great work to perform."

The events of this exciting, unforgettable day catapulted Heber J. Grant from a life of relative obscurity to the center stage where the fast-paced drama of The Church of Jesus Christ of Latter-day Saints was being enacted. He was to perform there for a period of sixty-three years, a record exceeded only by one of his successors, President David O. McKay, who served for sixty-four years. His term of service was to span the horse-and-buggy, kerosene, gaslight era to the age of airplanes, automobiles, radios, and television. He was to see the Church emerge from a struggling, persecuted, much-maligned sect to the strongest, most respected young church in the world. He was to live through the dark days of the so-called Mormon underground, and to see the civil liberties of his people suspended, the properties of the Church expropriated, and many of his brethren imprisoned because of their religious beliefs and practices. He was to witness the violent political struggles to eliminate the dominance of local affairs by federal carpetbaggers and to gain statehood for Utah. And thrice he was to see his beloved country embroiled in foreign wars that took the lives of countless thousands of young men. More important to him, he was to see the Church strengthened and enlarged, the proselyting effort accelerated, and thousands of new church buildings constructed, including the first temples built outside the United States. And, interwoven through all these important events of church and state, he was to see his own character mature, his personal enterprises prosper, and his family ties become secure through the love of his wives and progeny.

Chapter 7

A Season of Doubt

Notwithstanding the many hints of his destiny he had received throughout his life, Heber was stunned and thrown off balance by the summons to the apostleship. The fact that it was embodied in a formal, written revelation, received through the man he sustained as God's mouthpiece on earth, cast an entirely different light on the matter than if he had merely been invited to become a member of the Twelve. And the opening words "Thus saith the Lord" produced in him feelings of awe and unworthiness.

Once the euphoria created by the call began to wear off and Heber could objectively appraise the significance of what had taken place, he was beset with many doubts and anxieties. Why had the call come to one so young and seemingly so unprepared? Having served such a short apprenticeship learning the mechanics of church government, could he command the respect and devoted allegiance of brethren who had spent long years sharpening their leadership skills? Would he be able to fulfill adequately the many calls to expound the doctrines of the Church, to inspire confidence, and to motivate? There were good days when, elevated by a satisfying experience or a word of encouragement or praise, a surge of self-confidence would obliterate the doubts, filling Heber with a sense of peace and assurance. Then, just as quickly, these calm feelings would be replaced by gnawing apprehension.

Three months passed during which Heber lived an almost mechanical existence. He carried on his business affairs, filled the needs of his family, and went through the motions of discharging his apostolic responsibilities.

He attended stake conferences and other meetings where he was invariably called upon to speak and where he always gave a good account of himself, conveying a message or leaving an impression that elevated his listeners and helped them to change and to improve. Many of the Saints who heard him and who had known his father were impressed with the similarity in appearance and style between the two. The natural eloquence and earnestness they observed in the young apostle reminded them so much of his brilliant father. Some speculated that because of his spare physique and his tendency to drive himself in work, Heber would share with his father the fate of an early, spectacular eminence and a premature death. Those who held this view did so in ignorance of the tough, resilient constitution with which the young apostle had been endowed, and of the destiny that had been marked out for him.

As the new year dawned, Elder Grant was cheered by an assignment to accompany his fellow apostle, Brigham Young, Jr., on a mission to the Indians, in the course of which they were to set in order the affairs of the Church in the Mormon colonies lying to the south and east. He looked forward expectantly to serving as the companion of this able leader, who was then a mature forty-six and had served as an apostle for eighteen years, fourteen of them as a member of the Council of the Twelve. Perhaps during the several months they were to be together in daily intimate association Heber would be able to gain some insight, some inspiration to help lay at rest the nagging concerns that troubled him.

Setting off on January 6, 1883, the two apostles traveled through Colorado, southeastern Utah, and New Mexico, exhorting the Saints and installing new leaders as needed. Their trail eventually led them to the Mormon community of Sunset, Arizona, where they spent some time finalizing their plans regarding the principal work that had brought them into the wilderness. Despite the fact that they had been sent on a mission to the Indians, their contacts with the red man until now had been only occasional and accidental. In Bluff, at Durango, Santa Fe, and Albuquerque, and

again at the Winslow depot they had seen Indians, and
at each encounter they had been reminded again of the
object of their strenuous trip: to seek out, befriend, and,
if possible, convert to their beliefs the Lamanite brethren
who occupied such a central role in their whole system of
theology.

The Book of Mormon, from which the Church's
nickname was derived, contains prophetic promises concerning the Indians and the sacred covenants they will
be required to make and keep if they are to attain the
high destiny predicted for them. So these missionaries
came among the Indians, not in a spirit of condescen-
sion, but out of a sense of duty, to awaken them to a
knowledge of their origins and to help lead them to a
state of perfection.

With four teams and several riding mules, Elders
Young and Grant, Lot Smith, Joseph H. Richards, and
Thomas Brockbank departed from Sunset on Tuesday,
February 20, 1883, to commence their historic journey
into the heart of the Indian country. Their immediate
destination was Tuba City, an Indian village named
after famous Chief Tuba who, six years before, had attended the dedication of the St. George Temple with his
longtime friend and teacher, Andrew S. Gibbons. While
at the temple, Chief Tuba had also received his endowment. Gibbons, one of the missionaries to the Indians
who had crossed the Colorado River with a vanguard
party in 1858, had reported that Chief Tuba received
the endowment understandingly. Consequently, the
brethren now traveling toward Tuba knew they were going among a people who were intelligent and basically
friendly, and who had been cultivated for a quarter of a
century by a corps of dedicated missionaries. But they
could not help recalling that only a few years earlier a
promising young Latter-day Saint, George A. Smith, Jr.,
son of a member of the Council of the Twelve, had been
killed by an Indian who had asked in a friendly way to
examine his gun, and who had then shot him in cold
blood. This young martyr had been memorialized in the
thoughts of his brethren when the artesian well near
which he was murdered was named the George A.

Spring, one of the many distinctive points of interest the party would visit during their travels in the barren yet beautiful land. Names like George A. Spring, Coyote Springs, and Camp Echo were to acquire new meanings for the travelers as they visited them. For example, Elder Grant was enthralled by the acoustical properties of Camp Echo. "There (were) 3 distinct echos each time we hollowed," he wrote. "The last echo was the best and a sentence of eight or ten words could be heard distinctly."

Once among the Indians, the two apostles and their associates presented the message they had been sent to deliver and, whenever possible, planted seeds of friendship and understanding that they hoped would bear fruit for their brethren who would follow. In addition to the basic message embodied in the Book of Mormon and instructions about the power and love of God, these emissaries taught the Indians fundamental principles intended to improve their conduct.

Each day in this new and fascinating land provided Heber with fresh insights into the character and traits of the people he had been sent to teach. He also gained an appreciation of the difficulties of travel and communication in such a rugged, undeveloped country and an understanding of why the work here had progressed so slowly and would, for the time being at least, continue at that pace.

But while his work was absorbing and in many ways satisfying, there was still an uneasiness within him, a vague sense that all was not well, that a basic lack existed that made him less than whole, less than the confident, self-assured emissary he wanted to be and should be. After all, he had been called as an apostle, a special witness of the divinity and mission of the Lord Jesus Christ. Yet, repeatedly since his call in October, there had been a negative, questioning spirit within him that seemed to compete for ascendancy over the forward-looking, self-confident, and faithful spirit that customarily dominated his being. Intermittently that negative spirit whispered to him that he was unworthy to be an apostle, that he ought to resign. And when he would bear testimony that Jesus is the Christ, the Son of the living God, the Redeemer of mankind, there would often come the insidious whispering "You lie. You lie. You have never seen him."

In his moments of quiet reflection, Heber realized that these thoughts, these impressions, originated with his archenemy, Satan. He knew this because of the similar experience he had had as to the meaning of his patriarchal blessing. In that instance the nagging, recurring doubts had been banished, and the adversary put to flight when, in effect, Heber had said, "It is enough; I will tolerate you no longer."

Perhaps Heber had some premonition, as he arose one morning late in February, that his season of agonizing doubt was near its end. If so, he must have also sensed that it would have to be brought to a head by some power or agency beyond his own competence. The curtain of doubt that now enshrouded him seemed so massive, so stifling, that it would not yield to the mere injunction "go away," as it had in the earlier instance. This veil would be rent only by the power of God.

It was cold on the Navajo desert as the missionaries crawled from their warm bedrolls. The smoldering embers from last night's cheerful fire were brought back to life with dry kindling and gentle fanning. Working efficiently, the brethren busied themselves around the campsite, their breath leaving white clouds on the crisp air. Everything about this environment was invigorating, from the bite in the clear winter air to the rugged, varicolored formations surrounding them on all sides, to the uncertain expectancy about what the day would bring amidst a people who had produced both a Chief Tuba, an endowed Latter-day Saint, and the nameless, faceless killer who had gunned down young George A. Smith. Perhaps this incident was in the mind of Heber later in the day when, upon reaching a fork in the trail, he turned in the saddle to face his companion, Lot Smith, and asked, "Lot, is there any danger from Indians here?" "None at all," came the answer. "Go ahead and follow the crowd," Heber told his friend. "I want to be all alone."

With that, the young apostle followed a narrow but

well-marked trail, extending through an immense gully
that the white-tops could not traverse, to a point on the
other side, where the trail converged again with the
wagon road. His object in being alone was to meditate
and pray and to reflect upon the unusual turn his life's
course had taken. There still rested upon him the op-
pressive weight of uncertainty as to why he had been
called to the position he now occupied. He had not yet
received the assurance he needed that the call had divine
sanction.

The respite that he had sought so diligently was not
ushered in with fanfare. It came quietly, yet with a sud-
denness and an emotional intensity that ever after were
to produce in him feelings of elation and excitement
when he reflected upon the experience. His own words
best describe what occurred as he rode on the remote
trail deep in the wilderness. "I seemed to see, and I
seemed to hear, what to me is one of the most real things
in all my life," he wrote. "I seemed to hear the words
that were spoken. I listened to the discussion with a great
deal of interest. The First Presidency and the Quorum of
the Twelve Apostles had not been able to agree on two
men to fill the vacancies in the Quorum of the Twelve.
There had been a vacancy of one for two years, and a vacancy of two for one year, and the conference had
adjourned without the vacancies being filled. In this
council the Savior was present, my father was there, and
the Prophet Joseph Smith was there. They discussed the
question that a mistake had been made in not filling
those two vacancies and that in all probability it would
be another six months before the Quorum would be
completed. And they discussed as to whom they wanted
to occupy those positions, and decided that the way to
remedy the mistake that had been made in not filling
these vacancies was to send a revelation. It was given to
me that the Prophet Joseph Smith and my father mentioned me and requested that I be called to that position.
I sat there and wept for joy. It was given to me that I
had done nothing to entitle me to that exalted position,
except that I had lived a clean, sweet life. It was given to
me that because of my father's having practically

sacrificed his life in what was known as the great reformation, so to speak, of the people in early days, having been practically a martyr, that the Prophet Joseph and my father desired me to have that position, and it was because of their faithful labors that I was called, and not because of anything I had done of myself or any great thing that I had accomplished. It was also given to me that that was all these men, the Prophet and my father, could do for me. From that day it depended upon me and upon me alone as to whether I made a success of my life or a failure." (*Gospel Standards,* pp. 195-96.)

Heber was never able to describe adequately the nature of this watershed experience and the impact it had upon him; suffice it to say that it completely altered his life. It created in him a rocklike confidence in himself and his ministry that was never to be moved or shaken. It gave him a new perspective by showing the concern for the work on both sides of the veil. Perhaps more important than anything else, it brought the realization that, while his call was traceable to the intervention of powerful advocates beyond the veil, their influence ended with his call, leaving him to demonstrate that their confidence was not misplaced.

When Heber rejoined his companions, it is doubtful they detected any significant change in him. However, a look deep inside would have revealed that he was not the same. The amiable young man had been transformed into an apostle, a change so significant it may be said accurately that Elder Heber J. Grant's apostolic career dates from that hour, not from the time of his formal call.

While much work still lay ahead for the two apostles to complete on their mission, it was anticlimactic for Heber. The last leg of their mission was to take them through the Mormon settlements in eastern Arizona and ultimately into the Zuni nation and the eastern part of the Navajo reservation. Their route extended through a string of newly planted settlements whose names sounded like the roll call of the Mormon hierarchy: Woodruff, Snowflake, Taylor, and Erastus. They also visited Nutrioso and Round Valley, ending up in St.

Johns, a town site on the Little Colorado River that the Saints had purchased from two Jewish merchants for a herd of cattle. Heber and his party, on arriving at St. Johns, likely felt that they had reached the end of the world. Time and again the stubborn, persistent St. Johns pioneers had built dams to impound the waters of their meandering river, only to have them washed out due to the lack of rock footings to anchor the fill dirt. It was a perseverance like that of Nephi of old that enabled them first to survive and then to flourish in the wilderness. And while it could hardly be said that St. Johns blossomed like the rose, it nevertheless had an oasislike quality about it for the itinerant party that arrived there on March 30, 1883, for a conference of the Eastern Arizona Stake.

Isolated from the main body of the Church, the Saints there looked upon stake conference as their major religious and cultural event. The expectations of those who had thronged into St. Johns were heightened because they knew the apostles would be present. Their rigorous existence and the tough discipline of their lives had prepared them for the straightforward, unadorned counsel they received from the visitors. Along with their doctrinal sermons and practical counsel, the two apostles handled organizational and procedural matters, including the call of a corps of missionaries to work among the Indians.

The traveling party, augmented by the addition of Richard Gibbons, John Kartchner, Jesse R. Smith, and Isaac Turley, left St. Johns on Wednesday, April 4, headed for the Zuni villages and Fort Wingate. Just as the party prepared to mount up, St. Johns bishop David King Udall handed Heber a welcome packet of mail that included letters from his wife and mother and from fellow apostles Francis M. Lyman and John Henry Smith. These evoked nostalgic memories of family and friends, from whom he had been separated for three months, and a desire to return to them, especially to see his new daughter, Florence, who had been born in his absence.

Work among the Zunis was cut short because of their

preoccupation with spring planting. Moving on, the party visited a small Mormon settlement, appropriately named Navajo. Near Fort Wingate they counseled with a high Navajo Chief, Manuelito, whose name reflected the ancient Spanish influence that still clung to the area, and whose person reflected the best qualities of his race. "He is a fine-looking Indian," recorded Heber, "stands abt 6 feet high and is remarkably well built." Chief Manuelito willingly granted permission for the Latter-day Saint missionaries to proselyte among his people.

The apostles had originally planned to remain in this area for several weeks. They decided against it on discovering the scattered condition of Manuelito's people, who had no fixed habitation but roamed at will, remaining in one place only until the forage or game became scarce. Also, the travelers were weary after weeks of living on the ragged edge of civilization, and of late the incessant wind had almost become a morale factor, especially when it riled up the dust and sand. Such conditions were upsetting even to those who endured them regularly; to men like the two apostles, who ordinarily enjoyed the amenities of more gracious living, they were particularly stressful. An added burden was a painful attack of rheumatism that afflicted Elder Young. These, together with a feeling that their mission had about run its course, prompted the brethren to travel directly from Manuelito's camp to Wingate Station where they boarded a train for Albuquerque.

The party recuperated at this lonely railroad town for three days, during which time they weighed the alternatives of returning home or of going on to southern Arizona. The scales were tipped in favor of returning home by Brothers John W. and LeGrand Young, whom the apostles met in Albuquerque and who felt that Elder Young's physical condition was so poor as to warrant return. The ambivalence Heber felt toward this decision is reflected in this entry: "We have been talking of going home and taking all things into consideration among others brother B. Young's health, finally concluded to do so. The question came up about going home Tuesday evening and has been talked about ever since. I have stated from the first that to consult my own feelings I would say go on and carry out our programme and visit Southern Arizona. Bros. John W. & LeGrand have thought it best for us to return from the first. I finally concluded that all of the brethren thought it best for us to return and I said 'Let's go home.' Although my business needs me and I will be delighted to go home I must say that I dislike starting before our programme has been completed."

The decision having been made, the brethren lost little time carrying it into effect. They arrived home on Monday, April 23, 1883, completing an arduous mission that had occupied three and a half months, that had introduced the youngest apostle to the rigorous ministry he was to fill during the remainder of his life, and that, once and for all, had put to flight any lingering doubts about the divine nature of his call and the course his future life was to follow.

Chapter 8

The Imperious Mandate

From the day the Savior instructed the first
apostles just before his ascension, the apostolic
mandate has been clear. Reduced to its ele-
mental content, that mandate is: GO—go to
all the world and preach the gospel to every creature.

Heeding that injunction, the apostles of Jesus Christ
in all ages have toiled mightily to spread the gospel
through most of the civilized world. A wandering, nomadic existence seems always to have been the lot of
these special witnesses as they have traveled to countries
all over the globe, sharing the message of the true gospel.

Although he may not have realized it at the time, it
was to this kind of restless life that Heber Grant had
been called by President Taylor on that electrifying
October day in the Council House. His three-month
mission by rail, white-top, and horseback into the remote Indian country to the south was a preface to the
far-ranging and exhausting travels he would undertake
before the close of his apostolic career. The difficulty, the
extent, and the frequency of his travels over a period of
more than sixty years made him one of the foremost
world travelers of his generation.

At first his trips were usually to communities near
Salt Lake City, where he would instruct, reprove, and
encourage the Saints at quarterly stake conferences. Being a junior member of the Twelve, both in terms of
service and age, he at first often drew the more strenuous
and, in the eyes of many, the less desirable assignments,
jestingly characterized by some of those who followed
him in the apostleship as the "Phoenix in summer and
Alaska in winter" cycle.

However, the variety and depth of his business

activities and acquaintances caused Heber to travel more extensively in the early stages of his career than other apostles did. Thus, on May 18, 1883, he left by train for Chicago to attend to business and church affairs. It was his first trip to the East. His business objectives were to cement relationships with his insurance contacts, to induce them to deposit funds in Utah, and to negotiate an agency contract with a grocery jobber. Leaving Chicago, he traveled through Niagara Falls, Buffalo, and Erie to New York City, where, in addition to his business contacts, he renewed acquaintances with his uncle Augustus and his boyhood friend, Richard W. Young. Although the purpose of this trip was mainly business, he never missed an opportunity to instruct the Saints he met or to kindle friendships with nonmember business acquaintances or strangers.

Like any young father and husband who has been away on an exciting trip to distant places, Heber was met at Salt Lake's impressive Union Pacific Depot by his wife and three babies. But he barely had time to become reacquainted with his family and to pick up the threads of his church and business affairs at home before he had to travel to San Francisco to seek the favorable adjustment of a claim of one of his insurance clients, H. B. Clawson, whose business had been destroyed by fire on the night of June 21, 1883. An explosion of powder stored in Clawson's store spread the fire to neighboring buildings, including the Council House, which were heavily damaged or destroyed. A firebrand blown by the explosion set the Tabernacle roof afire, but it was extinguished before it caused substantial damage. Since the presence of powder on the Clawson premises violated the terms of the policy, Elder Grant was fearful that the insurance company would not pay the claim. This anxiety did not reckon with his skill and persuasiveness as a negotiator; the insurance officials in San Francisco gave all that he asked for. Typically, he did not take personal credit for this achievement. "I left the meeting feeling about as happy as a man possibly could," he wrote in jubilation, adding, in a more subdued tone, "my feelings were those of gratitude to our Heavenly Father as well as joy to know that Bro. Clawson would get his money."

Within days after returning from the West Coast, the young apostle was off on an extended trip into eastern Utah, where he was both to strengthen the people spiritually and to encourage them "to turn out and vote." A voting registration oath was required under the Edmunds law, but because such a small percentage of the Latter-day Saints were actually practicing plural marriage, the oath had little practical effect in nullifying their voting power. It was, however, psychologically intimidating to them, and this required constant effort on the part of the leaders to keep the Saints stirred up and motivated to exercise their franchise. This duty was not at all uncongenial to Heber's feelings, given his natural bent for politics and his persuasive, outgoing personality. Afterward he was able to vent his latent desire for public office when he was elected to the territorial legislature, the city council, and as a delegate to the territorial convention.

After trips into Davis, Tooele, and Utah counties in late summer and early fall, Heber prepared to join his companion, Elder Brigham Young, Jr., on another trip into Arizona to complete their mission that had been cut short by Elder Young's illness. The two apostles had arranged to rendezvous in Colorado Springs, where Elder Young had gone earlier for a brief vacation with his family. As Heber traveled alone, enjoying the mountain scenery that flashed by outside the Pullman window, he was caught up in a reverie, the mood of which is reflected in these thoughts from his journal: "Perhaps my realizing that I was leaving home for some time had something to do with the enjoyment of my ride through Salt Lake and Utah Counties. I certainly looked at the comfortable homes of our people and the lofty mountains on the east and the pleasant gardens and the farms and the fields with much more interest than I remember ever having done before in the many times I had passed and repassed over the same section of the country. While I am most partial to Utah scenery when the fields, gardens and side hills are green and the mountain tops covered with snow, yet I am free to confess that the

scenery of today has been pleasing to me with the snow
on the mountains but not enough on the side and foot-
hills to any more than cover the ground and not
sufficient to hide the beautiful autumnal tints on the
shrubbery. I cannot pass an opinion as I am not posted
on the subject but am persuaded that Utah in many
places can rival the far famed Switzerland when it comes
to 'autumnal tints.' "

The apostles spent a few pleasant days in Colorado
Springs, then plunged into the Arizona wilderness,
where they alternated in instructing the Saints and be-
friending the Indians, a ministry that was to occupy the
next two months.

During this trip, Heber celebrated his twenty-
seventh birthday. Of this event he wrote: "I have had
quite a number of ups and downs during the past
twenty-seven years. I should not care to live my life over
for fear of not doing any better. . . . The desires of my
heart this day are to live the life of a true servant of God,
to faithfully discharge the duties of my office in the
church, to do my duty to my fellowmen and especially
by my family. My heart is full of gratitude to God for
the wife, mother and children I am blessed with and I
hope to live worthy of them."

Also during this trip, Heber spent his first Christmas
away from home. In an entry written at Manassa while
the apostles were working their way toward Salt Lake
City, he could not hide the loneliness he felt: "Today has
not been a very merry Christmas for me and so far as I
am able to remember it is the first Christmas I have ever
spent away from home."

After returning from his second trip south, Heber
spent several months of relative inactivity, brought
about in part by an illness that kept him homebound for
almost a month and caused him to miss the April
general conference. He was sufficiently recovered to be
able to attend the dedication of the Logan Temple in
mid-May 1884, and toward the end of that month was
strong enough to undertake an arduous journey north
into the Snake River basin of Idaho with the president of
the Twelve, the indomitable Wilford Woodruff, who at

that time had served under the call of the imperious mandate for almost half a century. This pair, representing the oldest and youngest members of the Council of the Twelve, both in age and in years of service, made an interesting study in contrasts. President Woodruff, who was seventy-seven years old, gray, and weathered by time and experience, had been in the apostolic harness and had done some of his most effective proselyting work overseas many years before his young companion was born. Short and powerfully built, President Woodruff lacked the taste for business and commerce that was almost the lifeblood of his tall, spare companion, and, aside from his ministerial labors, was most content when tending his garden or orchard or writing in his voluminous journal, which spanned the five decades of his Church membership.

It was a source of inspiration and enlightenment to Heber to hear firsthand about the rise and growth of the Church from one who had been a confidant of the Prophet Joseph Smith and an eyewitness of many early significant events. The several weeks these companions spent together were ever to stand out in President Grant's mind as an essential link with the past. It was abundantly clear from the accounts of the older man, whose powers of observation and precise expression had been sharpened by a lifetime of teaching and faithful record-keeping, that the drama of the Restored Church had not been performed to an empty house. It had been enacted on center stage before a crowded audience. And Heber's narrator was an eyewitness of these events, a witness whose credibility was without chink or blemish. One could not gaze into the steady blue-gray eyes of President Wilford Woodruff, eyes alight with intelligence and energy, and question the truthfulness of his words. The testimony he bore that God is a living reality, that Jesus, his Son, is the Redeemer, and that Joseph Smith was and is a true prophet strengthened the convictions of the youngest apostle.

The brethren went by train from Salt Lake City to Market Lake, Idaho, where they were met May 30 by stake president Joseph Ricks, their guide and companion

for three weeks of traveling by team through the
Mormon settlements along the Snake and Teton rivers.
Following their customary pattern, they held meetings
wherever Saints were found in sufficient number. At
Rexburg, Wilford, Parker, Cedar Buttes, Lewisville,
Heath's Ranch, and Eagle Rock, the visitors exhorted
the members to be faithful and diligent and to live their
religion. They also gave practical advice about their
farming and ranching operations and their businesses.
Anything concerning the welfare of the people was
deemed by the apostles proper for counsel, commendation, rebuke, or exhortation.

The visitors were pleased with what they found in
the small Mormon communities. Everywhere the fruits
of industry were evident. Well-cultivated fields and orchards, neat homes and outhouses, and fat animals and
poultry were to be seen everywhere. Most important, the
people were energetic and self-confident, anxiously engaged in laying the groundwork of a kingdom they expected would one day be led in person by their monarch,
Jesus Christ. So impressed was Heber with the thriving
appearance of the King's City, Rexburg, that he
recorded a detailed description of it, concluding:
"Rexburg is only a little over one year old and the
amount of labor that has been done in this length of
time, considering the limited number of men that have
done it, is really remarkable."

Following his return from Idaho, Heber enjoyed a
brief respite with his family at Soda Springs in southern
Idaho. Then in mid-September he set out for a two-week
swing through southern Utah, where conferences were
held at Orderville, Milford, Panguitch, and Kanab. At
Orderville, he and his companion, Brigham Young, Jr.,
held meetings that they had expected would be difficult
and stormy, but that developed into councils of peace
and high spirituality. It was in this place that a plan of
communal living, the united order, had been inaugu-
rated several years before. Based upon the subordination
of personal wants to the interests of the whole, this novel
experiment, which had its origins in a revelation received by the Prophet Joseph Smith, had been tried with

varying degrees of success in other places. Nowhere, however, had it been carried on as long or with such success as in this remote community whose name implied its main purpose. But reports of dissension and misunderstandings had prompted President Taylor to instruct the two apostles to observe the feelings of the people and, if necessary, dissolve the communal organization.

Because of the briefings given them, the two visitors were prepared for the worst and were pleased and somewhat surprised at the way matters turned out. Much of their success can be traced to the perception with which they approached the problem, a model for anyone who seeks to bring harmony out of group dissension.

"We called upon the people to express their feelings freely," Heber recorded, "as to whether they wished to continue in the United Order or not. We informed them that our mission was to assist them in doing whatever they wished to do. . . . The sisters as well as the brethren were called upon to state their feelings." This airing of the problems revealed that most were in favor of continuing with the communal effort but only if "the present system [were] changed and more responsibility . . . placed upon the individual members."

Once the pent-up aggravations and hostilities had been vented and the problems brought into focus, a feeling of peace and accord came upon the Saints. Of the meeting that followed, Heber said: "We had an excellent spirit present. I can't recall attending a meeting where I felt that more of the kind and peaceful influence of the good spirit was present than I did this evening. It was decided by a unanimous vote to continue working in the United Order under the system of stewardships as found in the Doctrine and Covenants." In summing up the results achieved in Orderville, he observed reflectively: "I have been thankful that our labors were successful. I don't know but what I should say we accomplished our mission without any labor. My heart is full of gratitude to think our Heavenly Father prepared the saints to continue to work unitedly without any counsel on our part. My mission to Orderville will always be one of the

events in my life which I can recall with feelings of satisfaction and pleasure."

A relatively quiet three-week interlude followed the
journey south, during which elaborate plans were formu-
lated for what would prove to be one of the most
unusual excursions of Heber's long career—a somewhat
perilous trip to the Yaqui Indian nation in Sonora,
Mexico. Reflecting the intense pressure generated by the
Edmunds Act, he defined the purpose as follows: "Our
trip into Sonora is for the purpose of visiting the chief
man of the Yaqui Indian Nation and to try and find a
place on the upper Yaqui for a settlement. One of the
objects for wishing a settlement in Sonora is that when
our brethren are indicted for polygamy [they] can locate
in [it] and thus save the trouble of a law suit, in other
words to find a place for a City of Refuge."

These words were written on November 25, 1884, in
the then scruffy border town of Nogales, Arizona, where
the expedition was being grouped for the journey into
the heart of lonely Sonora. Heber and his companion,
Brigham Young, Jr., there assembled twenty-one men
from the Salt River and Gila Valleys to accompany
them into Mexico. Names familar to anyone acquainted
with the early history of the Latter-day Saints in
southern Arizona studded the expedition roster: a Mc-
Donald, a Peterson, and a Kimball from Mesa; a Rogers
and a Collett from Lehi; a Merrill from St. David; and a
Brinkerhoff from Thatcher.

Once all preparations had been made, the visas
cleared, the equipment insured, the military-style organization perfected, and the necessary maps and interpreters collected, the expedition crossed the border into
Sonora and commenced its tedious desert journey
toward the Yaqui nation. Heber's journal entry for
November 27, 1884, reveals the excitement and the personal historic sense this trip inspired: "Yesterday for the
first time in my life I put foot on the soil of a foreign
country."

The novelty of traveling in a foreign land sharpened
his perceptions. He was fascinated by the oranges, dates,
and figs growing in the oasislike communities along the

way. However, due to an epidemic of yellow fever then raging in Sonora, the travelers avoided entering these villages when possible. The natural desert vegetation, the Joshua trees, saguaros, and other cacti also drew his attention. One day's travel was enlivened by an encounter with a herd of wild bulls.

Passing through Magdalena, the party reached the capital city of Hermosillo, where the apostles conferred with the governor and other civil and military leaders. One Mexican officer ventured the chilling prediction that it would be "sure death" to go among the Yaqui. A base camp was established outside Hermosillo from which some of the brethren, led by Elder Young, traveled to Guaymas on the Gulf of California and thence into the heart of the Yaqui nation. Heber was asked to remain in charge of the base camp.

The ten days Heber's party remained in camp were trying ones. Boredom, added to concern about the yellow fever epidemic that had reduced Hermosillo's population by about five thousand, made the wait seem inordinately long. Heber's discomfort was intensified by painful boils, which made walking difficult and sleep almost impossible.

When at last Elder Young returned, he too had boils and was otherwise in poor health. This, along with the disappointing outcome of the negotiations with the Yaqui chiefs, caused the apostles to leave Mexico in a dispirited frame of mind. Traveling by train and white-top, they covered the distance from Hermosillo to Salt Lake City in five days, arriving home on December 20, in time for Christmas.

The almost ceaseless travels of Elder Grant during the first several years of his apostolic ministry were an accurate index to his future. Like the other members of his quorum, past and present, he was constantly in motion. There was no obstacle, no adversity, no inconvenience that could deter him; and no worldly attractions could entice him from the duty, the mandate, that had called him out of the world and set him on an exhilarating course that would slacken only with his death.

Chapter 9

The Underground

Heber J. Grant's induction into the Twelve occurred only months after the dark shadow of the Edmunds Act fell upon the Church, signaling the end of thirty-five years of comparative peace and heralding the opening of one of the stormiest chapters in Mormon history.

The Saints' search for immunity from the penalties of the Edmunds Act was not a malignant intent to subvert the law. Instead, it was a delaying, rear-guard action to buy time, during which they hoped to prove through legal means that the act, and the extraordinary means used to enforce it, were unconstitutional, infringing upon their rights and singling them out for special punitive treatment. It was only when all legal remedies had been exhausted, and the inexorable force of the law, as enlarged by the Edmunds-Tucker Act of 1887, had disenfranchised them, escheated the properties of the Church, and scattered or imprisoned their leaders, that they capitulated.

As the Mormon leaders prepared for the night of darkness brought on by the Edmunds Act, they adopted methods and strategies intended to help them avoid prosecution and imprisonment.

The older leaders, such as the First Presidency—John Taylor, George Q. Cannon, and Joseph F. Smith—who had openly lived in polygamy for years, were the most vulnerable, since evidence of their actions was readily available from many sources. These leaders dropped from public view to the underground, where they lived guarded, surreptitious lives, making only occasional and unannounced public appearances. Presidents Taylor and Cannon moved covertly from place to place, mostly

in Salt Lake and Davis counties, frequently using dis-
guises and pseudonyms and usually moving under the
cloak of night. President Smith, on the other hand, took
up temporary residence in Hawaii, living among the
members he had been instrumental in converting years
before when he had served as a teenage missionary. The
First Presidency gave direction to the Church as best
they could from the remote seclusion of their hideaways.
They depended largely on the Twelve to act as couriers
or mouthpieces for them, carrying or reading their
messages to the Saints. The general conferences, which,
during the crusade, were usually held either in Logan or
Provo, provided the best forum for the reading of these
messages.

During the first nineteen months of his ministry as an
apostle, Heber was admirably suited to perform these
duties for the First Presidency, as he had but one wife.
Thus he could move about with freedom and without
fear. This was only a temporary condition, however,
since he had planned from childhood to live in
polygamy.

The step into polygamy was a difficult one for Heber
to take. Naturally shy with women, it was an enormous
personal adjustment for him to undertake the delicate
maneuvers of a courtship with one woman while married to another. Always chivalrous toward Lucy and
sensitive to her feelings, he sought her consent before going forward. With Lucy's full approval he was sealed in
1884 to Hulda Augusta Winters and Emily Harris Wells
in the Endowment House. A year after these sealings,
Emily went to Liverpool, England, where, a few months
later, she gave birth to Heber's daughter. His journal
failed to record, except obliquely, the sadness he felt at
sending Emily away to England and his concern in not
being able to recognize and honor his polygamous wives
openly. It did not reveal, except dimly, the feelings of
anger he had toward the enemies of the Church. All this
and much more never found its way into his journal, at
the time, at least, because he was fearful it would fall
into the hands of enemies who would use it to convict
and imprison him as a polygamist. Those fears were

grounded in concern for his family and the Church as well as the personal abhorrence he had for prison and the loss of personal freedom.

But while his personal difficulties and fears were largely concealed, Heber's journal etches a clear picture of the apprehensions that gripped his brethren during this night of darkness. These men were hounded by implacable adversaries whose goal seemed to be the subjugation of the Latter-day Saints and the extinction of the Church. The brethren were prosecuted ruthlessly and imprisoned by the hundreds despite the unsettling effect this had upon family life and the economy.

While the brethren were able to keep up their spirits and self-confidence in the face of great difficulties, it often required unusual effort to endure the humiliation heaped upon them by men who never lost an opportunity to cast aspersions on them because of polygamy. A guard who insulted Heber when he visited Elder Lorenzo Snow in prison is a case in point. This man once had been caught in the act of adultery, yet he badgered the brethren, insinuating that their polygamy was a degradation and his promiscuity a virtue.

In contrast to this immorality, the following entry from Heber's journal reveals the nature of the feelings he had toward his wives: "From my experience of the past three years I am convinced that plural marriage is the *greatest trial* on earth for any woman to endure and having come to this conclusion I have made up my mind *firmly* with the help of my Heavenly Father to do *all* in my power to make the trial to my wives as light as it is possible for me to do. Thank God that I have wives with faith in the gospel and who desire to do all they can to aid me in my endeavors to perform the duties of life devolving upon me." In commenting on a problem faced by one of his wives, the concerned husband noted: "I am thankful to feel that I have her confidence and love, and trust that I may always retain these. I pray with all my heart and soul that no word or act of mine may ever cause her to regret the step she took when uniting her life to mine for time and eternity."

These tender sentiments reflect the character of a

man who was determined to live the highest laws of morality. This character was typical of most polygamists; it was the source of much of their strength. It was rooted in a conviction that strict morality is essential to attain exaltation, a status in which they hoped to share with the Savior all that the Father has. The doctrine of plural wives was not something they had sought after; it had been given to them by divine command. They understood it was a requirement of exaltation. This explains the tenacity with which the Saints clung to the practice for more than a quarter-century after the first anti-polygamy law was enacted in 1862. It explains their willingness to endure every type of indignity and humiliation, including imprisonment and, if necessary, death, to demonstrate their worthiness to receive the prize they sought.

The main thrust of the Edmunds Act of 1882 was political. Its authors believed that the voting registration oath it required and the vigorous enforcement of its criminal sanctions would siphon political power from the Latter-day Saints to their enemies and leave the Mormons leaderless. According to this plan, the residue of the Saints would supposedly be pliable and submit placidly to the ring of gentiles and apostates who had devised the act.

It soon became evident that this scheme was based upon a gross miscalculation. It did not reckon with the adroitness and tenacity of the Latter-day Saints, and with the depth of commitment of their leaders. While directing the Church from the underground presented vast problems of communication to the First Presidency, these difficulties were not insoluble. Indeed, it was discovered, somewhat to the surprise of the Mormon elders, that leadership by remote control had much to recommend itself. The mechanical difficulties of working through subordinates and the lack of personal contact were offset by an increase in devotion produced by the external pressures, and by a certain energetic ferment that seemed to arise from the mysterious aura of men living subterranean lives. Thus the words of a hunted, beleaguered prophet, whose absence alone spoke elo-

quently of his convictions, often carried more weight
when read by a devoted subordinate who had just come
from his presence than if he had delivered the message in
person. As long as the lines of priesthood authority
remained intact and the Church's facilities and resources
were undisturbed, the work strengthened and went forward as before.

To increase the internal strength he knew would be
necessary to weather the storm of the Edmunds Act,
President Taylor undertook three important initiatives.
First, through the Twelve and other trusted subordinates, he urged the Saints to vote and make their
influence felt at the polls. Hence they retained a strong
voice in local governmental affairs, except in federally
appointed offices where, generally speaking, Mormon-
hating carpetbaggers were in control. Second, he required those who held positions of important leadership
to live in polygamy. This closed the ranks on this important issue and ensured that the leaders were of one
voice and one mind on it. And third, he reinstituted the
School of the Prophets, an organization created by Joseph Smith in Kirtland, Ohio, in the 1830s. The purpose
of the school was to train and discipline the high leaders
of the Church in important doctrinal and spiritual matters. It was largely the influence of the school that had
enabled the Prophet to develop such cohesiveness and
esprit de corps among his followers, thus establishing the
Church solidly and setting it on the course President
Taylor was then steering. Having been a member of that
school, and having seen the profound influence it had
exerted, President Taylor felt the need to invoke its aid
in this crisis. He therefore assembled the First Presidency, the Twelve, twenty stake presidents, and four
others in the Endowment House on Friday, October 12,
1883, at which time he performed the ordinances and
gave the instructions pertaining to this unique body.

The events of the school had a profound effect upon
Heber J. Grant and the other brethren who attended,
steeling them for the trying days of the underground
ahead and providing an impetus to direct them
throughout their lives. Of these meetings, the young

apostle wrote: "Today has been an eventful one in the
history of our church—viz. it has witnessed the reorganization of the School of the Prophets. Our meetings since
Monday have been as interesting if not the most interesting to me of any I have ever attended in my life. They
have been times of rejoicing, a feast of fat things for the
lovers of the gospel. For several days when I met any of
the brethren that had attended our meetings in the
Social Hall, at Prest. Taylor's office, or in the Endowment House, they were almost sure to make some such
remarks as 'what splendid times we are having'; 'our
meetings are glorious'; 'I rejoice that I am worthy of attending these meetings' etc. etc. I shall try with the help
of our Heavenly Father to live in such a manner that the
blessings pronounced on me this day . . . may always be
the truth."

Within a few months another spiritual milestone was
reached, as the Logan Temple was dedicated in May
1884. Built at great sacrifice over a seven-year period,
this edifice symbolized not only the faith and diligence
of the Saints but also their reach for divinity and the
sense of responsibility they felt toward their kindred
dead. Assembled for these impressive services were the
First Presidency, the Twelve, and other General Authorities. At the time, the anti-Mormon crusade had not
yet shifted into high gear, so the Brethren were able to
move about with comparative freedom.

The dedicatory services were held in the assembly
room on the top floor of the temple, which seated about
fifteen hundred. The room was filled at each of the
several dedicatory sessions with members from many
areas of the Church. Because of the relatively large seat-
ing capacity and the controlled access to the temple,
several general conferences were held there during the
succeeding years of the crusade.

A few months after the dedication, the pressures had
become so intense that it was necessary for the First
Presidency and the Twelve to discontinue the weekly
council meetings they had held for years. By the first of
February, 1885, conditions had deteriorated to the point
that members of the First Presidency were forced to dis-

continue their public appearances entirely. During this
period President Taylor became a literal exile in his own
country, under the necessity of living an entirely covert
life.

Also during this period, the anti-Mormon crusaders
realized that the Edmunds Act needed more teeth if it
were to achieve its intended purpose, so they began to
agitate for amendment. The punitive amendments they
sought, ultimately incorporated in the Edmunds-Tucker
bill of 1887, included the creation of a federal board to
control voting registration and the election machinery of
the territory; abolition of the Perpetual Emigration
Fund Company; abolition of woman suffrage; dissolution of the Church as a corporation; abolition of the
Nauvoo Legion; establishment of an odious test oath for
voters; and provision for escheat of most of the Church
properties.

The Church carefully monitored the congressional
committee meetings that considered proposals to amend
the Edmunds Act of 1882. Church attorney Franklin S.
Richards spent much time in Washington during these
days, keeping his ear to the ground to detect the shifting
tide of opinion toward his people. Becoming convinced
that the Edmunds-Tucker bill would be passed with its
repressive measures against the Latter-day Saints intact,
he warned the Brethren: "Wisdom that church dispose
of as much of its property as possible."

Acting on this advice, the Church leaders imple-
mented a plan that had been previously discussed and
approved. It involved the creation of numerous local
"Church Associations" to which many of the ecclesiastical facilities and assets were transferred. In many
cases, these were used to construct and maintain academies. In addition, the Church began to divest itself of
its nonecclesiastical holdings. This aspect of the divestiture made it possible for Heber J. Grant to realize one of
his many boyhood goals. He spearheaded the move to
create a syndicate that acquired the Church's interest in
Zions' Cooperative Mercantile Institution (ZCMI).
When this transfer was completed and he had been
elected to the board as one of the principal stockholders

of the restructured company, he reflectively noted: "On the 11th [April 1886] I attended my first meeting as a director of ZCMI. I was duly elected a few days before. When a young man one of the dreams of my life was to be a director of this institution & I made up my mind to try and get there before I was thirty years of age, but when I was called to Tooele in October 1880, I dismissed all such hopes from my mind and they had not entered again until since my election. I find myself a director and lacking a little over [seven months] of being thirty."

The prediction of the Church attorney and the fears of the Saints were realized when on March 3, 1887, the Edmunds-Tucker Act became law without the signature of President Grover Cleveland. Most knowledgeable members recognized that its enactment sounded the death knell of polygamy in the United States. The disincorporation of the Church and the power provided by the act to escheat its properties were like giant pincers, inexorably bringing the Church and its leaders to their knees on this vital issue.

Once the power to deliver a crushing blow was in their hands, the government lawyers moved quickly. By July they had marshaled the facts and prepared the pleadings so that on the 26th of that month the escheatment action was filed in the courts. Ironically, President John Taylor, who had resisted the mounting tide so long, died the day before; and two days before, the Latter-day Saints had celebrated the fortieth anniversary of the arrival of the pioneers in the Salt Lake Valley. Most Saints considered President Taylor to be a victim of the callous zeal of the crusaders, and the bleak prospect ahead caused some to wonder how many more anniversaries they would be privileged to celebrate. There was widespread speculation about a mass exodus beyond the borders of the United States.

Once the ponderous legal machinery had been set in motion, it was only a matter of time until its purpose was achieved. All of the main assets of the Church, including the sacred temple block, were ultimately possessed by the court-appointed receiver. It was a travesty to the Saints that they had to pay an annual rental to the receiver for the use of the buildings they had sacrificed so much to construct. Moreover, the harassment of polygamists by the crusaders accelerated and intensified as they commenced to use the new tools of repression provided by the Edmunds-Tucker Act. The perverse ingenuity of local officials brought new terror to the beleaguered Mormons.

When the United States Supreme Court upheld the constitutionality of the Edmunds-Tucker Act in a test case, the handwriting on the wall was clear. The Church had been disincorporated; its properties were escheated; the Perpetual Emigration Fund, which had fueled migration to the United States, was no more; most of the key leaders were in prison, on the underground, or under indictment; and the members on the whole were dispirited and weary after almost thirty years of continual harassment and intimidation. During this period nearly thirteen hundred Latter-day Saints were imprisoned rather than renounce their wives and the solemn covenants they had made; and they faced the dreary prospect of more of the same, except on a magnified scale.

Facing this reality, and after long, prayerful strugglings, Wilford Woodruff, who had been sustained as the fourth president of the Church in the preceding year, made this historic entry in his journal under date of September 25, 1890: "I have arrived at a point in the history of my life as the president of The Church of Jesus Christ of Latter-day Saints when I am under the necessity of acting for the temporal salvation of the Church. The United States Government has taken a stand and passed laws to destroy the Latter-day Saints on the subject of polygamy, or patriarchal order of marriage; and after praying to the Lord and feeling inspired, I have issued the following proclamation which is sustained by my counselors and the Twelve Apostles." Then followed verbatim the "Official Declaration" or "Manifesto" by which the practice of polygamy was suspended among the Latter-day Saints. This was unanimously adopted by the Saints at the general conference held in the first week of October 1890. In a lengthy, well-reasoned sermon delivered at the conference session where the Manifesto was approved, President George Q. Cannon presented the doctrinal reasons to support the action. He cited Doctrine and Covenants 124:49, relieving "the sons of men" from a godly mandate in circumstances where they "go with all their might and with all they have to perform that work, and cease not their diligence, and their enemies come upon them and hinder them from performing that work." Surveying the nightmare of the past twenty-eight years, during which the Church had been under constant, unremitting pressure from the enemies of polygamy, the venerable leader declared, in effect, "It is enough; God has accepted your offering." Finally, to settle the minds of those who may have been troubled at the thought of turning their backs on a principle that had been given to them by heavenly mandate, he pointed out that the voice that commanded had the power to rescind. It was true that two different men were involved—Joseph Smith, who had uttered the command, and Wilford Woodruff, who had revoked it—but they were merely acting as agents, as mouthpieces, for the same principal, Jesus Christ, whom they recognized as the actual head of the Church. Consequently, the word of Wilford Woodruff directing a cessation of the practice of polygamy was as binding upon the Saints as had been the word of Joseph Smith ordering its commencement. The failure of many to grasp this basic distinction produced violent aftershocks for over a decade following the Manifesto, the destructive effect of which reached even into the highest councils of the Church.

Chapter 10

Aftermath

The removal of a principal cause of the persecution directed toward the Latter-day Saints did not eliminate the deep wounds and the trauma it had inflicted. While the Manifesto barred future polygamous marriages, it did not affect those that had already been contracted. Thus in the eyes of the Church those already living in polygamy at the time, who had contracted their plural marriages with Church approval, were accepted in fellowship although they were in violation of the law and still subject to its criminal sanctions. The brethren who were unwilling to put away their polygamous wives were, therefore, still under the necessity of living covertly to avoid prosecution. In time, however, the crusade lost its venomous tone and the laws were enforced more realistically and, toward the end, with a little compassion. Even Chief Justice Charles S. Zane, who was in the forefront of those who had enforced the laws with pitiless rigidity, softened his attitudes, as shown in a statement printed in the December 13, 1890, issue of the *Deseret News Weekly*. "It is idle now," said the Justice, "to think of disfranchising the Latter-day Saints. They are an industrious, temperate people, as a rule; and my observation has led me to believe that they are law-abiding since the church took its stand under the law against plural marriage." He even joined in a petition for amnesty, which was granted by President Benjamin Harrison in January 1893. A much broader amnesty was granted by President Grover Cleveland on September 25, 1894.

In the meantime, the legal machinery ground ever so slowly to reverse the process of escheatment, to reestablish the Church as a corporate entity, and to reinvest it with title to its properties. When this had been accomplished, the Church was ready once more to pursue, without undue impediment, its ambitious goal of converting and perfecting the world.

As these momentous happenings took place, Heber J. Grant was heavily involved not only in helping untangle the legal snarls that the antipolygamy laws and the Manifesto had produced, but also in some of the most trying days he was to experience in his personal life.

At the time of the Manifesto, Heber was the father of nine children, eight daughters and a son. Lucy, his first wife, had borne five girls: Susan Rachel, fondly called Ray, age twelve; Lucy, whose nickname was Lutie, age ten; Florence, seven; Edith, five; Anna, four; and baby Heber Stringham, the pet of the family, two. Augusta had given birth to a baby girl, Mary, the year before. By 1890, Emily had given birth to two daughters, Martha Deseret, called Dessie, age four, and Grace, age two. There were to be only three children added to Heber's family after the Manifesto, all through Emily: Daniel Wells, who was born in 1891 and died four years later; Emily, born in 1896; and Frances Marion, born in 1899.

It was not a simple matter to care for this large and expensive family. It was tantamount to financing three separate households. Since the Church provided only a nominal living allowance for the General Authorities, Heber had to generate most of the funds to cover his burgeoning expenses. While he had a natural talent as an entrepreneur and businessman and did exceptionally well at it, the increasing financial drain, the economic depression resulting from the crusade, and the uncertainties arising from the Manifesto and its aftermath exerted ever-increasing pressures. Added to this, of course, were the frustration and trauma, even the tragedy, inherent in the personal lives and relationships of such a large family.

It was about the time of the Manifesto that Lucy's health began to fail. Although she was only thirty-two years old at the time, her body and spirits were worn from having given birth to six children in the thirteen years of her marriage, from the tension of polygamy, from the fear that her husband and supporter would be imprisoned, from the mounting terror of the crusade, from the burden of filling the role of both mother and father during her husband's long absences, and from the uncertainties looming up in her dimly lit future. All these things, plus the ravages of a debilitating illness, combined to convert the once healthy and radiant Lucy into an almost helpless invalid. Once during the three years of her illness she was hospitalized for six consecutive months.

Heber was very solicitous toward Lucy during this critical period. He spent almost every spare minute at her side, giving comfort and encouragement. During her long hospitalization, he often spent the night at the hospital so he would be near if she needed him. No effort or expense was spared in giving her the best care available.

As time wore on and it became apparent that Lucy might not recover, she and Heber passed through a Gethsemane that brought untold physical pain to her, and to him, some of the greatest spiritual and mental anguish he was ever to endure. His poignant journal entries during the period reflect his tender love for his companion, the depth of his sorrow, and his mounting concern as the reality of her impending death bore in upon him. "Lucy is quite poorly this afternoon," he wrote on November 23, 1892. "I have shed some bitter tears this afternoon as Lucy feels that she cannot get well and as she suffers so much she has little desire to recover. She has eaten almost nothing for nearly two weeks and in chatting today with her sister Julia, we both felt that she can't possibly live long unless there is a change in her condition. I fasted and prayed for Lucy this morning."

While the concerned husband seemed to know deep down that Lucy's time was near, he resisted the idea and continued to bend his powerful faith toward a recovery. He wrote: "Lucy feels that she cannot possibly get well and we have had some serious conversations today and have both shed tears at our contemplated separation. I can't help fearing that her life is not going to be spared & yet it is impossible for me to get the impression out of my mind that her life is going to be spared to me and her children. In case of death she does not want her children separated and wants me to see that they all learn how to do some kind of work so that if they ever have to earn their own living they will not be at a loss to know how to do so."

Lucy's children were most distraught over her illness. While they tried hard to keep up the appearance of bravery and cheerfulness in the presence of their mother, this was not always possible. A touching entry made by their father on December 4, 1892, reflects the agony and dismay that Lucy's illness produced in her children: "This has been a sad day for me, as Lucy has been quite poorly. Ray and all of the children except Florence who is sick have been down today. Lutie has been down a number of times. She came down about five thirty and while kissing her mama she broke down and cried like her poor little heart would break. She has been with Lucy so much of the time during her sickness and has been so hopeful that she can't stand it to see her mama getting worse by the day and to have the fear that she is not going to recover. Ray cried while she was here but was careful not to allow her mama to see her. It is a fearful trial to me to think of our darling children being left without a mother. This afternoon between three and four Lucy said she felt that she was being held here by faith and that her sufferings were more than she could endure and she would be very thankful to be released."

The grieving husband and children clung to their ailing wife and mother for another month, during which her energies abated and her generative fires began to flicker out. At the end her body took on an almost skeletal form because she could not eat and assimilate food.

When it became obvious Lucy could not live, Heber accepted the fact sorrowfully and commenced to prepare for the end. After her comfort, his first concern was the children. Youth and inexperience had ill prepared them for the shock of losing a beloved parent. Lutie was especially distraught. She could not understand why her father, whose priesthood authority she had seen powerfully exercised in the past, could not now invoke

heavenly blessings to heal her mother. Heber's answer, a
reminder that death comes to all sooner or later, was
hardly satisfying to a twelve-year-old who passionately
wanted her mother to live.

Faced with the problem of reconciling his children's
anguish with the hard reality of a death he knew was im-
minent, Heber resorted to the device he always used in
times of distress. Apart from his children, he sought God
in fervent prayer. "I knelt down by the bed of my dying
wife," he wrote, "and told the Lord that I acknowledged
his hand in life or in death, in joy or in sorrow, in prosperity or adversity; that I did not complain because my
wife was dying, but that I lacked the strength to see my
wife die and have her death affect the faith of my
children in the ordinances of the gospel. I therefore
pleaded with him to give to my daughter Lutie a testimony that it was his will that her mother should die.
Within a few short hours, my wife breathed her last.
Then I called the children into the bedroom and announced that their mamma was dead. My little boy,
Heber, commenced weeping bitterly, and Lutie put her
arms around him and kissed him, and told him not to
cry, that the voice of the Lord had said to her, 'In the
death of your mamma the will of the Lord will be done.'
Lutie knew nothing of my prayers, and this manifestation to her was a direct answer to my supplication to the
Lord, and for it I have never ceased to be grateful."
(*Improvement Era,* June 1912, pp. 726-27.)

Lucy passed away on January 3, 1893, and was
buried three days later by a saddened but comforted
family. The older girls were mature enough to assume
much of the responsibility in caring for the younger
children, and with Augusta and Emily near, aided by
faithful domestic employees to help manage the
household, the children were kept together as Lucy had
desired.

With the passing of their mother, Heber made a special effort to spend extra time with the children to compensate for their great loss. It was with this in mind that
he planned to take the three oldest daughters, Ray,
Lutie, and Florence, with him on a trip to Chicago, New

York, Boston, and Washington. He wanted them to see the sights of these great cities, which he believed would "lessen the great sorrow which had come into their lives in the death of their mama." However, instead of being the fulfillment of a dream, a balm to heal the deep wound inflicted by their mother's death, the trip turned into a nightmare for the children and their disheartened father. While they were at Washington, hardly before the trip had gotten well underway, Lutie and Ray came down with diphtheria. Lutie was especially ill, her pulse beating only twenty-eight times per minute. Driven to his knees by a danger that was then a bafflement to medical science, and feeling alone and helpless, the harried father was supplicating the Lord, "shedding bitter tears, when the inspiration came that if I would send out for President George Q. Cannon and Bishop Hiram B. Clawson, who were then in Washington, that as they held the Priesthood, they could rebuke the disease, and that my daughter would live." Responding to the call, President Cannon and Bishop Clawson gave a blessing to the ailing girl, in the course of which President Cannon, who acted as mouth in the blessing, said something startling and wholly unexpected. "In blessing Lutie," Heber recorded, President Cannon stated "that the adversary had decreed her death and made public announcement of his decree. I subsequently learned that the lady who was the proprietor of the boarding house was a spiritualist, and that she had visited her medium and asked her to tell her what was going to happen in her home. The medium told of the sickness of two little girls, that the older of the two had been nigh unto death, but would recover. She told her that she saw the second little girl get worse and worse, and finally die. She described taking the body out of the house, and the coffin being put upon the railroad train, and the railroad train going hundreds and hundreds of miles toward the west, and then she described the train going over the high mountains and then stopping in a valley and the coffin being taken off the train and then taken to a burial ground upon the hillside, where she saw it lowered into a grave." (*Improvement Era*, June 1912, pp. 727-28.)

The near tragedy in Washington was only Act One in a drama that ended months later in Salt Lake City and that almost prevented Heber from participating in the dedication of the Salt Lake Temple in early April. While Ray and Lutie left behind in Washington the terrible memories of their illness, they brought with them the seeds of the disease that had taken them to death's door, infecting several of Heber's other children. So ill were they that it became necessary to hospitalize some of them, both to prevent a further spread of the disease and to provide the professional care lacking in the home.

Finally this optimistic journal entry signaled the end of the nightmare: "After the afternoon meeting on the 13th (of April) Prest. Cannon referred to my trouble with my children having the diphtheria in Washington and since I had come home to have some of the others come down and he prophesied that I should have my sins forgiven and soon be out of the deep water that I was now in on account of the sickness of my children. All of my little ones having been preserved to me and their lives spared from the disease of diphtheria, I feel to acknowledge that Prest. Cannon's promise has been fulfilled."

Lucy's death and the subsequent serious illness of her children made a lasting impression on Heber, deepening his spiritual sensitivities, mellowing his fiery temperament, and magnifying the qualities of love and solicitous concern for the welfare of others that were inherent in his character. These events were also a harsh schoolmaster, preparing him for yet another trauma that lay ahead less than three years away, the death of his namesake, Heber Stringham Grant, a son of promise in whom Heber set great store. The story of his precious son's death is best told in Heber's own words:

"When my son Heber was dying, notwithstanding I had builded great hopes upon his future life and he was my only living son, I never experienced a more peaceful, calm spirit, than was in my home. I was sitting by the little boy, expecting every moment would be the last. Between me and . . . Augusta was a vacant chair, and as I was sitting there, the impression came over me that my boy's mother was occupying the vacant chair, waiting for him to breathe his last. I turned to Augusta and spoke of the peaceful influence that I felt, that there was apparently no death in the room, and asked her how she felt. She said her feelings were the same as mine, and she had the impression that Lucy was in the chair between us, waiting for Heber's death. When Heber was dying, they came and woke me up. I had just finished having a dream. The dream was that while I was sleeping, a messenger came in company with my wife Lucy, and she instructed him to carefully take Heber out of bed, that she had come for him, and she wanted him to go with her, and the messenger was to take him so quietly that I would not be disturbed. In my dream, I jumped up out of bed immediately, and took hold of my boy. The messenger who was acting under Lucy's instructions to take him away had a struggle with me, and I succeeded in wrenching Heber away from him. But in doing so, I fell, and I fell upon him; and very seriously injured his limb, from which he had been suffering so long with hip disease. His cries of agony pierced my very soul, and I got to thinking, 'What if I have injured him, and made him lame for all the days of his life? It would have been better to have let his mother take him.' I felt quite sad to think I had not consented to my boy being taken by his mother. I walked out of the house and wandered around the streets, and happened to meet Brother Joseph E. Taylor. I told him of Lucy coming to the house to try to get her boy, and of the struggle that I had had with the messenger. He spoke of the fact that a mother has to offer her life upon the altar of sacrifice to bring her children into the world, and he said to me, 'Brother Grant, much as I like to keep my children on this earth, I believe if the mother of any of my children were to come for her child, I certainly would raise no objections. I do not think there should be any family quarrels over a matter of this kind.' I walked home with the feeling in my heart that if Lucy returned again, she could have her boy. I had just come to this conclusion in my dream when I was awakened, and the information was given to me that Heber was dying; and a subsequent impression which both Augusta and I received, that his mother was sitting between us waiting for death, was in confirmation of my dream." (*Improvement Era,* June 1912, pp. 728-29.)

Having received this spiritual assurance, Heber, who had built such great hopes on this son, hoping "to see him a missionary proclaiming the gospel of Jesus Christ and a power for good upon the earth," was able to see him die without shedding a tear. Years later in reflecting upon the incident, the grateful father noted with his customary fervor: "No power on earth could have given to me this peace. It was of God. And I can never speak of it or write of it without feelings of gratitude filling my heart, far beyond any power with which I am endowed to express my feelings." (Ibid., p. 730.)

Except for his two Emilys—his wife, who died in 1908, and his daughter, who died in 1929—Heber was not to experience again the sadness of death within his inner family circle. The other nine daughters and Augusta all outlived him. His ever-increasing progeny, grandchildren and great-grandchildren, with their companions and offspring, fulfilled an innate yearning to achieve the patriarchal status occupied by the ancient biblical prophets. All this helped to mute the scenes of tragedy and alarm that marked the years in the aftermath of the Manifesto.

Chapter 11

The Winds of Business

The dominant qualities in Heber J. Grant's makeup—forthrightness, self-confidence, faith, and persistence—were evident from the time he was a young boy. The startling incident when he shook his fist and vowed to buy back the family home, his perseverance in learning to write and to play baseball, and his determination to reach goals in matrimony, in business, and in politics all testify of the underlying character of the man who ultimately was to rise to the pinnacle of authority and power in The Church of Jesus Christ of Latter-day Saints.

Given this basic character, it is not surprising that the scriptural personage who exerted the most profound influence upon Heber was the one whose personality and works most resembled his own—Nephi of the Book of Mormon. The maturing young prophet assiduously followed the lead of this hero. He frequently wrote and spoke about him in the most laudatory, even worshipful, terms, as evidenced in these words he uttered from the pulpit of the Tabernacle at general conference in October 1899: "There is no character with which I have been familiar through my reading that has inspired me more than has Nephi of old. I can never read the life of that man without being inspired with a desire to be faithful, diligent and true to the Lord, that I may be abundantly blessed of the Lord, as was Nephi. If we all could be inspired with a determination to live as this man lived, there is no question in my mind but we would grow and increase in the Spirit of God, and in power and ability to do the will of our Heavenly Father on the earth."

Writing for the *Improvement Era* as an old man, he

voiced similar sentiments in different words: "If you have ambitions, dream of what you wish to accomplish, and then put your shoulder to the wheel and work. Daydreams without work do not amount to anything; it is the actual work that counts. Faith without works is dead, so the Apostle James tells us, as the body without the spirit is dead. There are any number of people who have faith, but they lack the works, and I believe in the people that have both the faith and the works and are determined to do things. Unto those of you who have worthy determination the Lord will open the way before you whereby you can accomplish the labor. There is no passage in all the Book of Mormon that has made such a profound impression upon my very heart, soul, and being, as the statement of Nephi when he went up to Jerusalem with his brothers to secure the brass plates of Laban. When they made a failure, and the brothers of Nephi wanted to go back to their father's tent in the wilderness, Nephi told them he would not go back, that he would stay there until they had accomplished the thing which the Lord required of them. And he announced to them that he knew the Lord made no requirements of men but what he prepared the way whereby the thing that was required might be accomplished. . . . I read the Book of Mormon as a young man, and fell in love with Nephi more than with any other character in profane or sacred history that I have ever read of, except the Savior of the world. No other individual has made such a strong impression upon me as did Nephi. He has been one of the guiding stars of my life." (*Improvement Era,* September 1941, p. 524.)

Heber was never one to savor a principle or idea merely as an intellectual exercise. He was an activist, not a scholar; a performer, not a spectator; a doer, not a dreamer. So the principle illustrated in the life of Nephi was adopted as his own and, when welded to his innate characteristics, produced unusual results. Two incidents following close on the heels of the Manifesto illustrate the electrifying effect of Heber's personality and iron will.

The State Bank of Utah was organized in 1890 with

Heber Grant as president and his brother-in-law, Heber
M. Wells, as cashier. The bank came into being because
Heber Wells once expressed regret that he had spent so
long a time as a Salt Lake City employee without opportunity to engage in business. That offhand remark
triggered Heber J. Grant's creative energies, and he suggested they organize a bank and install the brother-in-
law as one of its principal officers. In hardly any time at
all, the resourceful apostle had raised $500,000 from his
business and professional friends, the bank was organized, and Heber Wells was launched on a new career,
the impetus of which was to carry him into the
governor's chair.

As fate would have it, the fledgling bank was caught
almost immediately in the vise of the economic panic of
1891 that swept the country, skyrocketing interest rates
to one-half of one percent a day ($182\frac{1}{2}$ percent annually). Needing cash to meet the demands of its
anxious depositors, the bank decided to sell $100,000
worth of 6 percent ZCMI notes it held. With the money
market as it was, any hopes of selling the notes without
substantially discounting them was slim indeed. But the
young, resourceful bank president was determined to
make the attempt. He made arrangements to travel east
in search of a buyer for his notes, an errand one astute
observer likened to trying to sell snowballs at the South
Pole.

Before leaving, Heber discussed the purpose of his
trip with President Woodruff, who, unsolicited, said,
"You are going East on a very difficult mission. Sit down
on this chair and let me give you a blessing." The
President promised Heber that he would find the money
he sought and that more would be offered to him than
he needed. "I went out with a feeling of perfect
assurance that I would be successful," he recorded.

Heber's first stop was in Omaha, Nebraska, where he
called on the president of the Omaha National Bank
and asked him to purchase a $12,000 ZCMI note. The
older, more experienced banker laughed at the auda-
cious young man who presumed to sell 6 percent notes in
a market yielding $182\frac{1}{2}$ percent per year and, in a re-

proachful tone, advised: "You go home, call all your
banking friends together, and decide to lend a little more
than would be considered strictly safe, and the money
will circulate around and come back into your bank
again, and you can take care of your own bank." Mr.
Millard, the banker, whose advice corresponded with the
best money wisdom of the day, was taken aback by the
brash, almost impudent reply. "I told him it was money
I was after and not advice," Heber recorded, "and that I
had to go East for $100,000, and that I intended to get it,
and I would stop on my way home and tell him where I
got it!" After recovering from the shock of this startling
response, Mr. Millard replied, "Well, Mr. Grant, it will
be quite a long while before I see you."

At Chicago, Heber engaged in a similar dialogue
with a vice-president of the Merchants Loan and Trust
Company, except it followed a request that the bank
purchase *two*, not one, $12,000 ZCMI notes. "Young
man, have you read the morning papers?" the incredulous banker asked.

"Certainly," Heber answered.

"Have you read the financial sheet?"

"Yes," was the answer.

"What is money loaning at in New York?"

"One half of one percent a day."

"Well, do you expect to get any money at six percent
per annum?"

"Yes, I do," Heber replied, "because that is the rate
you charge your customers if their balances are good
enough to justify your making loans."

At this point in the conversation Heber received the
same little lecture on the philosophy of banking he had
received from Mr. Millard in Omaha, to which he
responded, "I did not come to Chicago to get that advice; I had the same advice from the president of the
Omaha National. I told him I would stop on my way
home and tell him when I got the money. I will do the
same with you." The Chicago banker smiled and said he
did not expect to see his visitor "for a long time."

In New York, the Nephi-like quality in Heber's
character emerged full-blown. Instead of giving up and

returning home as Nephi's brethren were inclined to do at the first signs of opposition, Heber increased the tempo and force of his demands. Here he again doubled his goal and, instead of asking an officer of the National Park Bank to purchase two ZCMI notes of $12,000, he asked him to purchase four. The reaction was predictable. "Why, Mr. Grant," the banker chided, "the idea of your coming into this bank with a panic on and money lending at one-half of one per cent a day and expecting to get a loan of $48,000 when we have never met before!" At that, Heber asked for a sheet of paper on which he scrawled his distinctive signature all across the page. Then, bringing his fist down on the counter, he demanded, "Do you know my signature?"

"Yes," was the startled reply.

"I did not come in here, sir, as a 'gold brick man,' a stranger to you. You know my signature; your bank solicited us to open a bank account. You do not seem to know how to treat a customer decently. I will tell you how we do business in the wild and woolly west. If a man offers us a note, if it does not suit us, we let him talk to our committee and see if he cannot furnish some additional securities or endorsements so we could be justified in making the loan."

When the banker, whose attitude toward Heber was now more conciliatory, explained that their heavy calendar would preclude a personal interview, Heber wrote a letter to the committee in which he explained the need for money, that ZCMI notes were solid and the company had never defaulted, that the notes had been endorsed by his own bank and by thirteen of Salt Lake's most prominent businessmen, and that other endorsements could be obtained if necessary. He concluded by writing, "If you do not want to buy . . . note[s] guaranteed by thirteen reputable men and a bank of a half million dollars capital, take my advice and do not do business so far away from home."

Heber Grant learned afterwards that when the president of the bank saw his letter and the notes in the committee meeting, he said, "What? Zions Cooperative Mercantile Institution, with all-seeing eyes in the corners, and 'Holiness to the Lord' printed over it? That is good for sore eyes. When I was the third assistant cashier of this bank, it was my business by instruction of the president to purchase commercial paper that was for sale, and I was instructed to buy all the notes offered of Zions Cooperative Mercantile Institution and I haven't seen one of their notes now for about ten years; they have got in a position where they do not need any help from us. We must not fail to buy these notes from Mr. Grant."

This breakthrough touched off a chain of events that enabled Heber to sell $88,000 worth of ZCMI notes without discount in just two days. Encouraged by this success, and more in jest than anything else, he sent a wire to the banker in Chicago who predicted he would fail: "I have been here forty-eight hours and I have $88,000. Can I send you the remaining $12,000 note? Kindly wire at my expense to H. B. Chaflin Company and ask them if they have loaned me $25,000 at 6 percent; the National Park Bank, $48,000; Kuntz Brothers, $15,000; and wire if I can count on you for the other $12,000 that I need to make up the $100,000." To his happy surprise, he received a return wire, "Send the note."

While this money helped to ease the financial problems of Heber's bank, it did not solve them. Responding to urgent pleas from home, he continued his quest for money and was able to obtain an additional $226,000 from some of his insurance associates on the strength of his personal signature alone. In the end, he received an offer of $48,000 more than was actually needed, thus fulfilling the prediction made by President Woodruff. "From the day that President Woodruff blessed me," Heber wrote, "and said I would get all the money I was going for and more if I needed it, I had a perfect assurance in my heart that his promise would be fulfilled, and it was fulfilled to the very letter."

In this episode and numerous others, Heber demonstrated the main characteristic of his hero, Nephi; he was prepared to undertake any task pointed out by divine mandate, regardless of how gloomy the prospects of success might be. Perhaps in no endeavor, however, was he more sorely tried than in his efforts to establish a sugar industry in Utah and the difficult problems of finance that followed. This story began in 1889 when President Woodruff decided to establish a sugar industry as a means of providing the Saints with a dependable money crop. To this end he appointed a committee, including Heber J. Grant, to look into the matter and submit a feasibility report. Having viewed the proposal in all its aspects, the committee unanimously recommended against it. Dissatisfied with the result, President Woodruff appointed another committee that also included Heber. "I begged to be excused," Heber said in a conference talk several years later, in 1919, "because I had already formed my opinion, had already signed my name to a report, but he would not listen to my request to be excused." The second committee also came in with an adverse report.

Had it been an ordinary business transaction, the matter likely would have ended there. But it was not, and it did not. "Never mind the report," President Woodruff said. "The inspiration to me is to establish the sugar industry." That decision having been made, the Utah Sugar Company was organized and Heber, along with others, was called to seek subscriptions for stock in the new company. At this point, Heber's whole attitude toward the project changed. It was not that he lacked confidence in his own business judgment. It was rather that he had more confidence in the inspiration of President Woodruff, whom he sustained as a prophet.

"I took individual letters to different men," Heber said, "asking them to subscribe. I delivered a letter to the late David Eccles . . . [who] had a comprehensive grasp of business affairs which to me was superior to that of any man I ever met. David smiled when the letter was presented to him, signed by President Woodruff and his counselors, asking him to invest five thousand dollars, or seven thousand five hundred dollars. He said 'Well, I would like to get off at the lowest figure. You can put me down for five thousand dollars.' Then he added, 'I hope they will buy lumber from me, so I may make a profit on a part of the five thousand dollars; and after I get the stock, if you can find someone who would like to buy it for twenty-five hundred dollars, I will be much obliged to you if you will come and get the stock.' " (Ibid.)

The events following the initial subscription of capital stock in the new company seemed destined to fulfill David Eccles's dire prediction. The contract for construction of a factory near Lehi, Utah, had been let when the panic of 1891 struck. Viewing with dismay the skyrocketing interest rates paralyzing the economy, the experienced businessmen on the board of the new company advised that it should take advantage of a fifty-thousand-dollar forfeiture provision in the construction contract, absorb the loss, and abandon the plans for a sugar factory. The answer from President Woodruff was disappointing but not unexpected: "From the day I received a knowledge of the divinity of the gospel of Jesus Christ revealed through the Prophet Joseph Smith, from the day that I went out as a humble priest to proclaim that gospel, although it looked like death in front of me, if the path of duty that the gospel required me to tread called me to face death, I have never turned to the right nor turned to the left; and now the inspiration of the Lord to me is to build this factory. Every time I think of abandoning it, there is darkness; and every time I think of building it, there is light. We will build the factory if it bursts the Church."

The stubborn persistence revealed by this statement explains why the Utah Sugar Company ultimately succeeded. There were many rocky places in the road ahead that the company safely negotiated, chiefly because of the tenacity and will of President Woodruff and Heber J. Grant, who, once the journey was commenced, never turned to the right nor to the left but followed implicitly and enthusiastically the direction of his file leader.

As an epilogue to the drama of Heber's business activities and traumas in the early 1890s, it is fitting to turn to his efforts during the last six months of 1893 to prevent a failure of his bank. The panic of 1891 had made depositors uneasy about the stability of all banks. They watched the banks very carefully and at the first sign of difficulty demanded their deposits. Banks that overextended their resources in making time loans were thus put in jeopardy when there were excessive withdrawals. The State Bank of Utah, which apparently was overextended for such a time of fiscal uncertainty, encountered a serious threat in the summer of 1893. In an an attempt to ward it off, Heber went east to try to borrow money from his banking and insurance friends. So tight was the money market, and so insistent were the demands at home, that Heber remained away almost continually for several months, scurrying from place to place seeking the funds necessary to keep his bank afloat. The urgent wires and letters that passed between him and Heber M. Wells, who was on the job in Salt Lake City, paint a suspenseful picture. Wrote Heber Wells on July 1: "I haven't given up the ship or anything of that sort, but I have called a meeting of our directors to meet in conjunction with Zions board tomorrow [Sunday] to decide after hearing our exact condition whether we had better attempt to open on Monday. . . . It is a grave question whether we had better open on Monday at all as I do not believe we could get through the day. . . . Before you receive this it is possible—nay probable you will hear of our suspension."

After a hectic day on Monday, the harried banker was able to write Heber with a little, but not much, optimism. "We are still alive and see each others face, I mean Geo. M. [Cannon] and I. The day has been an easier one than the most hopeful could have thought. Our deposits went up $10,000, our loans went down $18,000 and our reserve increased $20,000." An indication of why the bank did not close on Monday as the letter of July 1 had indicated is found in this statement in one of Heber Wells's letters: "The committee met at 1 p.m. Sunday at the BP's office. I read them your telegram saying you were vehemently opposed to closing etc. and after a two-hour conference, we decided to open without saying anything to the clearing house."

A week later he seemed to see a light at the end of the tunnel when he wrote, "I am much more comfortable now than I was a week ago at this hour. During the week our reserve has increased $48,100. Of the amount you are responsible for $37,500 and we at home have managed to get in $10,600."

But this seeming confidence was misplaced. Actually, the storm that threatened to swamp the new bank had barely begun. A month later, during a brief visit to Salt Lake, Heber J. Grant attended a meeting where the financial conditions were discussed, of which he wrote: "The present financial situation was considered and some little feeling was manifested by those present. I was not able to keep from crying when I spoke as I felt that nothing but the blessings of the Lord would keep us from failure."

Some insight into the extent of the load he carried at this critical time is found in this entry written the latter part of August, after he had returned to New York. "I feel to thank the Lord with all the power of expression that I am capable of that I have been able to stand the pressure of the past month, that is the last half of it, as I left home soon after the middle of the month. I think that I should have broken down with the mental strain which has been upon me had it not been that I had more or less education in being anxious during the months of May, June and July."

The anxieties and pressures this entry reflects clouded the vision and optimism that usually characterized Heber's outlook, and these worries drove him to his knees in humble, entreating prayer. "When the end will come is more than I am able to tell," he wrote, "but it looks at the close of the month of August as if two or three more days would see the State Bank of Utah and the Zions Bank with closed doors. I do hope and pray with all the power which the Lord has given me that He will assist us so that this will not have to happen."

That humble prayer was to be answered in a miraculous way, by a process that had now become common. "Saturday morning Sept. 2nd [1893] I got up after but two or three hours of sleep," he wrote, "and I recalled the blessing that I had from Prest. Joseph F. Smith in which he had promised me that I should meet with success far beyond what I had expected and as I had not met with any success I told the brethren that I knelt down by my bed and asked the Lord with faith for a fulfillment of the promise of the servant of the Lord to me. I got up feeling cheerful and with an assurance that I should be blessed in getting the money that was needed and a feeling that it would be the mind and will of the Lord that our banks should close in case I was not able to get the money we needed. I walked down town with no idea of where to go or what to do. I walked into the office of Blake Brothers & Co. where I met Mr. John Claflin and I told him frankly of our condition and that I was willing to make any sacrifice in order to save the banks I was interested in. He offered to loan me $400,000 provided I would give him $100,000 commission. I finally agreed to take half this amount and to pay half the commission that he asked. I had told the Lord in my prayers this morning that I was willing to make any sacrifice that might be necessary even if it was $50,000 if He would open the way for me to get the money needed and I had also told Him that I was not able to do anything and that He must open the way for me to get the money if the banks were to be saved and the promise of Prest. Smith to me was to be made good. . . . I felt to testify that the Lord had made good the promise of His servant to me at the time that it looked as if it were impossible for me to get any money."

Like the assault waves of an army charging again and again over the battlements, Heber and his brethren were repeatedly threatened with financial ruin during the years between the Manifesto and statehood. In the interval between each wave they would regroup, bind up their wounds, and steel themselves for the next assault. Acknowledging their incompetence to solve the intricate problems of finance that daily became more complex, the postulates of which altered with the fluctuations of the market, they retreated into the security of their faith in God where, like their ancient kin, the children of Israel, they needed only to look and listen and follow, one step at a time.

Always on the cutting edge of this warfare was Heber

J. Grant, whose experience, personality, and determination equipped him admirably to bear the brunt of the attack. He was indomitable. While the din of battle occasionally deafened him and temporarily interrupted the normal channels of heavenly communication, his head soon cleared and his spirits revived, enabling him to hear the signals assuring ultimate victory. Thus, the State Bank of Utah survived the financial devastation of the 1890s to become a stable lending institution. Later it merged with two other banks to become the Utah State National Bank.

One must not imagine, however, that Heber emerged from this conflict unscarred. At the height of battle it became necessary for him to incur heavy personal indebtedness, mortgaging his home and other property. The debts thus assumed were to burden him and his family for several years and were not to be lifted until shortly prior to his departure for a mission to Japan in 1901. And as might be expected, the manner in which he acquired the means to satisfy these debts illustrated again his simple faith and his discipleship toward his hero, Nephi of old.

Chapter 12

Politics and Statehood

When the Latter-day Saints first arrived in the valley of the Great Salt Lake they made no serious attempt to differentiate between civil and ecclesiastical authority. Nor was there a need for them to do so, since most of the inhabitants, except for the Indians who lived apart, were members of the Church and were willing to submit to the direction of their priesthood leaders. Thus, bishops and high council courts, which today restrict their jurisdiction to strictly ecclesiastical matters, for many years adjudicated disputes and declared rights and duties in a wide variety of cases that today would be handled by civil courts.

This pattern created much fuzziness in the minds of the Saints as to the line of demarcation between matters of church and state. It could be difficult, for example, to differentiate between the pronouncements Brigham Young made as the president of the Church and those he made as the governor of the territory. Nor were the Saints too concerned about drawing that line as, for the most part, they were content to take his direction whether he gave it while wearing his Sunday or his everyday hat.

Any confusion by the Saints on this point was compensated for by the gentiles, who drew the line with meticulous precision. Any real or imagined incursion by the Church into matters of state was met with loud and incessant protest. The mere presence of an LDS official in a civil office gave rise to suspicion and criticism by the gentiles, who were concerned above almost everything else about being in subjection to the dominant church.

It was only natural, therefore, that members and

nonmembers divided into two political parties, the
People's party and the Liberal party. For years these two
groups engaged in lively, sometimes acrimonious com-
petition for local political offices, the principal territorial
offices being appointed, of course, by the federal government.

During the almost fifty years of Utah's territorial
status, most nonmembers opposed statehood out of
concern that the preponderance of Latter-day Saints
would bar them from many elected state offices. This opposition was strengthened by the fact that the gentiles
exerted more influence in national affairs than the Saints
did, guaranteeing that most appointees to territorial
offices were non-Mormons.

Once the polygamy issue was swept away by the
Manifesto, it became plain that statehood could not
much longer be withheld from Utah. The only serious
impediment seemed to be the concentration of the Saints
in a single political party, the consequences of which
boded ill for the gentile population. Since the gentiles,
with their predominant influence in Washington, might
thus bar statehood, the leaders of the People's party,
most of whom were committed members of the church,
dissolved the party in June 1891.

At that time, leaders of the Church encouraged the
Saints to affiliate with whichever of the two national
political parties was most congenial to their views and
principles. Most were inclined toward the Democratic
party, including Heber J. Grant, who, not long after the
dissolution of the People's party, actively affiliated with
the Democratic party and in 1891 served as chairman of
its finance committee.

The reason the Latter-day Saints preferred the
Democrats grew from the fact that the three main anti-
polygamy laws, the Morrill Act of 1862, the Edmunds
Act of 1882, and the Edmunds-Tucker Act of 1887, were
the handiwork of Republican politicians. The last of the
three had become law without the signature of a Democratic president, Grover Cleveland. It was only natural
that the Saints would disfavor the party that they felt
had heaped such abuse upon them for so long.

A trend away from support of the Democrats started
a few years after the Manifesto, when they began to drag
their feet on statehood for Utah and the Republicans
began to support it. But Heber never completely severed
his ties with the Democratic party, although his strong
views on the protection of home industry through high
tariffs, on Prohibition, and on government spending
collided with his party and caused him frequently to
support Republican candidates whose views on these
and other political issues coincided with his own. So
often did this occur that he was inclined to refer to
himself as a political independent, a role more consistent
with his status as an ecclesiastical leader.

Heber never completely lost his yen for political
office, although from time to time he goodnaturedly dis-
paraged politics. His real attitude toward politics and
political office, at least the attitude he held in his
younger years, is reflected in this remark he made during
the October 1934 general conference: "Do you think I
would not like to have been the first governor of the
State of Utah, where I was born? If you do you are mistaken. I do not know of anything that I should have
liked better than that at that particular time."

The events behind this statement and others related
to it were complex and produced one of the most explo-
sive conditions within the hierarchy of the Church
following the days of Joseph Smith. The drama commenced to build shortly after the Manifesto. To allay
fears that the Church intended to dominate politics,
fears that arose when the People's party was dissolved,
the Church's leaders made a statement of political intent
through an interview with a reporter of the Salt Lake
Times. This was widely interpreted to mean that church
leaders would not become actively engaged in politics,
either as advocates or candidates, an interpretation that,
as to the General Authorities, was confirmed in October
1892 when President Woodruff recorded a decision that
"none of the presidency, twelve, or the presidents of
seventy" were to "take the stump to make political
speeches." Later, it was realized that this would prohibit
the services to the state of many able men, and it was

therefore decided to allow church officials to accept political preferment.

It was against this background that Heber received an invitation from the Democratic party to run for governor in the first state election held in 1895. "I went to President Wilford Woodruff," he later reported, "and handed him the telegram. I said: 'How shall I answer that?' " Heber probably suspected what the answer would be, although he was taken aback by the abruptness of it. "What are you bothering me with your affairs for?" President Woodruff asked. "Haven't you got enough inspiration as one of the Apostles to know what your duty is?" At this Heber beat a hasty retreat, pausing only long enough to say, "Thank you. If you had wanted me to run, you would have said so. Good-bye." (*Conference Report*, October 1934, pp. 125-26.)

On two other occasions Heber was again urged to run for a high political office, the United States Senate, but declined without giving the matter serious thought, remembering the response he had received from President Woodruff the first time.

While this marked the withdrawal of Heber J. Grant from the political arena as a potential candidate, it did not end his career as a political student or activist. Through most of his life he spoke out vigorously on political issues that had moral implications, that affected the economic well-being of his people, or that, in his judgment, threatened the fabric of constitutional government. But he never again was a candidate or an active political worker.

The incident involving Heber and President Woodruff had a happy outcome because, once he learned the president of the Church disfavored his candidacy, the young apostle withdrew without question or remonstrance. This was not the case, however, with two other General Authorities, Moses Thatcher of the Council of the Twelve and B. H. Roberts of the First Council of Seventy, who, without consulting the Brethren, had agreed to run for the U.S. Senate and Congress, respectively, on the Democratic ticket. There does not appear to have been a sense of rebellion in

either of these leaders when they agreed to be candidates
in the first place. They had simply misread the signals
when the Brethren had modified the rigid policy of 1892,
believing that this left them free to seek political office.
They failed to recognize, however, that the question was
not merely one of involvement in politics, but of the rejection of their ecclesiastical calls that a preoccupation
with politics would entail. Thus, in the eyes of the
Brethren the issue was not whether these men could or
should engage in politics, but whether they would be
permitted to accept responsibilities that would hamper
or destroy their ability to serve the Church.

To implement their design, the First Presidency and
the Twelve adopted what was later to be known as the
"Political Manifesto," defining the circumstances under
which leading officials in the Church might properly become involved in a nonecclesiastical activity, political or
otherwise. It stated: "We unanimously agree to and promulgate as a rule, that should always be observed in the
church and by every leading official thereof, that before
accepting any position, political or otherwise, which
would interfere with the proper and complete discharge
of his ecclesiastical duties, and before accepting a nomi-
nation or entering into engagements to perform new
duties, said official should apply to the proper authorities and learn from them whether he can,
consistently with the obligations already entered into
with the church upon assuming his office, take upon
himself the added duties and labors and responsibilities
of the new position. *To maintain proper discipline and order in
the church,* we deem this absolutely necessary; and in
asserting this rule, we do not consider that we are infringing in the least degree upon the individual rights of
the citizen. We declare that in making these requirements of ourselves and our brethren in the ministry, we
do not in the least desire to dictate to them concerning
their duties as American citizens, or to interfere with the
affairs of the state; neither do we consider that in the re-
motest degree we are seeking the union of church and
state." (*Comprehensive History of the Church* 6:334.)

The effect of this was to present an ultimatum to

Elders Thatcher and Roberts. Their reaction to it would determine whether they would retain or lose their status as General Authorities.

The political thicket in which Elder Roberts had become entangled almost overwhelmed him in the first two months of 1896. He had adamantly resisted the entreaties of his brethren to comply with the political manifesto, not because he denied their priesthood authority, but because he felt this issue lay beyond the scope of that authority. It had not been an easy decision to make. Behind him stretched thirty-nine years of struggling achievement during which he had emerged from the obscurity of an unnoticed birth in Lancashire, England, in 1856, to the eminence of a General Authority. Called as a member of the First Council of Seventy in 1888, he soon achieved wide recognition as one of the leading speakers and writers in the Church. He recognized that the stand he had taken would inevitably cause a fatal rupture in his relationship with the First Presidency and the Twelve, shattering his hopes for a brilliant and rewarding ecclesiastical career. And while, intellectually, he was convinced of the rectitude of his position, he still had a vague, subconscious feeling that he might be wrong, for he knew of the spiritual perceptions of the men whose counsel he now seemed to reject.

So Elder Roberts oscillated back and forth, pulled alternately by the power of his brilliant intellect and by the inner whisperings and impressions that often had charted his life's course: he felt certain, then uneasy; now confident, now distraught. The urging and adulation of some of his political friends, accompanied by a slow but constant withdrawal from the companionship and influence of his fellow General Authorities, finally brought him to the painful decision to reject the political manifesto. Word of this reached the Brethren, prompting several abortive attempts to dissuade him. By March 12, 1896, a seeming impasse had been reached; Elder Roberts showed no signs of yielding. It was felt by the Brethren that one final approach should be made, and Elders Francis M. Lyman and Heber J. Grant were assigned to make it.

At the outset, the meeting of the three brethren seemed only perfunctory. Inquiry by the two apostles revealed that Elder Roberts was still adamant in his intention not to yield to the political manifesto. Elder Grant wrote: "He [Elder Roberts] said he was willing to have us take immediate action in his case." With an air of finality, Elder Roberts rose from his chair, put on his coat, and walked toward the door. At that moment, his career hung in the balance. He had reached a fateful crossroad. One branch led toward a life of public service in the rough-and-tumble of the political arena. The second led toward a life that at once would be more peaceful and more turbulent than the other; more peaceful because of the close, constant association with men and women who shared his views of life's meaning and purpose; and more turbulent because of the subtle, unseen, and sometimes terrifying powers with which he would have to contend as a leading church official.

As he reached the door he turned to say goodbye, and in doing so, said he wanted his brethren to know that the action to be taken against him "was causing him the deepest sorrow notwithstanding he had been able to control his feelings; and he did not want [them] to think that he failed to appreciate all that he was going to lose." At that moment of crisis, Heber J. Grant saw an opening, a glimmer of light, that convinced him the battle was not yet lost. Like the superior salesman he was, he took advantage of it and commenced to make the greatest sales appeal of his life: "I said to him that matters were just beginning to be interesting and asked him to be seated. We chatted for some two hours and brother Lyman and I seemed to be blessed with ability in our talk to impress brother Roberts. He said when we got ready to part that he would not like to have us report to the brethren tomorrow to take action in his case, but that he would be pleased to think the matter over during the night and would write to us his decision in the morning."

To the persuasive eloquence Heber had brought to bear upon the problem, he added his fervent faith and prayers. "With all my heart," he wrote, "I pray that the

Lord may bless brother Roberts this night and that he
may decide to bow to any decision that his brethren may
render in his case."

The efforts of Elders Grant and Lyman that night
proved to be as fruitful as any they had exerted in their
long lives of faithful service to the Church. Elder
Roberts changed his views, forsook his political ambitions, and retained his place among the General Authorities. Thus was preserved for the Church one of the
most prolific and effective writers it was to produce.
Most of B. H. Roberts's best literary works poured from
his pen after that crucial night.

Important insights into the character of Heber J.
Grant and the genius of his leadership are gained from
the journal entry he made after the Roberts affair had
been successfully concluded: "I feel to thank the Lord
that He has caused brother Roberts to humble himself. I
feel that nothing but the influence of the Lord could
have brought about this condition of mind in brother
Roberts. I feel that he is an honest and true man, and I
feel to thank the Lord with all my heart that I have been
an instrument in His hands in connection with Brother
Francis M. Lyman in reaching his heart and causing
him to go to the Lord. We were greatly blessed in our
talk with him last night and I feel impressed today that
the right thing to do with men who are a little off in
their acts is to go to them alone and not bring them up
before a council of the priesthood and humiliate them."

Relating how he happily spread the good news of
Elder Roberts's turnabout, Heber concluded: "I made a
copy of the letter from brother Roberts, and I did not
walk across the road to read it to Brother Franklin D.
Richards, but I ran over there, and found him and
brothers Geo. Teasdale and Geo. Reynolds in his office
and I read them the letter from Bro. Roberts and tears of
joy came into their eyes. I read it to Prest. Wilford
Woodruff before I left his office and tears came into his
eyes."

Tears also filled the eyes of the Brethren over the case
of Elder Moses Thatcher, but these were tears of sadness,
not joy. For many complex reasons, he refused to accept

the political manifesto, was dropped from the Council of the Twelve, and was later stripped of his priesthood offices.

Generally regarded as one of the most intellectually brilliant men in the Mormon hierarchy, Elder Thatcher played a leading role in ecclesiastical and civic affairs during most of his adult life. Called at age twenty-eight, he served for eleven years (1870-1881) as the president of the Mexican Mission. Following his call to the apostleship he undertook a special mission to Mexico City, where he was instrumental in arranging for the settlement of many Latter-day Saints in northern Mexico. A Mormon village in Arizona bearing his name symbolizes the stature he attained in the eyes of his contemporaries.

Elder Thatcher was almost fifteen years older than Heber and entered the Council of the Twelve three years before his younger associate. Widely recognized as one of the most astute and progressive businessmen in the territory, a judgment with which Heber concurred, he soon gravitated to positions of power and influence. Elder Thatcher also had a talent for diplomacy and negotiation that showed to the best advantage in his dealings with the Mexican government and in the complicated mosaic of territorial politics before statehood. His immense talents, the powerful position he held as a member of the Twelve, his impressive business and political credentials, and his comparative youth augured well for a distinguished life and ecclesiastical career.

All this was evident to everyone, including Elder Thatcher, who, as the list of his past achievements lengthened and the hope of future eminence grew, began to make unfavorable comparisons between himself and those senior to him in the highest circle of Church leadership. This was the seed that, once having taken root, grew and spread until it distorted his judgment. He honestly felt that he was right and his less richly endowed brethren were wrong. And so it was that his personal qualities of brilliance and self-confidence fueled both Moses Thatcher's spectacular rise and his dramatic, tragic fall.

The brethren labored diligently with Elder Thatcher
as they had with Elder Roberts. In fact, they devoted
even more time and prayerful attention to him because
of the weightier influence of his office in church affairs
and the increased furor that would attend his fall. Numerous delegations from among the Twelve were sent to
call on him to try to convince him of the need to follow
counsel and to accept the political manifesto. All of
them failed. Indeed, the only effect they seemed to have
was to confirm his obstinacy. No rancor or bitterness was
manifested on either side of this controversy.
Throughout its course, those involved acted toward each
other as gentlemen and brethren whose honest views
were in collision.

As the April 1896 general conference approached,
the relationship between the First Presidency and the
Twelve and Elder Thatcher reached the point of
rupture. By this time, the controversy had become a
cause célèbre throughout the Church. It was widely
known that Elder Thatcher had openly questioned the
authority of the Brethren to prohibit his involvement in
activities that conflicted with his apostolic calling.

With the issue so clearly drawn, the authorities had
no choice if they hoped to maintain the discipline
necessary for effective church government. In this dilemma, neither their personal regard for Elder Thatcher
nor the deterioration of his health could or would deter
them from taking the steps necessary to preserve the integrity of the Church.

An insight into Elder Thatcher's condition at this
time and the feelings of his brethren toward him is found
in this entry from Heber J. Grant's journal for Friday,
March 13, 1896: "Called on brother Moses Thatcher
this evening and found him very low indeed. He told me
he would consider it a great blessing from the Lord if he
could be layed at rest. He felt that he wished to rest and
was satisfied with his measure of life and the great pain
and struggle which he had had during the past five years
had worn him out. He told me that he felt impressed
with the idea that he had a cancer in his stomach. He is
a wonderfully sick man and it looks to me that he can

not live long unless there is a change for the better."

In less than a month from the time of this visit, Elder Thatcher's name was dropped from the roster of the Twelve and he was not presented for sustaining vote at the April general conference. When this comparatively mild, though shocking, disciplinary action failed to bring about the desired conformity in Elder Thatcher's conduct, the Brethren took a second, more ominous step. In the autumn of the same year, he was summoned before the Twelve for "a settlement of his differences with them and the other general authorities of the church." (B. H. Roberts, *Comprehensive History of the Church* 6:334-35.) When he ignored this summons, the Twelve had little recourse but to sever him from the Twelve.

Still recalcitrant and unwilling to yield to the authority of the priesthood, Moses Thatcher was confronted with his third and most portentous trial when, in July 1897, he was charged with unchristianlike conduct before a high council of the Salt Lake Stake. Facing possible excommunication, he at length came to his senses and frankly acknowledged that he was in error.

While this traumatic episode did not insulate the Church against the buffetings of politics, it did solve once and for all the question of when and under what conditions it would be appropriate for leaders of the Church to become engaged in politics.

Chapter 13

A Call to Japan

Once the battle of statehood had been won, and as the pressures generated by the polygamy issue continued to subside, a sense of calm and gratitude settled upon the Church. And now that things were relatively peaceful in the heart of Zion, the Brethren began to turn their attention to other parts of the vineyard. Elder Brigham Young, Jr., expressed strong feelings on the subject: "For some time I have felt impressed that valuable time is being lost in not carrying the gospel to all of the nations of the earth where it is possible to do so. Of late I have often times asked myself the question, are we not sacrificing the spiritual labor in order to build up the country materially? The spiritual things of the kingdom must have our first attention, and all other matters must be secondary. While it is necessary to look after the body still it is the spirit of man which giveth life. I ask myself the question have I been as important a factor in bringing to the attention of all men the truths of the gospel as I might have been? I feel that the most important duty devolving upon us as apostles, is that of seeing that the gospel is carried to all men."

Elder Franklin D. Richards was similarly impressed that "the gospel should be carried to all the nations of the earth." He added a statement that foreshadowed a major turning point in the life of Heber J. Grant. "Something should be done in Japan," he said. "The question of opening a mission in Japan (has) been discussed many times. . . . The last time it was under consideration, the matter was referred to apostle Abraham H. Cannon."

But before the Church could open its doors in such

faraway lands, it needed to become financially stable at home. The next four years saw a turnabout in the Church's financial affairs even more dramatic and far-reaching than the incidents a few years before when Heber had almost single-handedly rescued his bank from insolvency.

The stage was set against the background of economic forces that had been paralyzed by the difficulties of taming a wilderness, contending with the fight against polygamy, and surviving the crushing effect of the panic of 1891, not to mention the financial chaos created by the escheatment of Church properties and the lengthy, complex, and expensive efforts to recover them. All this had sapped the Church's resources and reduced it to a scrounging hand-to-mouth existence.

It was this bleak prospect that faced President Lorenzo Snow when he assumed leadership of the Church upon the death of President Wilford Woodruff on September 2, 1898. He immediately adopted the stop-gap measure of issuing $1,000,000 worth of short-term 6 percent bonds. Realizing that this was merely a temporary remedy, and did not get at the root of the Church's financial ills, President Snow searched for a more permanent, enduring solution. As he prayed and reflected, he discovered the answer in a revelation on tithing received by his predecessor, Joseph Smith. So simple in concept, yet so profound in its effect, President Snow concluded that this law, if practiced correctly by the members, held the answer to all of the Church's financial problems. Realizing the power of the principle and the dedication of the Saints, he knew that the key to success lay in teaching and motivating them.

He launched his campaign at St. George in the spring of 1899 while on a speaking tour through southern Utah. Thereafter for many months he seldom if ever failed to dwell on this principle in his public addresses. The other General Authorities picked up the theme, and soon the whole Church was inundated with thoughts and promises about keeping the law of tithing. To the oratory, President Snow added another element that lent a powerful impetus to his campaign; he elicited public commitments from the members to observe the law of tithing. President Snow first used this effective device at a general meeting of the leadership of the Young Men's Mutual Improvement Association in Salt Lake City in May 1899. Following a powerful sermon on the law of tithing, this resolution was presented to the assembly: "Resolved: That we accept the doctrine of tithing, as now presented by President Snow, as the present word and will of the Lord unto us, and we do accept it with all our hearts; we will ourselves observe it, and we will do all in our power to get the Latter-day Saints to do likewise." The resolution had an electric effect upon those in the congregation, who rose to their feet and shouted "aye" in acceptance.

While the inspired action of President Snow lifted the Church out of the morass of debt in which it had become mired, Heber continued to struggle with the personal indebtedness he had had to assume in order to keep his businesses afloat during the recent panic. These were exceedingly trying times for a man who had always taken pride in his self-sufficiency, in his ability to care for his family in style and comfort. So pinched did his finances become that it became necessary for members of his family to go to work in low-paying clerical jobs in order to defray living expenses.

It was in these circumstances that Heber attended one of the weekly temple meetings in 1900 where a frequently discussed subject was again broached. "We have decided to open a mission in Japan," President George Q. Cannon began. As these words were spoken, Heber experienced a repetition of what had occurred almost twenty years before when George Teasdale greeted him on the Tabernacle steps. He recalled that "it came to me as though a voice spoke, 'You will be called to preside there.'" With that shocking insight, he tuned out the rather lengthy discussion that followed, and engaged in one of those inner debates for which he was noted. "I cannot go to Japan," he said to himself, "seeing that I will lose a little over five thousand dollars a year income," a significant factor to a man who was heavily in debt. Then the contrary argument came into his mind: "One time I was over one hundred thousand dollars worse off than nothing, and it was miraculous the way the Lord blessed me. I would be ashamed not to go on a mission if I were wanted." With this, he made up his mind to accept the call when it was offered, without making excuses. Then later, as President Snow talked, the thought came to Heber that "it is not an excuse to tell your condition financially." "Shut up, Mr. Devil," he recalled thinking. "If I should tell my condition financially there isn't a man in this room that would let me go to Japan. That is the best excuse I could possibly make."

So, when it was finally announced that Elder Heber J. Grant had been selected to go to Japan, he accepted without reservation, adroitly parrying questions the Brethren put to him about his financial condition.

As the Brethren filed from the temple, Elder John W. Taylor asked Heber to remain behind. "Heber," he said, "you have made a financial sacrifice today that is the equal, financially speaking, of Abraham offering up Isaac. The Lord accepted the offering and provided the ram in the thicket to save Isaac. The Lord has accepted your offering. I know your condition financially, and I prophesy that you shall be blessed of the Lord and make enough money to go to Japan a free man financially."

At first, Heber was almost stunned by the implications of this prophecy. "I had just made a calculation a short time before," he later wrote, "and with the small income my wife was making by doing a little typewriting, of thirty dollars a month, in her very limited spare time; my daughter Rachel working for sixty-five dollars a month; my daughter Lucy for thirty dollars a month; and myself for a little over five thousand dollars a year, that in ten years I would be free with the world financially, and the thought of being free in one year was overwhelming."

But so frequently had he seen the powerful, energizing effect of such prophetic utterances, and so impressed and thrilled was he by the substance of what he had been told, that he was almost instantly imbued with the inner feeling that the prediction would be fulfilled.

Wrote he: "I turned to Brother Taylor with tears in my eyes and said: 'I know that you have prophesied what will come true, and I am overwhelmed with gratitude that I am to be free financially in a year.' "

But Elder Taylor had not quite yet played out his role. He added, significantly, "I am inspired to tell you how to do it. You are not to plan to make money, but you are to get down on your knees every morning and tell the Lord you want to make some money that day, and then go out and get it, and you will be astonished how easily you will make the money."

Moving with his accustomed speed, Heber followed his friend's injunction without delay. "I went home for my lunch and went to my bedroom," he wrote, "and prayed to the Lord, expressing unbounded gratitude for the prophecy, and thanked Him for giving me an assurance that it would be fulfilled. I told Him I did not want to wait until tomorrow to make some money; I wanted to make some that afternoon." An impression came to him while he was praying that, when acted upon, yielded unexpected revenue.

This incident ignited a burst of energy and a string of financial dealings that, in a few short months, were to erase Heber's heavy obligations and to send him to Japan debt-free. "Just before going to Japan," he wrote, "I paid my tithing on my profits for the four months, and the amount was forty-six hundred dollars. I had earned over two hundred percent more in only four short months than I had previously earned in any four months, and went to Japan a free man, financially." (*Improvement Era*, December 1941, pp. 713ff.)

As the burden of debt was lifted from Heber's shoulders, it was replaced by an air of lighthearted gaiety that even the prospect of being separated from his family for a time could hardly conceal. As he went about the busy tasks of preparing to leave for Japan, there was not the slightest tinge of sadness or regret on his part or that of his family.

Accompanied by Louis B. Kelsch, Horace S. Ensign, and Alma O. Taylor, Heber left by train for Vancouver, British Columbia, on July 24, 1901. At the depot to see the missionaries off was a large group of associates, friends, and family headed by Joseph F. Smith, who was to become the president of the Church within a few months. Amid much happy well-wishing, the train pulled out at 11:00 P.M. and, within minutes after its departure, Heber had assembled his companions in the drawing room of the sleeping car, where they sang three favorite hymns whose lyrics aptly expressed basic Mormon doctrines and whose tunes, sung with volume and gusto, assured the passengers that this was not to be a dull trip. As the strains of "Truth Reflects Upon Our Senses," "Do What Is Right," and "God Moves in a Mysterious Way" floated through the car, the erstwhile sleepers likely had alternate feelings of enjoyment, amusement, and annoyance at this nocturnal serenade.

The incident typified Heber's ministry in Japan. It was to be happy, active, and exuberant. As he reflected the following day, "I was never happier in my life, and there was never a feeling of deeper gratitude in my heart than there was last night as our train pulled out of the depot."

In Vancouver, the missionaries boarded the *Empress of India*, which departed for Japan at 5:30 A.M. on July 30. This being Heber's first sea voyage, he was naturally enthralled by every aspect of his new environment: the large ship, containing all the elements of a compact luxury city; the efficient, purposeful crew; the brisk air; the sea birds and marine life. All these, coupled with excitement about the new missionary adventure that lay ahead, filled him with a happiness and anticipation clearly reflected in his first journal entry made at sea: "Wednesday July 31st 1901: Have spent the day walking the deck, having walked about five miles. Wrote a little on my cousin's letter. Did a little visiting and some pitching of rope quoits. It has been very smooth indeed all day. . . . We have been away from home one week, and I have been as contented and happy and as thankful as ever in my life."

The following day, however, he received his first nauseous insight into real life at sea. It heralded the beginning of a siege of seasickness that was to follow him to

the end of his voyage. "Am not feeling well this morning," he wrote. "It was with difficulty that I was able to
remain at the breakfast table." He did not fare so well at
lunch and had to rush from the table before he had
finished. It was then that he commenced a fruitless
search for a place on the ship where he would be free
from the constant rolling and pitching that produced his
nausea. Although he failed, he did find that there was
less movement in the barbershop, which was amidship
and below deck, and to this sanctuary he retired often to
seek relief.

Arriving in Yokohama after a somewhat turbulent
crossing, the missionaries put up at the Grand Hotel,
from which they made their first contacts. They made
tentative arrangements for translation and publication
of some Church literature and looked for permanent
lodgings. At this point they experienced much opposition, inspired largely by the ministers of other Christian
sects who had learned of their coming and, being misled
by false reports of the Church, were determined that it
would not get a foothold.

Once he and his companions had settled in, Heber
felt the need to offer a special prayer, dedicating Japan
for the preaching of the gospel. In this he was to follow a
pattern that had been set long ago by his predecessors in
the apostolic ministry.

The day selected for the significant event was Sunday, September 1, 1901. The four missionaries found a
secluded spot in the woods outside Yokohama and at
about eleven o'clock they began their solemn meeting.
Elder Alma O. Taylor, the youngest of the four, who
served as clerk of the meeting, prepared detailed minutes
of the proceedings, which reported the following:

"After the four prayers had been offered up we knelt
again in a circle and brother Grant offered up the dedicatory prayer. His tongue was loosened and the spirit
rested mightily upon him; so much so that we felt that
the angels of God were near for our hearts burned within
us as the words fell from his lips. I never experienced
such a peaceful influence or heard such a powerful
prayer before; every word penetrated into my very bones

and I could have wept with joy. The following is an outline of the prayer as I remember it: (a) An appeal unto
the Lord to hear the words that would be uttered. (b) An
expression of thanks for the preservation of our lives for
the testimony of the gospel that we had in our hearts
and for the great blessing of being considered worthy in
the eyes of the Prophet of the Lord to go as messengers of
life and salvation unto a people who had never heard the
Gospel. (c) An entreaty for the forgiveness of our sins. (d)
Dedication of the land for the proclamation of the truth
and to the bringing to pass of the purpose of the Lord
concerning the gathering of Israel and the establishment
of righteousness upon the earth. (e) By the power of the
priesthood and in the name of Jesus Christ, Satan was
commanded to release his hold upon the minds of the
people, and rebuked in his efforts to overcome the work
of the Lord in this land. (f) Words of praise unto the
Lord for preserving the people of this land from the
power of the great and abominable church and that He
had blessed them with sufficient knowledge to see the
shallowness of the man-made Christianity which was
sought to be introduced among them. (g) Petitioned the
Lord to touch the hearts of the people that they might
know that we were men of virtue, honor, and devotion
and that we had come among them to do them good;
that their minds might be directed into channels of religious thought and their hearts prepared to recognize
the truth when it was declared unto them, being even as
sheep quick to recognize the voice of the shepherd. (h)
Thanks for the talents with which we had been blessed
and dedication of them unto the work of the Lord. (i) A
request that we might be endowed with every qualification needed in the opening of this mission. (j) A prayer
for the church and priesthood. (k) A personal mention of
the goodness of the Lord in preserving the life of Apostle
Grant during the severe attack of sickness which he had
some years ago been called upon to pass through, and
when he was given up to die by nearly all his friends. He
felt that the Lord had restored him to come upon this
mission. (1) Thanks for the companions he had; for the
integrity of Brother Kelsch who had been in the mission

field for the past ten years, but was willing to come to
this land and labor for the salvation of souls; for the
ready heart of Bro. Ensign in responding cheerfully to
the call to go out and preach the Gospel, in spite of the
fact that he had but lately returned from a mission to
Colorado; for his youthful compassion 'even Alma' who
in spite of his youth had been favored of the Lord with
much intelligence and knowledge and a love for the
truth which caused him to accept joyfully the call to
come to this land. . . . (m) Words of gratitude for the
love which we had for each other and the unity that
existed among us. (n) A request that the three Nephites
would visit us and assist us in our work; and (o) Spoke of
the righteousness of Lehi and the great faithfulness of
Nephi in doing whatsoever the Lord commanded him.
Also spoke of those, who because of iniquity, had been
cut off from among the Nephites . . . [and expressed the
feeling] that the blood of Nephi and Lehi had been
transmitted unto the people of this land, many of whom
have the features and manners of the American Indians
who are a remnant of the Lamanites. Asked the Lord,
that if this were true, that He would not forget the integrity of His servants Lehi and Nephi and that he
would verify the promises made unto them concerning
their descendants in the last days, upon this people, for
we felt that they were a worthy nation."

Not only were the three elders who listened to this
prayer profoundly affected by it, but Heber was moved
almost to the point of tears. "I am not as a rule gifted in
prayer," he wrote in his journal, "but on this occasion
my heart burned within me and it was with difficulty
that I was able to refrain from shedding tears of joy
while I was offering it."

After the dedicatory prayer, the brethren sang "O
My Father," then bore their testimonies, each one in his
turn. "More than once while the brethren were speaking," Heber wrote, "tears of gratitude filled my eyes for
the rich outpouring of the Good Spirit which I felt in our
midst."

The spiritual emotions this experience inspired were
always to remain with the four elders who shared them.

The inspiration of that day was to stand out like a promontory in the comparatively fruitless months of proselyting that lay ahead. Time and again, the elders would turn to this prayer—the wellspring of their Japanese ministry—like thirsty travelers in a parched land, to revive their spirits and to take new sightings on their goals.

Chapter 14

Missionary Struggles in Japan

I t was no easy task to blaze a missionary trail in the exotic land of Japan. Deep-rooted differences in language, race, customs, and religious bent posed problems of communication that were perplexing even to a man of Heber J. Grant's optimistic temperament. The brethren strove mightily to scale these barriers, but often they seemed insurmountable, especially when set against the background of what seemed to be a giant conspiracy by the other Christian sects, who closed ranks momentarily in an effort to freeze out the Mormons. However, inured from childhood to the reproaches of enemies and detractors, Heber was not discouraged in the least from using every device and following every lead that might help advance his cause. He made friends with employees and executives in the U.S. Consulate. He laid the groundwork for the publication of an "Address to the Japanese Nation," over which he and his companions toiled for many days. He made arrangements for a man to act as a sort of press agent for the brethren. In addition, he exploited his wide business experience and connections by making the acquaintance of influential American businessmen and professional men in Japan. It was through these contacts that he was able to arrange for a tour through part of Japan to Tokyo and Kanazawa. This was no pleasure trip; it was more in the nature of a reconnoitering excursion to learn the lay of the land and to feel the pulse of the people.

Heber was enthralled by the sights and the sounds of this small, energetic country, which less than fifty years before had been opened for the first time to occidental influence by the treaty negotiated by Commodore Perry. In this short period the Japanese people, so intelligent and hardworking, had made giant strides toward making their nation one of the foremost industrial powers in the world. Being a businessman and entrepreneur, Heber was especially interested in the manufactories he observed. At one silk factory, he took delight in computing the time required by the female workers to produce the finished silk products, and marveled at their cheerful resignation to the many hours they spent at their workbenches.

Heber was also taken up with the unfailing courtesy and kindness of this people, their dedication to family traditions, and their unflagging work habits. And the Japanese countryside was a constant delight to him. Judging from the superlatives used in some of his journal entries, he was often amazed by the beauty and charm of a country scene, a grove, or a well-tended garden, wishing his artist friend John Hafen were present to capture the sight on canvas for his family and friends to enjoy.

For some time after his arrival Heber did not attempt to learn the Japanese language, feeling he could work through interpreters and would better use his time doing the public relations and motivational work for which he was best suited. After several months, however, he began to feel uneasy about his inability to communicate directly with the Japanese in their own tongue, and he sought counsel from the First Presidency. His intuition suggested what their answer would be, although it is plain from a journal entry made in late November that he was not enthusiastic about the tedious labor that he knew learning a complicated language like Japanese would necessarily entail. "In writing to my wife Augusta in the morning before the arrival of the Presidency's letter," he recorded, "I mentioned the fact that I had had no word from them as to my learning the language . . . and that if they decided for me to learn the language that I felt as Nephi of old that the Lord did not require a work of any of His children save he prepares the way for them whereby they could accomplish the thing that He required and I felt I could do what ever was wanted and that I would do my best."

By this time, the missionaries had established their

headquarters in Tokyo and were working as a four-man team as they had done from the beginning. The feeling grew among them, however, that it was wisdom to separate, although Heber regretted breaking up the quartet that had been wont to gather around the piano in the parlor of their boardinghouse to serenade the guests. The matter having been decided, Elders Ensign and Taylor paired off and commenced to work independently, making periodic reports, of course, to their mission president.

While Heber was severely limited in proselyting due to his language deficiencies, he was never idle. Nor did he spend time sight-seeing or souvenir hunting. He was always busy, not only out of habit but also because he felt the need to set the proper example for those who looked to him for leadership. He took pride in the fact that he was always striving to advance the work in one way or another.

One activity that claimed much of his attention was answering the libelous attacks on the Church made by other Christian denominations that had preceded the Latter-day Saints into the country and had, over several decades, developed a significant power base, especially with the news media. The *Japan Mail*, one of the most influential newspapers in Tokyo, often opened its pages to these enemies, and there they mixed fact with fantasy and fiction to draw a grossly distorted caricature of the Church and its teachings. Realizing that these falsehoods, if not corrected, would irrevocably poison the public mind against his message, Heber spared no effort in making prompt rebuttal whenever possible. Working with an assistant who regularly monitored the Tokyo newspapers for him, he prepared answers that, more often than not, he was able to get into print, either for a monetary consideration or by the gentle persuasion he could exert through his newfound friends in business and government.

Once he had decided to learn Japanese, Heber established a regular schedule of study and recital. This required an almost heroic effort on his part because of the lack of enthusiasm he had for learning the language, its unbelievable complexity, and the deficiencies in his scholastic training. However, as he applied himself persistently to this onerous task, he found that it became progressively easier, even as one of his favorite maxims had foretold. "I have found the task of studying less tiresome during the past week," he wrote on January 26, 1902, "than any time since I arrived in Japan."

By February Heber and his companions had been in Japan for six months, a sufficient time to give them a clear insight into the problems and challenges of the work there. He began to feel that if he could share these insights in person with his brethren, whose combined knowledge comprised a vast store of missionary expertise, it would be possible to accelerate and strengthen the work far beyond what he could hope to accomplish alone. Beyond this, he regretted having been away from home at the time of the death of President Snow and the subsequent reorganization of the First Presidency. And, of course, there was the powerful attraction of his family, whose personal association he had missed, albeit without any real sense of homesickness. As these thoughts took root in his mind, there formed a desire, which soon gave birth to a plan, to return home in time for the April conference. "In the morning before getting up," he recorded on February 11, "I got to thinking of how I would have enjoyed being home when the presidency was reorganized and how I would enjoy being at conference in April and how much better I could explain matters in this mission to the Presidency than I can write, and I finally said to myself that I did not see any reason why I should not take a trip home."

While some indecision followed this entry, accompanied by the usual internal debate in which Heber often engaged as he weighed the pros and cons of an issue, the plan reached fruition on March 11, 1902, when he departed for home on the steamship *Galic*. On the dock waving their goodbyes were Elders Kelsch, Ensign, and Taylor, along with brothers Nakazawa and Kikuchi, the precious fruits of seven months of proselyting in Japan. Both of these converts had been ordained elders shortly after their baptism. And while they were later to wither and fall from the Church for lack of a deep-rooted conversion, nevertheless as they stood there waving while Heber's ship pulled away from its berth, they represented to him tangible, heart-warming evidence that ultimately the teachings of the Church would take hold among this remarkable people.

Having just returned from the exotic Orient, Heber was a celebrity in Salt Lake City. He was much in demand as a speaker throughout the city and was a favored dinner guest. Everywhere he spoke, he delivered essentially the same message—one of love for the Japanese people and for his companions in the ministry. Time and again he emphasized that his corps of missionaries had deliberately slowed the conversion process to avoid baptizing persons who lacked knowledge and commitment. "We have made no effort whatever," he said, in the April 1902 general conference, "to try and baptize people. Many have come and applied for baptism—ten young men at one time; many have written us letters and asked to be baptized into the Church; but we have realized that they did not understand the Gospel, and we had no desire to baptize and seal the Holy Ghost upon a person who would be likely to lose the Spirit and turn around and fight the Church." But although the harvest had been meager, Heber had supreme confidence in the ultimate success of the Church in Japan. Said he: "I have the assurance in my soul that there is to be a wonderful work accomplished in Japan; that there will be many, yea, even thousands of that people that will receive the Gospel of Jesus Christ." These prophetic words were to see fulfillment in the astonishing growth of the Church in Japan after World War II.

Perhaps the most significant influence his mission had exerted upon Heber thus far was to increase his patience and to enlarge his sense of love and appreciation for others. "I never expected," he told the conference, "that it would be possible for a man of my temperament and disposition, who from a boy of fourteen years of age has been actively engaged in business, to forget it, and that I could content myself in a foreign land studying a language that put me to sleep every time I tried it, and yet be happy. But I was. There was the sweet spirit of God with us, and many times in our little meetings we shed tears of joy, because of the outflow of the Spirit of God. If I had the privilege of picking the Church over for three companions I could not be better satisfied than with those that I have. I had my choice, and I have not been disappointed."

But more impressive than anything else to the audiences who heard Heber speak about his mission to Japan was the fervor of his testimony, the sense of undeviating commitment to the Church and its teachings that his words conveyed: "I rejoice in the knowledge that the work of God is onward and upward and that each of us who is true and faithful will be saved. I rejoice that this Gospel is going to all the nations of the earth. I rejoice in being a messenger of the plan of life and salvation. God has blessed me with a knowledge. I know that He lives. I know that Jesus is the Christ. I know that Joseph Smith is a prophet of God. I know that I shall live forever, and that if I am faithful I shall be exalted. I know that this same blessing will come to all of you, if you are faithful."

During the three months Heber remained in the United States after returning from Japan, he carried on his family, church, and business affairs in the usual way, but they took on a new dimension for him. He savored the experiences of each day, looking on them with the new eyes his absence had created. His joy in having his loved ones about him every day, in counseling regularly with his brethren, and in handling the daily grist of business with its stimulating challenges and rewards was almost unbounded. It was not that he disliked the mission field; on the contrary, he loved proselyting and was anxious to return to his small but dedicated corps of missionaries, with whom he kept in regular contact by mail. But in living abroad he had come alive to many things that for so long he had taken for granted, so it seemed in a sense as though life began anew when he picked up the threads of normal existence upon his return.

But as the weeks wore on, Heber became restive and anxious to take up again the labors that, for the moment, occupied the center of his thoughts and desires. In counseling with the Brethren, it was decided that his wife Augusta and their daughter Mary, along with several young elders and the wife of Horace Ensign, should return with him. The group of young men favored with this choice call included John W. Stoker, Frederick A. Caine, Erastus L. Jarvis, and Sanford Wills Hedges.

On June 26, 1902, a special meeting was held in the Salt Lake Temple Annex, where instructions were given to the missionaries who were scheduled to depart for Japan the following day. Especially impressive was the counsel given by President Joseph F. Smith: "Become convinced if you are not already convinced, become convinced that Jesus is the Christ, that He lives and is the Redeemer of the world. Know ye that Jesus Christ himself appeared to Joseph Smith and renewed his convenant with men in the world, and Joseph Smith was the agent chosen through God through which this covenant should be renewed to the world. Learn this great and glorious truth, for it is a truth, and this is the truth that you go to preach to the world."

To emphasize the nature of their work and the relationship he bore to them, he concluded with this admonition: "Now another thing, my brethren and sisters. I am a weak man, a very weak man, I have many faults, many imperfections, and many shortcomings. I am by no means perfect, by no means perfect; but the Priesthood that God my Father has given to me is not imperfect, it is truth. Though you may see my weaknesses and my imperfections, and may look upon me with some degree of contempt likely in your minds, do not for a moment allow yourselves to look with contempt or lightly upon the position that God has called me into. Don't you do it, for though I may be a weak instrument in the hands of the Lord, the Lord has put me in the place I stand in the order that he has established."

Heber and his party caught the eleven P.M. train out of Salt Lake City the following night. After intermediate

stops in Portland and Seattle, they traveled by steamship to Victoria, B.C., where they boarded their
passenger ship bound for Yokohama. The voyage was
about the most pleasant one Heber was ever to take. Except for one morning, he was entirely free of seasickness
during the fifteen days at sea. With gratitude he noted,
"I felt to rejoice exceedingly for the great improvement.
We had a pleasant voyage. The wind blew a little, and
we had a little fog but as a rule the weather was all that
could be expected. The steamer is a very steady one
indeed. Our state rooms were all located on the upper
deck, and so we had plenty of air and the fact that we
did not have to go down to our rooms to sleep I think
had much to do in keeping our party from being sea sick.
None of the party suffered to any extent from sea sickness and most of them escaped entirely."

The presence of Sister Grant radically altered the
complexion of missionary work in Japan. Augusta, the
consummate homemaker, created an atmosphere in the
mission headquarters reminiscent of the friendly hearths
the elders had left behind. Here they could always be
assured of a friendly welcome, a home-cooked meal, and
the kind of motherly encouragement that caused them
to work ever more purposefully.

Periodically Heber called them together in the
mission home so he could hear their reports, impart
counsel, and provide motivation. At this point in his
career, after more than twenty years as a member of the
Twelve, he had learned to wear his apostolic mantle
gracefully. In most instances, he directed the affairs of
the mission through the principle of consensus. In this
was mirrored his training in the high councils of the
Church where the Brethren constantly seek for that
unity which the Master requires of his disciples. It also
reflected his extensive experience in directing corporations where success depended upon the input of all
charged with developing or executing company policy.
A record of a missionary meeting held in Tokyo in June
1903 carries definite overtones of a board of director's
meeting; absent is every vestige of dictation or arbitrari-
ness. "At the meeting this afternoon," Heber wrote, "I

spoke in English and all of the elders including Oyama spoke in Japanese. Between Sunday School and afternoon meeting we had a little council meeting. We discussed first whether we should ask for more elders to be sent to Japan, and the decision was unanimously in favor of doing so. Second shall we have another tract. Same decision. Shall we change the field of labor of Bros. Jarvis and Stoker. Decided that they had better remain where they are, at least for the present."

In meetings of this kind, Heber was playing one of the most important roles he was to fill as a mission president. He was training impressionable young men in the art of leadership. He was training those who would hold the reins of leadership in the next generation, and he never missed an opportunity to teach them the skills on which their success as leaders would hinge. An entry from the journal of Elder Alma Taylor during this period clearly reveals this aspect of Heber's leadership. In summarizing instructions his mission president had given to the brethren, Elder Taylor wrote: "Would feel satisfied if the brethren were only able to make friends of the people. One of the purposes of calling young men on missions was to open up communication between heaven and the missionary in order that when he returns home to Zion he may be worth something to the church and the Lord. He stated that Prest. [Andrew] Kimball of the Saint Joseph Stake always kept as many of the young men as possible in the mission field for the reason that he needed strong men to help in the building up of a new country and realized that the best way to get them filled with the spirit is to have them on a mission for two or three years. Even if we do not baptize a soul we will be repaid for all the sacrifices we make in the abundance of other blessings we will receive. When the power of the evil one was threatening the church, when many of the prominent men were apostatizing, when the saints were receiving their bitterest persecution, the Prophet Joseph Smith sent the apostles on missions so that when they returned they would be filled with the power of God and be prepared for their mighty labors at home. If we can do our duty and go home with the proper spirit, we have obtained much and our labors will have been in no wise vain."

Heber's work routine varied little after Augusta and Mary joined him in the field. An early riser, he began the day with prayer and scripture study. He continued his struggling efforts to learn the Japanese language, having almost daily sessions with a tutor. He kept alive his government, business, and professional contacts and handled an ever-increasing volume of correspondence with his brethren, family, and friends at home and with his missionaries in the field. Wherever he went, he served as an ambassador of goodwill for the Church, planting seeds of friendship and understanding that years later would take root and produce beneficial fruit.

But despite every exertion he and the missionaries put forth, they could not generate enough enthusiasm and commitment in their proselyting contacts to produce convert baptisms. They were hampered by the high standard of worthiness Heber had imposed, by vast differences in cultural and religious background, by the heated animus of the other Christian sects, and by the unbelievable complexity of the language. It was also a source of consternation to Heber that the two converts who had gladdened his heart as he waved goodbye to them on leaving for home in April 1902 had proven to be unconverted. One of them was interested only in using his membership for personal gain, and the other showed himself as having no real conception of the principles the elders had taught him. In the meantime, only one additional convert had come into the fold, and Heber held out no optimistic hopes for him.

This meager harvest was a sore disappointment. Heber's training and background had geared him for the kind of proselyting results the early missionaries had experienced in the United States and England, where it was not uncommon for converts to be measured by the hundreds and thousands. It was painful for him to recall that his beloved associate Wilford Woodruff had reaped a harvest of hundreds of converts during a period of a few weeks in England, a comparison that produced some feelings of inferiority and frustration. Of course, reason

convinced him that comparing the two missions was un-
realistic because of the vast differences in their composition, but the great disparity in the yields was still a cause
of some concern and anxiety.

As the weeks and months wore on with no discernible
evidence of a change in proselyting fortunes, there
emerged in Heber's thinking and attitudes a new philo-
sophical aspect, a resigned and patient quality that was
to color his personality and conduct through the remainder of his life. It was almost as if he had received an
infusion of the Oriental character, a calm and detached
wait-and-see attitude, which, when merged with the aggressive do-it-now habits he had practiced from infancy,
set him apart from all his contemporaries. Ever after he
seemed to show in his character the presence of these two
competing qualities.

Deprived of the fruit of convert baptisms, Heber laid
ever-increasing emphasis on the other prime object of his
ministry—the training and development of his missionaries. He saw instinctively that the influence for
good emanating from this effort would be extensive,
even eternal, in its scope. The motivation and incentive,
the skills and abilities he might plant in the young elders
under his charge would be transmitted by them to their
families and associates and, in turn, by them to their
descendants. Vast consequences emerging at some time
in the remote future might thus be traceable logically
and directly to his doings of the moment.

For this reason, Heber never lost an opportunity to
train and inspire the missionaries. Frequent training and
testimony meetings were held, usually in the mission
home in Tokyo. These were special occasions for the
missionaries, as they received a once-in-a-lifetime opportunity for intimate association with an apostle of the
Lord. In most mission fields of the day, the mission
president had responsibility for so many missionaries,
with the attendant administrative work and often the
responsibility for member districts and branches, that his
time for personal contact with each missionary was
greatly restricted. In the case of Japan, the situation was
different because of the exceedingly small missionary

force and the nonexistent branch and district organizations. Thus the president was able to devote long, productive periods to this activity.

As September 1903 approached, Heber felt the need for a commemorative service of some kind to mark the second anniversary of the dedication of the land for the preaching of the gospel. It was decided that nothing would be more fitting than to travel to the secluded spot outside Yokohama where the dedicatory prayer had been offered. Having gathered in Tokyo for the occasion, the entire mission force, including the Grants and their daughter Mary, Elders Horace Ensign and Joseph Featherstone and their wives, and Elders Alma Taylor, Erastus L. Jarvis, Fred A. Caine, John W. Stoker, and Sanford W. Hedges left by train on September 1. Upon arriving in Yokohama, they made their way to the nearby hill, which had become sacred to them because of its association with the dedicatory services. After resting and making the necessary preparations, they began a lengthy and inspiring meeting that included bearing of testimonies by all present, interspersed with favorite hymns. Inasmuch as Heber was soon to return home, the remarks he made on the occasion were in the nature of a valedictory. The faithful scribe, Alma Taylor, included this summary in his journal: "Prest. Heber J. Grant was the first speaker. He expressed his pleasure at being present—referred to the time when the four who first came to Japan were strangers in a strange land—they were not familiar with the customs of the people, opposed by the papers, refused lodgings at a boarding house, and in every way opposed by those who wanted and tried to get them prohibited from preaching in Japan. Spoke of the particularly bitter attitude of the 'Japan Mail,' the editor of which wilfully lied about them and their position towards the doctrine of polygamy, which doctrine Pres. Grant had personally assured him they did not intend to teach or promulgate—asserted that the feelings that fill the hearts of pioneers can only be understood by the pioneers themselves—felt that the four first elders were abundantly blessed of the Lord and many times melted to tears by the manifestations of the Spirit of God. Prest.

Grant said that he treasured sacred remembrances of the
spot of ground upon which we were assembled not only
because it was the place of the dedicatory prayer, but because of having come there in company with Elder
Kelsch and in the course of the prayers they offered up
received many blessings and promises which dispelled
the feelings of sadness that were then filling his heart. . . .
Prest. Grant referred to the fact he is only blessed with
the spirit of prayer on rare occasions, yet nevertheless
sincere in offering all supplications to the Lord. Remarkably blessed in making the dedicatory prayer two years
before. On that occasion Elder Kelsch brought a copy of
the prayer offered on the Mount of Olives when Orson
Hyde dedicated that land unto the Lord for the return
of the Jews but Prest. Grant declined to read it feeling
that he wanted to be influenced by the whisperings of
the Spirit rather than by what someone else had asked
the Lord, and felt to acknowledge the influence of the
Spirit in enabling him to offer an acceptable prayer.
Prest. Grant felt that since the time of the dedication
much good had been accomplished. He referred to the
home going of Elder Kelsch and the little he seemed to
have done here and to his own contemplated return and
the slight labor he felt to have done, but stated that, as
in the case of Elder Kelsch, all who come to this land
and return in a short time will be interested in the
progress of the work and do much by calling the attention of the Saints to this mission. . . . He felt that the
Presidency and the apostles were satisfied with what he
had done here—and was glad that Elder Ensign who
had had some experience in missionary labors before
coming to Japan was to be left in charge and that Elder
Ensign's wife was here with him. He said that all should
give to Elder Ensign the loyal support which he himself
had received while presiding here."

Later, in reflecting on his service with Heber, Elder
Taylor observed: "In my opinion, it is unreasonable to
think that the Lord ever intended the peculiar equipment with which President Grant is endowed should be
stranded for long in a morass of verb conjugation and
chop stick technique." And, comparing the meager

harvest in Japan with the rich yields in England and Hawaii, he concluded, "One can readily understand why the Japanese Mission tested to the utmost the fortitude and faith of its founders." (*Improvement Era,* November 1936, p. 691.)

The extent to which Heber was tried and tested by his service in Japan is best inferred from his later sermons and writings. Speaking in the Salt Lake Tabernacle during the October 1903 general conference he confided: "When I received my release, I felt I could not come home; that I must stay at least six months more; and the first night, instead of being happy, as one usually is when released to return home, I felt sad, for the first and only time in Japan. I did not go to sleep until three or four o'clock in the morning, and I felt I must cable home and ask permission to remain."

In the bright glare of day, Heber thought better of this nocturnal impression, and dismissed it as having come from a spirit of pride. "I disliked to have to tell you that I had been there 15 months and done nothing," he said. "I wanted to stay six months more, to get some results from the active labor we had done there, so that I could come home and say I had done as well as other apostles who had gone out on missions. . . . It was pride and not the Spirit of the Lord, that prompted this feeling."

In the self-deprecatory, amusing way that always endeared him to his audiences, Heber then reviewed the meager fruits of his Japanese mission. "We have baptized only three people so far," he said, "and two of them I am afraid are no good." Of one of them he added, "Oh! he believed it all—ready to give his life for it. I found out afterwards that he wanted to borrow some money from me to start a patent medicine establishment." Of the second, he reported, "He wanted fifteen hundred dollars from me to start a job printing office, and when he didn't get it, his faith oozed out."

Another penetrating insight into the trauma Heber suffered from his Japanese ministry is found in the account he gave years after the event: "When in Japan, feeling that I was not accomplishing anything, I went out into the woods and got down on my knees and told the Lord that whenever He was through with me there, where I was doing nothing, I would be very glad and thankful if he would call me home and send me to Europe to preside over the European Mission." Only a few days after he offered this fervent prayer he received a cable from the First Presidency: "Come home on the first boat." (*Improvement Era*, July 1936, p. 396.)

Obedient to that directive, Heber, Augusta, and Mary sailed from Yokohama aboard the *Aki Mari* on September 8, 1903. They arrived in Salt Lake City in time for the October general conference, during which an announcement was made that opened another exciting chapter in Heber's life and fulfilled the premonition he had had as he prayed in Japan before returning home.

Chapter 15

European Mission President

The incident that triggered Heber's speculation and yearning that he might preside in Europe was the death of Elder Brigham Young, Jr., on April 11, 1903. Elder Young's passing vacated the office of president of the Council of the Twelve Apostles, a vacancy that would be filled by the next senior apostle, Elder Francis M. Lyman, who was then presiding over the European Misssion. Heber assumed, naturally and correctly, that Elder Lyman would return home to direct the affairs of his quorum, and he would thus need to be replaced in Europe. It was this assumption that had inspired Heber's heartfelt prayer in Tokyo, a prayer that saw fulfillment when, before the conference, President Joseph F. Smith called him to suceed Elder Lyman as president of the European Mission.

True to the practice of confidentiality in such matters, Heber had not divulged the call to his family. They were taken by surprise when, at the end of the final session on Tuesday, October 6, 1903, President Joseph F. Smith casually announced that Elder Heber J. Grant would succeed Elder Francis M. Lyman as president of the European Mission.

The emotional impact of this unexpected announcement on Emily Wells Grant, Heber's third wife, who had remained home during his mission in Japan, is shown in the reminiscences of her youngest daughter, Frances Grant Bennett: "The words went through her like an electric shock. She stumbled out of the meeting as best she could, not wanting to see or talk to anyone and not even waiting for Father to take her home. She managed, somehow, to get home; and when he joined her there a few minutes later he found her in tears."(*Glimpses of a*

Mormon Family, Deseret Book, 1968, p. 1.) Joy soon replaced her sorrow, however, when an incredulous Emily was told that she and the girls would be permitted to accompany Heber into the mission field.

Had Emily known then what she was later to learn, the sounds of her joy may have been muted, if not muffled entirely. The difficulty lay in selling the family home, uprooting six girls ranging in age from four to twenty, transporting them and their many valises, trunks, and miscellaneous baggage across a continent and an ocean, and settling them in a new home in a foreign land. With this impressive entourage of femininity, it stretches the mind to realize that Elder Grant was to leave four daughters behind, two of them married and two teenagers.

Fortunately, the Grants were able to make a ready sale of Emily's home to her sister and brother-in-law, Edna and Tom Sloan, and Heber purchased an adjoining lot with the promise that, upon their return, he would build Emily a new home. As fate would have it, the planning and building of this dream home were to occupy Emily's last days shortly after her return from England, as a deadly illness was to carry her to an early grave in 1908 at age fifty-one. For the time being, however, the Grants were busily engaged in preparations to enter the mission field.

For many years the Church had maintained a European Mission home at 42 Islington Street in Liverpool, in a once proud and respectable neighborhood that had deteriorated badly and, at the time of the Grants' arrival, was almost a slum area. Here Emily had lived during her first stay in England while her father, Daniel H. Wells, presided as mission president. But time and events had radically altered the character of the neighborhood.

Fortunately, the Grants were never to occupy the Islington Street quarters, as they carried instructions from the First Presidency to purchase a more commodious, well-situated mission home. They checked into a hotel from which Heber and Emily commenced a search for suitable, permanent housing. Unable at first to find anything to satisfy their special requirements, they leased temporarily a comfortable two-story, four-bedroom home at 9 Hartington Road, where they remained for several months. In the meantime, Heber used the Islington Street building as his office. At length a place that met their unique specifications was found for sale at 10 Holly Road. A red brick, mansion-type building, surrounded by an impressive wrought-iron picket fence, the Holly Road home included a large drawing room on the main floor, which doubled as a chapel for the Saints in Liverpool; a mezzanine with living quarters for the elders; a spacious second floor that comprised the private apartment for the Grant family; an attic; and a spacious basement in which a print shop was installed, including the press that had published the first *Millennial Star*. The first editor of this famous early Church publication, Parley P. Pratt, had included a copy of his poem "The Morning Breaks, the Shadows Flee" on the front of the first issue of the *Star* in Manchester, England, more than sixty years before. The sentiment of this poem seemed to typify Heber's feelings as he faced this new day in his apostolic career.

It seemed very natural for Heber to succeed his friend Francis M. Lyman as mission president; he had succeeded him as the president of the Tooele Stake and had later followed him into the Council of the Twelve. A dozen years later he would succeed him as the President of that Council. His long acquaintance with President Lyman had conditioned him to expect that affairs in the European Mission would be in perfect order. As he later observed: "I knew from my experience . . . that he would have all the holes filled up, the bridges made and the roads in good condition. I knew that I would find the mission well-organized and everything in fine shape with a good foundation on which to build." (*Conference Report,* April 1907, p. 36.)

What Heber found was a corps of 114 missionaries in the British Isles whom he would personally direct, and many other missionaries who would be indirectly supervised by him through mission presidents in Holland, Belgium, Switzerland, France, Germany, Austria, and Scandinavia. In addition, he assumed the editorship of the *Millennial Star*, which was circulated weekly to the English-speaking members under his jurisdiction, and he was responsible for the printing and distribution of the numerous tracts and books used by the mission in proselyting. Some idea of the enormous production that rolled endlessly from the mission print shop is gained from the fact that during the first eleven months of Heber's presidency of the European Mission, over 3,800,000 tracts or books were printed there. This mountain of literature was delivered by the indefatigable missionaries with a perseverance and consistency that reflected the character of their leader.

With one notable exception, the conditions Heber found in England were the opposite of those in Japan. Here he was working among a people who spoke his language, whose religious and cultural backgrounds were similar to his own, who had descended from the same racial stock, and whose legal and social mores were like his. Furthermore, he found a smoothly functioning organization for proselyting, based on precedents and initiatives that extended back for seventy years, and an ongoing system for administering the local congregations.

The one familiar problem Heber encountered in England was the unfavorable treatment of the Church and its doctrines by the press. In Britain, as in Japan, he found an almost complete absence of factuality in news reports about the Church. If anything, matters were worse in England because the British papers were generally unwilling to open their pages to rebuttal, and because the distortions and falsehoods that had flooded the British Isles for decades had created a climate not merely of indifference, but of open hostility. So poor were the Church's press relations in England that Heber later reported that in the almost three years of his ministry he was unaware of a single instance in which anything favorable to the Church had found its way into the English press. This does not mean to say he did not try to alter this pattern. On the contrary, he labored mightily toward that end, but he failed in it—a failure that underscored the importance of the little Church press that was kept going almost around the clock in a futile attempt to stem the tide of adverse publicity.

Once Heber had established his family in comfortable circumstances and had the reins of administration firmly in his grasp, he began to move out into his field of labor to perform the work for which he was specially qualified.

His first trip of any consequence was to Holland in the early part of February 1904 to attend the semiannual conference of the Netherlands-Belgium Mission in Rotterdam. Following a practice that was to characterize his term as mission president, he took two members of his family along, both for his companionship and for their education. Edith and Grace were the ones favored to make this trip.

Heber and the girls made their headquarters at the mission home with the president of the Netherlands-Belgium mission, Willard T. Cannon, and his family. Gathered in Rotterdam for the conference were President Cannon's thirty-three missionaries, members of the Church from throughout the mission, President Hugh J. Cannon of the German Mission, and President Levi Edgar Young of the Swiss Mission.

Despite his exceedingly heavy schedule of meetings, Heber found time to expose Edith and Grace to the culture of Rotterdam with a visit to a museum and art gallery. There he was very much taken with Rembrandt's *Night Watch* for which, he was surprised to learn, an Englishman had offered seven and a half million dollars but was turned down by the proud Hollanders, who considered this masterpiece to be priceless. It was also a source of considerable interest to him that an artist who sat painting an excellent copy of the *Night Watch* was willing to sell it for only three hundred dollars.

However, the visiting apostle did not permit this cultural excursion to divert him from the main purpose that had brought him to Rotterdam. Of the many meetings held during the conference, the most significant one, the one that held out the best prospects for increased success in proselyting, was the one held on Saturday

with the missionaries and the visiting mission presidents.
This meeting lasted five hours, during which all of the
missionaries gave activity reports, the visiting mission
presidents spoke briefly, and Heber capped the meeting
with a two-hour discourse in which he gave "instructions
on everything that [he] thought might be of value to
them in their missionary labors."

The exceptional record in convert baptisms compiled
in Europe during his administration attests to his effectiveness in directing missionaries. Out of his vast
experience as an apostle for over two decades, as a stake
president, and as a mission president, he was able to
prescribe changes in procedures and attitudes that
spelled success.

But Heber's role at the conference did not end with
the marathon report meeting on Saturday. On Sunday
there were three general sessions, at which he hoped to
strengthen the Saints who were already in the fold and
to lead the attending investigators along the path of
conversion.

It was with some trepidation that Heber took his
place at the pulpit Sunday morning in Excelsior Hall,
the customary meeting place of the Rotterdam Saints.
Before him sat an audience of about five hundred, of
whom he later wrote: "With the exception of the large
audience in the Metropolitan Temple in San Francisco,
I never have faced such an intelligent and large audience
out in the world." Not only was the size and composition
of the audience intimidating, but it was also unsettling
to have to communicate through an interpreter.

As anticipated, he was awkward in speaking at the
morning and afternoon sessions and did not feel he had
accomplished much. But of the evening session, he wrote
with some enthusiasm: "I was greatly blessed of the Lord
and the few minutes I spoke I had a great liberty as
though I were not talking through an interpreter and
was able to bear a strong testimony regarding the Gospel
of Jesus Christ and the divinity of the mission of
Joseph Smith. . . . I had a burning desire to bear my
testimony to them and I feel truly gratified to the Lord
that He granted me the privilege of doing so."

This trip to Holland was representative of many other trips Heber and his family would take during their stay in Europe. That same year they enjoyed beautiful scenery and cultural attractions in France, Switzerland, and Scandinavia, but their major purpose was always to further the Lord's work, and they worked diligently to strengthen the missions they visited.

One especially noteworthy event occurred in Scandinavia when Heber visited there in the summer of 1906. It happened that he and his party, which included his wife Emily and Nephi Anderson, the associate editor of the *Millennial Star,* found themselves in Stockholm on the fourth of July without any plans to celebrate. Moved by a patriotism that often showed in his conduct, Heber asked, "What would you like to do to celebrate our country's natal day?" Receiving no suggestion that seemed quite appropriate to the occasion, he proposed something that startled them for its novelty and audaciousness. "I would like to call on King Oscar," he said. Seeing that this spur-of-the-moment suggestion found enthusiastic acceptance among the group, he advised them to get ready while he prepared a letter of introduction. "To His Majesty, King Oscar of Sweden and Norway," it began, "I am here with a party of Mormons. This is the day of all days—our natal day—that we as Americans celebrate. I hope you will waive formalities and grant us an interview. I have letters of introduction from both of the United States Senators from Utah to our Minister to Sweden and Norway, asking that he arrange for me to have an interview with you. I enclose a letter from the Governor of the State of Utah, which I hope will be sufficient to cause you to waive formalities and grant my party and myself an interview."

Armed with these credentials, which hardly satisfied the strict requirements of diplomatic protocol, Heber and his party started out with a gaiety and self-confidence that might have marked a Sunday afternoon social call in Salt Lake City. It was not that he was ignorant of the amenities of social intercourse; his expressed hope that formalities could be waived negated that idea. The event was rather a reflection of the

honest, down-to-earth character of the man who made
the request. The spirit and object of the interview are
best conveyed through his own words. He later wrote:
"King Oscar at the time was on a little island, about a
half hour's ride from Stockholm. When we reached the
king's castle on this island, a soldier was walking back
and forth in front of the castle, with a gun over his
shoulder. I said 'When he comes here and turns I will
follow him, and when he gets to the end of his beat I will
by that time be talking to somebody at the front door,
and he will not shoot me as he will think I would not be
there unless I had a right to be.'

"The first person who came to the door undoubtedly
talked Swedish only, but pretty soon another man came
who could talk perfect English, and he asked me, 'What
can I do for you?' "

One can imagine the shock that the answer produced: "I wish to see the king." "No one can see the king
without a proper introduction," the attendant
responded. Then followed a dialogue that was reminiscent of the confrontation Heber had had with the
banker in New York when he was trying to sell the six
percent ZCMI notes: "I said, 'Did the king tell you to
deliver that message to me?' He said, 'No.' I said, 'You
return to me my letter which I sent the king from the
governor of the great state of Utah, or an answer from
the king that he will not receive me.' He came back and
said, 'The king will step out on the lawn here and receive
you.' "

Of the extraordinary interview on the lawn of King
Oscar's castle, the indomitable apostle later wrote: "The
king received us . . . and asked a few questions in
Swedish, which were interpreted by the editor of the
Swedish Star. Then the king said, 'How many of you
understand Swedish?' There were only two or three in
our party who did, and he changed to perfect English.
He then said, 'Mr. Grant, the various religious people
here wish me to prohibit the Mormons from proselyting
in my kingdom. I have sent my personal representatives
to the United States without announcing that they were
my representatives, to interview my former subjects,

where there are large numbers of them, and they report to me that in no other part of the United States are my former subjects so contented, so happy, and so prosperous as in Utah, and so long as I am King of Sweden your people shall have religious liberty."

In the early part of this same year, Heber took an interesting swing through Italy with Emily, Dessie, and Grace. Although the sights and sounds of ancient Rome were intensely fascinating to Heber and provided mental images he was to call forth again and again, he was affected more by the impressions he received as he contrasted the vigorous, simple, and young organization he represented with the extensive, tradition-laden church he found headquartered in the Vatican. Nor could his mind avoid a comparison between the fantastic splendor of what he saw and the spartan ministry of the humble fisherman, Simon Peter, who centuries before had taught the Savior's principles in simplicity and plainness to the ancestors of the Romans who then possessed the Eternal City. These comparisons brought home forcefully the idea that the deviations from Christ's teachings, so evident in the Rome of Heber's day, resulted from tradition, human error, and miscalculation, and not from any defect in the precepts Peter and his brethren had taught. All this brought to the modern apostle a recognition of the need to adhere to first principles, to retain the basic simplicity of Christ's teachings, and to avoid man-made innovations. "Never," he wrote, "have I been more profoundly impressed with deep gratitude for the gospel than since I came on this trip; and this trip to Rome, the headquarters of Catholicism, has increased this feeling. The simplicity of the gospel in comparison with the display has never been made so forcible to my mind. I would not have missed this trip for anything."

Two other events that occurred in the last few months of Heber's European mission deserve special mention. On August 7, upon his return from a trip to Belfast, Ireland, he found waiting for him a letter from President Joseph F. Smith, written from New York, advising that he, President Smith, was en route to Europe and was due to arrive that day in Antwerp. "I immediately left for London," Heber wrote, "and took the night train and steamer from Harwich to the Hook of Holland." In Rotterdam the following day, he recorded, "I went to the hotel where I had the pleasure of meeting brother [Charles W.] Nibley's father and mother and two sisters and President Joseph F. Smith and wife Edna. I was indeed delighted to meet this party, especially Pres. Smith."

This expression of love for his leader was heartfelt, notwithstanding the question President Smith had raised years before about the wisdom of calling Heber as the president of the Tooele Stake. Any lingering doubts President Smith may have had about the depth of Heber's conviction had long since evaporated. The call President Smith had extended to preside in Europe demonstrated his confidence in Heber; the success Heber reaped as a mission president had vindicated that confidence.

As for Heber, he regarded President Smith with an admiration that bordered on awe. To him, this great man was the embodiment of what one might look for in a prophetic leader. He was intelligent, spiritually minded, industrious, honest, and absolutely reliable. Although he was unbending in matters involving the exercise of his ecclesiastical authority, a quality thought by some to manifest an overly stern and austere character, he was childlike in the love and affection shown toward his family and associates.

As these two spiritual giants embraced in Rotterdam that August, they likely did not realize that within a dozen years they would speak their last earthly farewell and the prophetic mantle would pass from the older man to the younger along with the fatherly benediction President Smith was so accustomed to using in addressing Heber: "God bless you, my boy."

Within two months after his rendezvous with President Smith in Rotterdam, Heber received authorization from Salt Lake City to purchase another mission home, still larger and more functional than the one at 10 Holly Road. Located at 295 Edge Lane, across from

Wavertree Park, this impressive new home, called Durham House, was to serve the Church for many years to come and would become the focal point of many a missionary's reminiscences. Heber's pride in his business acumen found satisfaction in the knowledge that this building cost two and a half times as much as the Church paid for it.

Approval to purchase Durham House was also a signal to Heber that he was soon to be released. This thought filled him with the mixed emotions that come upon most missionaries as they plan to return home. He was at once pleased with the success that had attended his labors and dissatisfied they had not been more productive. He looked forward to renewing close relationships with his family and associates at home, while regretting genuinely the severance of the close ties that had bound him to the missionaries and Saints in Europe. He yearned for the clear mountain air and open spaces of the American West, while knowing deep within he would miss greatly the crowded, ancient cities of Europe with the civilized encrustation of the centuries that lay upon them. Especially would he miss the periodic visits to the cavernous museums and art galleries, where he had been impressed with the artistic qualities of western man and had gained a new appreciation for the meaning of the word *excellence*.

As he inventoried the fruits of three years of dedicated missionary labor, Heber counted not only the hundreds of conversions that had come about either directly or indirectly through his efforts, but also the new insights he had gained into the secrets of leadership; the broadened perspective of the world and its people; the new acquaintances who would play leading roles in Church affairs in the future when he would assume the presidential chair; the treasured memories he would often recall in the years ahead to support the thesis of a sermon or lesson, to entertain, to counsel, or to admonish; and last, but far from least, the increased love and cohesion introduced into his family circle through the active participation of Emily and the girls in his missionary labors. It was with this rich store of achievements and memories that Elder Heber J. Grant returned home to Salt Lake City in December 1907, in time for the Christmas dinner he had looked forward to with eager anticipation.

Chapter 16

The Maturing of a Prophet

Heber's return from Europe was accompanied by the expected flurry of speaking engagements, the settlement of his family and personal affairs, and the reintroduction to his regimen of church and business activities. While in the mission field, he had been able to devote himself almost exclusively to a single activity at a time. Now, at home, he found so many things clamoring for his attention that sometimes he felt terribly fragmented and torn.

The most trying of all the burdens resting upon him during the period following his European mission were his family responsibilities. Having been away from his businesses for almost five years, he had to apply himself diligently in that area to generate the means to maintain his family and to repay the debts he had had to incur while in the mission field. There was the expense, too, of building Emily's new home, and, worst of all, the anguish of watching this beloved companion die ever so slowly. The cancer that ultimately took her life had been diagnosed not long after their return from Europe. The medical skills of the day held no remedy for her illness, and it was not in the providence of God that the many prayers and administrations for her recovery be granted. And so Heber's childhood sweetheart slowly wasted away while working consistently in planning and supervising the construction of her dream home on Second Avenue. Knowing the end was near, the concerned husband spent as much time with her as his heavy commitments would allow. They spoke frankly about the end and the settlement of Emily's affairs upon her death. It was heart-wrenching for Heber to watch the process of death slowly take this devoted companion.

And matters worsened for her when her mother, Martha Harris Wells, passed away. The funeral was held in Emily's home so she could be present. President Joseph F. Smith and Elder Orson F. Whitney, a member of the Twelve and Emily's former bishop, were the speakers.

Her mother's death and burial signaled a turn for the worse in Emily's condition. She failed rapidly. "Emily looks very, very bad indeed this morning," Heber wrote in his journal on Saturday, May 23, 1908. "Unless there is a change for the better, she certainly cannot live but a few days." This prophetic statement was fulfilled two days later when Emily slipped quietly away. "In the death of my wife," the distraught husband wrote, "one of the hardest blows of my life has come to me. However, I am consoled by the fact that our union is eternal, and that if I can live worthily, as she has done, that I am to have her throughout the countless ages of eternity. Her sickness and death [have] been very sad indeed, in fact, pathetic. To have our loved ones dying month after month, and not to be able to do anything for their relief or for their restoration, is hard to endure, in fact beyond one's expression to tell." He added reflectively, "To my mind, the saddest of all deaths is to have a mother taken away from her children, just at the time when they seem to need most her counsel and advice." Then followed the inspiring benediction that seemed so well to typify the simple faith and indomitable spirit of this giant of a man: "However, I feel to say in the language of Job, 'The Lord giveth and the Lord taketh away. Blessed be the name of the Lord.' My children are standing up under the blow very nicely indeed."

The final scene of this drama of death was enacted two days later when funeral services were held for Emily in her newly completed home and she was tenderly laid away. As fate would have it, the funeral took place on May 27, 1908, the twenty-fourth anniversary of her marriage to Heber. In a contemplative mood he wrote: "It seems rather strange that I should be attending her funeral on the anniversary of our wedding. I am sure that she would sooner be buried on this day, however, than any other day in the year. From the time we were

married, I have never been separated from her on the
27th [of May] . . . without writing her a letter, expressing
my appreciation of our love, and my gratitude to the
Lord for our union. We have practically celebrated our
wedding day monthly as well as annually."

The ordeal of laying a second wife to rest and arranging for the care of her motherless daughters added a new
layer of maturity to the apostle. This was an important
addition to his character, and it would take a vital place
among the credentials qualifying him to serve as a high
spiritual leader. The condolences he would send in the
future to those mourning the loss of loved ones; the
counsel he would offer to those suffering personal up-
heaval; the admonitions he would give to those who
were indifferent to the blessings of family life—all these
things and many others pertaining to human relationships would be rooted in his personal experiences
and would, therefore, carry a ring of authenticity and
authority. Paraphrasing a scripture that reflects the
maturing process through which even the Savior had to
pass: "Though he were an apostle, destined to be the
prophet, yet learned he obedience and wisdom by the
things which he suffered."

Heber's family life formed the matrix that fed his
many other varied activities. While he devoted a lion's
share of his time to his ecclesiastical duties and business
interests, the roots of his existence and the eternal hopes
he nurtured grew in the soil of his family. The theology
he expounded, which gave sense and meaning to life,
taught clearly that one's hope for exaltation lay in the
eternal union of man and wife, sealed by heavenly authority, and in the crowning jewels of children born to
that union. To him, church position and business attainment, while worthy of his best efforts, were but the
transitory means of reaching the ultimate end: to become perfect, to attain godhood, to qualify to share with
the Savior in all the Father has, and to experience "a
continuation of the seeds forever." These goals lay in the
direction of family love and solidarity. A grasp of this
underlying principle is essential to an understanding of
the motivations and drives that propelled Heber J.

Grant along his exciting but sometimes perilous road.

But the side issues, the subordinate aspects of his life, sometimes may have appeared to dominate his thinking and efforts. Certainly this was true in the years immediately following his release as president of the European Mission, when references to church and business affairs filled his journal.

On the ecclesiastical front, he was saddened to learn that bitterness toward the Church by the gentile community, generated by the titanic battle over polygamy, had not yet dissipated, notwithstanding the fact that the Manifesto had been in effect for seventeen years. The dissension and controversy that followed in the wake of the Manifesto arose from the widespread belief in gentile circles that it was a facade to mask the Mormons' intent to continue practicing polygamy underground while making a surface show of compliance. This idea gained some credence when two members of the Twelve, John W. Taylor and Matthias F. Cowley, resigned in 1905 while Heber was in Europe. They were formally disciplined in 1911 because of their unorthodox stand on the issue of polygamy; and while their views were rejected by the Brethren and were contrary to established church policy, uninformed enemies drew wrong inferences from their conduct and attributed false motives and aims to the leaders as a whole. Also, the refusal of the Brethren to cast off the polygamous wives they had married prior to the Manifesto was a source of misunderstanding and criticism. The pent-up enmities generated by this issue were brought to a head in the celebrated case of Reed Smoot, a member of the Twelve, who on January 20, 1903, was elected a United States Senator by a Republican legislature in the state of Utah. This action precipitated a frenzied national debate, the central issue of which was whether he was disentitled to serve in such an eminent position because the church of which he was a high official had once taught and practiced polygamy. It seemed irrelevant to Senator Smoot's enemies that he was not and never had been a polygamist, or that the teaching and practice of polygamy had been officially discontinued by the

Church more than a decade before. At this remote time and in the context of today's political and social climate, the ludicrous nature of the arguments raised by his enemies is apparent. "What we do deny him," some of them intoned in a protest entered in the senatorial hearings, "is the right either natural or political, to the high station of senator of the United States from which to wage war upon the home—the basic institution upon whose purity and perpetuity rests the very government itself." (*Proceedings in the Smoot Case* 1:1-25.)

Although it took a great toll in human effort and anguish over a period of four years, the bigoted attempt to deny Senator Smoot his seat failed; and on February 20, 1907, he took his place in the Senate, where he was to remain for over a quarter of a century. Heber, who had been away from home during most of the Smoot controversy, returned only two months before the favorable decision in the Senate and in time for the discussions surrounding "The Address of the Church to the World" that was delivered by the First Presidency at general conference in April 1907 and adopted by the unanimous vote of those present. While this unusual document appraised the role of the Church in its worldwide aspects, it focused especially upon the dramatic, controversial issues in which the Church had been involved recently: polygamy, the alleged Church control of the state, and the alleged dictation of the Church in political matters.

While the controversy over the Smoot case alternately simmered and boiled, Heber busily pursued his apostolic career. By this time, constant and unremitting travel had become a way of life for him. The month following his return from England found him and Augusta in Mexico, where they were ushered about by Heber's first cousin, Anthony W. Ivins, who within a few months was to be called into the Council of the Twelve. Numerous meetings were held throughout the Mormon colonies, and the visiting apostle often both spoke and sang. By this time he had gained some notoriety due to his persistence in learning to sing despite being tone deaf, and his audiences were often more eager to enjoy his musical talent than his forensic abilities.

While in Juarez, the Grants and the Ivinses had dinner with John W. Taylor, who still adamantly clung to his apostate views on polygamy and was drifting inexorably toward his excommunication four years later. Breaking bread again with his old friend doubtless evoked in Heber's mind vivid memories of the day when Elder Taylor had prophesied that Heber would go to Japan free of debt. That sacred experience had forged an immutable bond between the two men that was even to bridge the chasm opened up by Elder Taylor's severance from the Church. This bond immunized the friends against the animosities that often infect excommunicated members.

The swing into Mexico occupied almost two months, extending from mid-January to mid-March, during which time both Heber and Augusta were alternately sick and well. Notwithstanding, the apostle kept moving and active, going from village to village to instruct and motivate the Saints in the tough, sometimes thankless task of establishing permanent communities.

Somewhere in the midst of his ecclesiastical duties, Heber had to find time to attend to his growing business interests. Insurance, ZCMI, real estate, banking, and the sugar industry all required his attention, and at this time he was making an effort to add still another member to his collection of enterprises.

Conscious of the need and desire for rapid communication, and seeing a chance to both serve the public and make a profit, he became a principal figure in organizing and promoting the Utah Independent Telephone Company. However, a number of difficult factors created a complex legal snarl and prevented the enterprise from ever really getting off the ground. The March 14, 1908, journal entry that recorded the end of this difficult and unpleasant business venture also noted, in an offhand way, that Heber had written a letter to several who had joined him in paying off the mortgage on the home of a widow: "If they had seen the tears of gratitude which she shed when I handed her the checks necessary to cancel the mortgage, they would have been glad that they had been able to help in this matter."

An entry made two months before told of a similar incident involving a member of his quorum: "Orson F. Whitney expressed his gratitude to the Lord for the blessings of the year 1907. He spoke very feelingly his gratitude to me for having cancelled the mortgage on his home. He said that it had lifted a burden from his shoulders that had been for years sapping his financial life's blood. Tears of gratitude to my Heavenly Father came into my eyes while he was speaking for his blessings to me whereby I was enabled, without cramping myself at all, to cancel the mortgage on the home of brother Whitney."

Like a finely cut diamond, Heber J. Grant's life had many interesting and brilliant facets. One or the other showed most prominently depending upon the angle of observation and the direction and intensity of the reflecting light. In the aggregate, the roles he played in his family, businesses, and church combined to prepare him more completely to wear the prophetic mantle, his assumption of which lay only a few years ahead.

Chapter 17

The Propagandist

The word *propaganda* has fallen into general disrepute, chiefly because it has become associated in the public mind with those who manipulate opinion to advance a dictatorial regime or to promote false ideas. In its inception, however, the word was intended to describe the process by which religious principles were "propagated" or taught to the masses. In its original and classical sense, therefore, the word can be aptly used to define the means Heber J. Grant used to advance certain ideas with which his name has been linked over the years. In this classical sense, he was a propagandist of the first order. As if by intuition, he applied all the best techniques used by the professional propagandists of this day, including the techniques of repetition and dramatization. He refrained, however, from anything hinting of deception. Two causes that attracted his immense powers of persuasion and persistence in the years following his European mission were Prohibition and home manufacturing.

The emergence of Prohibition as a national issue coincided roughly with Heber's return from England. It was in 1906 that the first concerted efforts were made in the United States to illegalize the production and consumption of liquor. Because of his commitment to the Word of Wisdom, which he accepted unquestioningly as God's will revealed through a living prophet, and because he had seen the deteriorating effects of saloons and drunkenness both at home and abroad, Heber took up the issue as if it were his own and lent his powerful influence and effective oratory to the fight. At stake conferences, in general conferences, in sacrament meetings, and elsewhere, he decried the moral and physical degradations so often associated with alcohol. He advocated the enactment of legislation that would control or eliminate its use. Typical of the devices he used was this resolution he offered at general conference in October 1908: "Believing in the words and teachings of President Joseph F. Smith, as set forth this morning on the subject of temperance, it is proposed, therefore, that all officers and members of The Church of Jesus Christ of Latter-day Saints will do all in their power, that can properly be done, with lawmakers generally to have such laws enacted by our legislature, soon to be elected, as may be necessary to close saloons, otherwise decrease the sale of liquor, and enact what is known as the 'Sunday Law.'" On motion, the conference unanimously adopted this resolution.

The intensity with which Heber pursued this campaign is demonstrated in this journal entry made in connection with the April 1909 general conference: "President [Francis M.] Lyman remarked to me that I would no doubt be called on to speak this morning, and he suggested that I do not refer to the question of Prohibition. [He] said a great many people had remarked to him that they were getting somewhat tired of my constantly preaching upon this subject, and he would like to have me talk on the peaceable things of the kingdom."

Heber's first reaction to this suggestion was one of annoyance. He failed to understand why his friend would thus dissuade him from discussing what he considered to be the all-absorbing topic of the day. But he was too well-trained in church procedure, too habituated to following the mandates of his file leader, to hesitate for long in doing what he directed. "While waiting for my turn to speak," he wrote later in a contemplative mood, "the passage of scripture 'Obedience is better than sacrifice, and to hearken than the fat of rams' came to my mind, and I smiled and decided to follow President Lyman's advice."

Insofar as his general conference talks were concerned, Heber was for two years to honor the restriction placed upon him by President Lyman, though in

other forums and in many other ways he continued to
agitate for laws that would curtail the use of liquor. In
that period, he and other like-minded reformers were
instrumental in getting a local option liquor bill through
the Utah legislature, a fact noted by President Anthon
H. Lund in his general conference address in April 1911:
"Our legislature has given us a law on the liquor question, and there is a time appointed when the people will
be at liberty to express themselves on this question. It
seems to me that all through the settlements of Zion,
where we the Latter-day Saints are in the majority, the
sentiment should be to do all in our power to eliminate
the liquor traffic from our midst."

Emboldened by these words of a counselor in the
First Presidency and by the success of seeing the legislation he favored enacted into law, and having received no
further reminders from President Lyman, Heber again
picked up the theme of Prohibition in his general
conference talks. Now, however, the objective was
different. Now, instead of aiming his words at the legislators or those who might influence legislators, he concentrated upon those whose votes would bring about the
local option control of liquor. In the April 1911
conference he said: "I rejoice in the key note that has
been sounded here that, under the law that has been
enacted, we can and should do away with the saloon in
every community where the Latter-day Saints are in the
majority."

He then launched into a dramatization, one that was
to be repeated over and over again during the following
months and that was to exert a powerful influence upon
the Saints who would later vote on a local option proposal to ban liquor. The mere words standing alone do
not begin to convey the impression left by the powerful
voice and the magnetic personality and speaking style of
Heber J. Grant.

> *The Saloon Bar*
> *A bar to heaven, a door to hell—*
> *Whoever named it, named it well!*
> *A bar to manliness and wealth,*

A door to want and broken health;
A bar to honor, pride and fame,
A door to sin, and grief and shame;
A bar to hope, a bar to prayer,
A door to darkness and despair;
A bar to honored, useful life,
A door to brawling, senseless strife;
A bar to all that's true and brave,
A door to every drunkard's grave;
A bar to joy that home imparts,
A door to tears and aching hearts;
A bar to heaven, a door to hell—
Whoever named it, named it well!

His concluding statements about the matter remind us of the oratory of Heber's father, Jedediah M. Grant, as he admonished the people in his fiery sermons during the reformation. "I recommend," Heber urged them, "that you expel this door to hell from your communities. You have the the ability to do it; and if you do not do it, it will be your own fault. If, in years to come, the tears and the dishonor and the shame that are depicted in this little piece of poetry, come into your own home by the lives of your own children, a part of the sin will fall upon your own heads." (*Conference Report*, April 1911, pp. 23-24.)

While Heber and those aligned with him achieved a signal victory in the Prohibition fight at that time—and a few years later were to emerge victorious in the larger, national battle for adoption of the eighteenth amendment—there lay ahead a demoralizing defeat when the eighteenth amendment was repealed and the work of decades was lost overnight. But even that event, humiliating as it was to then Church president Heber J. Grant, who saw Utah cast the deciding vote in favor of repeal, did not still the powerful voice he raised against a practice that he foresaw would undermine the moral fiber of a great nation and bring misery and degradation to millions.

Later Heber was to add other items proscribed by the Word of Wisdom—tea, coffee, and tobacco—to the litany of evils that he constantly called to the attention of the Saints, admonishing them to discontinue their use. Never before nor since the era of Heber J. Grant has this subject been given such constant and intensive treatment. So pervasive was it that several generations of Latter-day Saints had drummed into their consciousness from infancy the urgent need to refrain from the use of these substances, both as a means of promoting robust health and of setting them apart as a distinctive, even a peculiar people. While it is true that the unusual theology they taught, based upon newly revealed and important scriptures, distinguished them from others and had a unifying effect, this was primarily in the spiritual and mental realms, and could not be reduced to something simple and objective around which the Saints could rally. It might be difficult, for example, to determine whether one has faith or has truly repented, because the elements upon which a judgment of those issues is based exist largely within the mind and the conscience, shielded from the view of others. On the other hand, the question of whether one does or does not drink liquor or smoke tobacco can be determined objectively with ease. Thus, the emergence of the Word of Wisdom as a chief index of orthodoxy, drawing a clear line between member and gentile, and a clearer line between valiant and indifferent members, provided a cohesive force important to the vitality and growth of the Church. And at the center of this force stood Heber J. Grant with his constant preachments, cajoling and exhorting the members to observe the Word of Wisdom. There doubtless were some who resented these repetitious sermons, as illustrated by President Francis M. Lyman's counsel, but there was hardly anyone in the Church who failed to grasp the message they enjoined.

Heber's enthusiasm for the Word of Wisdom during this period intertwined with another campaign to which he gave zealous devotion. Although home manufacturing did not carry the same moral overtones as the Word of Wisdom, its consequences were, to his mind, of such vast importance as to justify his best efforts in promoting it. Those consequences seemed to him to embody one of the principles cherished most by the Latter-day Saints, the principle of free agency. He reasoned that as long as his people remained dependent on outside manufacturing they were in economic bondage and, therefore, susceptible to being misled into conduct at variance with their religious principles. Regrettably, he had seen people whose normal character was benign and charitable become selfish and hostile at the scarcity or high cost of goods and commodities. Further, the home production of life's necessities seemed to promote the sense of initiative and rugged independence he felt should characterize the true disciples of Christ.

Whatever the incentives and motivations, the manner in which Heber single-mindedly pursued the goal of home manufacturing reminds us again of his adroitness and skill in molding public opinion. Repeatedly he would return to the theme in his general conference and other talks, emphasizing first one and then another aspect of the problem, cajoling, urging, and admonishing his listeners to patronize home manufacturers. These talks were laced with amusing and sometimes poignant stories, illustrating the main points to which he often turned: to the entrepreneur, "use your talent and means to develop local industry," and to the consumer, "if there is a choice, always buy home-manufactured goods."

Heber's talk at the general conference in April 1910 is typical of hundreds he delivered in support of this favored project. He stated: "From my childhood, I have been interested in home manufactures and I was very pleased with the remarks of our President on this subject. So far as I have the ability, I am anxious to make an impression upon the minds of my hearers today, that when they shall return home, from this conference, they will do so with a determination that in the future they will be more loyal in sustaining and building up our manufacturing institutions than they have been in the past." Having laid that groundwork for what was to follow, the speaker then launched into a series of stories and illustrations that added interest, amusement, and conviction to his words, stories that would be repeated and embellished throughout the Church in such a way as to make people remember and heed his words. "From the time that I was a boy of sixteen, until the factory closed, with only two or three exceptions, I never wore a suit of clothes that was not made of cloth manufactured at Provo," he continued. "I purchased a suit, once, while in California for six months, as my clothes became the least little bit shabby. I paid more than twice as much for it as I would have paid for a Provo Woolen Mills suit, and I was ashamed of it at the end of four months, and gave it away. I have worn many a suit of Provo goods continuously for three years, barring the time that it was at the tailors, being cleaned and pressed, and then I did not wear it out, and it didn't get shiny either; but I can't get a suit of clothes today, for ten dollars a suit more than I used to pay for a Provo suit, that does not shine and shine like everything in three months, instead of three years."

Then, warming to the subject with an enthusiasm and positive good humor that were peculiarly his own, Heber continued: "I remember, when the Wyoming legislature was here, that I was wearing a light-colored suit. I happened to be a member of the Utah legislature, and they gave a ball in the theater; so I had to buy a black suit, so as not to be the only 'white sheep' in the crowd, at that ball. But I gave the suit away the next day, for fear I might want to preach home manufacture when I had it on, and that the chips would fly back in my own face. Subsequently, when in New York for over six months at one time, I bought a suit there; but as that was in the panic of 1893, which wiped me off the earth, financially, I could not afford to give that suit away, so I wore it out. With these two exceptions, I wore nothing but Provo goods until the factory closed down."

After having put the audience at ease with these entertaining, amusing stories, Heber then shrewdly presented the sound logic supporting his plea for the members to purchase home-manufactured goods. "The way I figure it," he said, "the wool that would have made a suit of clothes, if shipped out of our country, will bring back one dollar to help enrich the community; but

if that wool were put into cloth, and the cloth into a suit
of clothes, at least twenty-five dollars of the value of that
suit would remain here and would be received by somebody for labor or in the increased value. We are told that
a dollar is to the world of finance what a drop of blood is
to the body—that it is the circulatory medium. I understand from doctors, that the heart handles about four
ounces of blood every time it beats; that it beats seventy-
eight times a minute, with the average individual—call
it eighty, in order to make it easy, and we have twenty
pounds of blood handled every minute, or practically
every drop of blood in the body. . . . It is going and going, circulating and circulating. It is the same with
money. Where the money goes out of a community, to
import goods into that community, the circulating medium is weakened; the life blood is taken away, and the
community becomes about as sickly as the individual
would be if you should bleed him, and take half of his
blood out of him. He would have a pretty light color."

A favorite story Heber used to illustrate his point was
one he told in the October 1913 general conference
about Bishop George L. Farrell, who "announced that
one reason why he bought home-made goods was because he loved Bishop Farrell." The bishop was quoted
as saying, "If I buy home-made goods my money stays at
home and it floats around and I get a chance to secure a
little of it occasionally. . . . At Smithfield, I saw a man
who had made some shoes for my children and I handed
him five dollars in payment. He saw another man at the
depot to whom he owed five dollars and he gave him the
five; and he saw another and he gave him the five; and
he saw another and he gave him the five, and when the
fourth man got it he came up to me and said 'Bishop
Farrell, I owe you six dollars; here is five on account';
and I put my home-made shoes back in my pocket."
Concluding the story, Heber said, "I am not vouching
for the exact language but I am vouching for the facts,
because I heard the talk. So five dollars worth of home-
made shoes paid twenty-five dollars worth of debts as
quick as I have been able to tell it to you, or as it took
Brother Farrell to tell it."

Heber's interest in making the Saints a self-sufficient people surfaced again in later years when he lent his extraordinary powers of persuasion and instruction to the welfare program. While he gathered about him an exceptional group of brilliant, able, and articulate men who perfected the mechanism and piloted it expertly over many a rough road, it was he who provided the initial thrust to launch it and who, adding the powerful weight of his prophetic office, pushed it along. His devotion to the causes of the Word of Wisdom and home manufacture had helped him develop those techniques of repetition and dramatization that ultimately made that most important program work.

Chapter 18

President of the Twelve

The Christmas of 1912 was a tranquil one for the Grant family. At home in Salt Lake City, surrounded by family and friends, they enjoyed the sense of peace and contentment that had seemed to settle upon the whole city.

Heber's busy schedule somehow included diversions to relax him and help him keep his life in perspective. Sports programs provided a special outlet for him, both as a spectator and as a participant. "Afternoon, played ball at the gym," is a typical journal entry, or, just as common, "Afternoon took Geo. Midgley to the baseball game. Butte vs. Salt Lake. Good game. 4-5 favor Salt Lake."

Reading was also a favorite diversion. "Day at cottage and in hammock reading," he wrote of an outing in Brighton. "Pleasant restful day." When he found a literary work that pleased him and was motivating and uplifting, he would buy it in quantity and distribute autographed copies to his family and friends. The little books *Heart Throbs, Great Truths,* and *As a Man Thinketh* were favorites of his, and were scattered widely among his acquaintances.

From his earliest days, Heber had enjoyed the stage. Whenever his crowded schedule permitted, he attended productions at the Salt Lake Theatre, where he had a special reserved box. When movies came into vogue, he attended them too, with almost but not quite as much interest and enthusiasm.

Another favorite diversion of the day was to go for an automobile ride. The novelty of the automobile had not worn off at this time, and it was a common practice among those who owned cars to go for a little spin in the evenings for the sheer enjoyment of driving and seeing the countryside. Heber was an enthusiastic participant in this pastime and frequently shared the experience with family members or aging friends.

It was also during this period that he became seriously interested in golf. For the early risers on the avenues of Salt Lake City it was not an uncommon sight in those days to see their illustrious neighbor, properly attired for the links, head out at the crack of dawn for a quick nine holes before breakfast.

This is not to say that Heber's life was devoid of problems at this time. He had his share of them. His position of leadership in the Church did not provide immunity from the difficulties that afflict all. The main difference between him and the vast majority of people was in the attitude with which he faced his problems. Whereas most people are intimidated or overwhelmed by trouble, Heber thrived on it, looking upon it as a means of testing his endurance.

The Job-like ailments that afflicted Heber at this time were boils and insomnia. The boils were not only painful and unsightly, but the internal disorders of which they were the outward manifestation also interrupted the rhythms of his entire system and likely produced or aggravated the insomnia. "Slept all night. First time for a long time," he wrote in his journal with a sense of relief and jubilation following a good night's rest. It had culminated a rather long period of sleepless nights during which he would turn fitfully for a time and then, unable to sleep, would rise to roam about the house, to read, to snack, and to meditate. More often than not he would dictate or write letters. This added significantly to an extensive correspondence covering every aspect of his life.

Heber was most faithful in maintaining touch with his family by letters and notes. Seldom did a child, an in-law, a grandchild, or a close relative pass a milestone without receiving a letter and often a check from him. Invariably the letters to his children were filled with sentiments of overflowing love, commendation, and gratitude, sentiments that always characterized his rela-

tionship with them. This letter he wrote to his daughter
Grace following the birth of her first child is typical:
"My darling Grace: I thank the Lord from the bottom of
my heart that you are a mother and that all is well. May
the Lord bless you, my darling daughter and also 'Miss
Mary Wells Evans' now and forever. I think it is
splendid to name your baby after our dear departed
Mary. If your daughter should be as sweet and lovable
as Mary was, we can ask no more." It was signed "Your
loving father."

The qualities of love, compassion, genuine interest,
and unqualified support this letter manifests reveal why
Heber J. Grant was so successful in his preeminent role
in life, that of husband, father, and patriarch. The
family letters that flowed endlessly from him helped
preserve the family solidarity that he confidently
believed would extend through the eternities. His business letters, in contrast, were usually terse and only long
enough to cover the essential points that brought them
forth. His ecclesiastical letters were, as a general rule,
more discursive, being used as a means to instruct, to
exhort, and to inspire.

As the years wore on, it seemed more and more
natural for Heber to assume a primary role in giving direction to his brethren. His innate tendency was to lead
out, as evidenced by his business enterprises where, from
an early age, he was a dominant figure. His call into the
Council of the Twelve had effected an anomalous
change in his leadership status, at once enlarging and
restricting the scope of his authority. His status was not
unlike that of a member of a board of directors whose
ideas and suggestions are heard at board meetings and
whose authority is extensive when acting in committee
assignments under direction of the board, but whose
power to dominate and give significant direction to the
affairs of the whole organization is restricted.

But as Heber gained seniority in the Council of the
Twelve, his influence became more pronounced and his
views carried more weight in the deliberations of that
body. Especially was this true as it became apparent
that, barring an unforeseen accident or untimely death,

he ultimately would assume the mantle of highest authority in the Church. And the fact that he was still comparatively young and basically in good health made it likely that once he had succeeded to the presidency, he would occupy the position for some time. Thus, as the time drew near for his ascension to that high place in church government, there would naturally be a tendency to defer to him in many matters. As to those junior to him in the Twelve, this deference foreshadowed the loyalty he would receive from them as their file leader in the years ahead; and as to his superiors, it demonstrated their concern that one who may succeed to the presidential office be prepared in every way.

On the part of Heber J. Grant, this change in status—which came about imperceptibly over the years—in no way altered his self-image or the attitudes he held toward his brethren. He failed to see in it any cause for self-congratulation or any reason to assume that it came in recognition of superior qualities of mind or character. Had there been a thirst for self-aggrandizement in his makeup, and none is evident from the record, it would have been quenched at his call into the Twelve, which brought the knowledge that ambition and self-preferment are at odds with service as a special witness of Christ's divinity. He would not have been long in that company before realizing that his life would be a lie and an affront to God were he to ignore the mandates of humility and oneness enjoined upon His disciples by the Savior.

Thus when Heber succeeded to the presidency of the Council of the Twelve on November 18, 1916, at the death of Francis M. Lyman, there was no cause for jubilation, no reason to engage in the rituals that often accompany a promotion or appointment in the world of business or politics. But the event was historic, marking as it did an important milestone in the ongoing drama of the Church. It marked the demise of one valiant servant who had exhausted his human energies in fulfilling the imperious mandate of the apostleship and the ascension of another who had served a thirty-four-year apprenticeship.

As the new president of the Twelve looked back upon the long road he had traveled since that day in 1882 when he had been electrified by the special revelation calling him to the apostleship, he was caught up in nostalgic reflections. "I then spoke briefly," he wrote of a meeting held in January 1917, "pledging my best efforts, as President of the Quorum of the Twelve, to do my duty. Referred to the fact that all of the members of the Council of the Twelve, except President Lund who is now in the Presidency, who were members at the time I was appointed had now passed away; and that in addition, three of those who had been ordained after I had become a member of the Council had passed away, and two had lost their standing." Then, reflecting a combined sense of loneliness and humility, he concluded: "Announced that I felt very lonely at having parted with so many of my associates during the past thirty-four years. I felt my lack of experience in comparison to that possessed by President Lyman, but told the brethren that I wished to follow his example of diligence and prayed for wisdom to make a success of my office."

The pressing demands of his new position provided Heber with little opportunity for leisurely contemplation of the past. There was too much to be done, too many initiatives to be taken, looking toward the proselyting and conversion of the entire world. The new president of the Twelve entertained no illusions about the task that faced him and his brethren in fulfilling the Master's injunction to preach the gospel to every creature. The resources and manpower of the Church, measured against the vast world population, the greatest portion of which had never even heard of the Mormons, made the task seem formidable, if not impossible. Cultural and linguistic barriers, government restrictions, problems of travel and communication, and limited financing all combined to make the task seem beyond the reach of human effort. As it was, however, Heber and his associates were conscious of a vast reservoir of power available to them that lay beyond human view or experience: spiritual power that could be drawn upon as they needed it and as they became schooled in its use. They knew that help would be available through the veil at the moment they had reached the extremity of their own skill and endurance. They also knew that the job ahead would not be accomplished overnight or even within the span of their own lives. All they could hope to do was to build upon the foundation laid by their predecessors, making sure that when the job was turned over to others, the building would be as sound as when they had commenced their labors, with the walls raised higher toward completion and with an ample supply of materials available with which to continue the work.

Just as important as these factors was the recognition that success in battle depends as much upon logistics and supply as upon the tenacity of warriors at the point of conflict. It was not only necessary that there be a corps of dedicated missionaries in the field, but that the sources from which they sprang also be kept pure and viable. Thus, the work of the apostles in strengthening the stakes at home, in counseling the local leaders, and in motivating the general membership at stake and general conferences was a vital aspect of their ministry.

Shortly after becoming head of the Twelve, Heber took steps that added an important element of strength to the stakes in Zion. On a visit to Parowan, Utah, he held not only the meetings typical of a stake conference, but also special meetings in most of the wards during the two days that followed. On Monday he made a whirl-wind tour to the Summit, Enoch, Paragonah, and Cedar City wards, holding meetings at 11:00 A.M. and at 1:30, 4:20, and 7:40 P.M. On Tuesday, he held meetings in the New Harmony, Kanarra, and Lund wards. He both spoke and sang at all these meetings, in two instances speaking for almost an hour. It is unlikely that a president of the Twelve had ever before visited in these small, outlying wards.

It is difficult to assess the effect of such an experience upon those who attended, especially upon impression-able young people whose parents likely set the stage by emphasizing that the visitor would probably be the president of the Church one day. And the young people

likely were briefed about his tenacity and will, his capacity to overcome obstacles and to achieve significant
things despite handicaps. Then to see him in person with
his distinguished appearance and energetic air; to hear
him sing "Beautiful Zion" or "Truth Reflects Upon Our
Senses"; to hear him quote "Let Each Man Learn to
Know Himself"; or to hear him bear a powerful testimony that God indeed lives and hears and answers
prayers, could not have failed to stir within them desires
to seek new goals and to generate confidence in their
ability to achieve unusual things.

After his experience in Parowan Heber said, "I
believe that it would be a good thing if the members of
the Council of the Twelve would spend a little time
when at stake conferences, making visits to the various
wards." After reporting his Parowan trip to the First
Presidency and the Council of the Twelve, he noted,
"President Smith remarked that he thought if the
members of the Twelve should do a little more visiting of
wards, when at stake conferences, it would be a very
good thing."

Given the discipline and unity of the leading councils
of the Church, there can be little doubt that after
December 1916, the customary practice of members of
the Twelve in visiting stake conferences was to schedule
separate meetings in wards where feasible. After all, had
not the president of their quorum led the way by
example, and had not the president of the Church endorsed the initiative and encouraged the Brethren to go
and do likewise? And it is undoubtedly true that this
word filtered down into the other leading councils of the
Church, the First Council of Seventy and the Presiding
Bishopric, who would have been as anxious as the
Twelve to follow the lead of their prophet, to get in step
with the spirit of the times, to move unitedly toward
their common goal of building the kingdom—of preparing a people and a habitation fit for the presence of
Deity.

These motivational concepts explained in large part
the vigor and enthusiasm with which Heber approached
his assignment as the head of the Council of the Twelve.

He never missed an opportunity to push the work along. It was his object to perfect the mechanism of the Church wherever possible. But he was careful never to exceed the bounds of his authority. He was meticulous to see that neither he nor his brethren of the Twelve encroached in any way upon the prerogatives of the president of the Church or the First Presidency. He never manifested any attitude toward his file leaders other than one of complete loyalty and subjection to their will. Perhaps nothing better illustrates this aspect of Heber's character than the remarks he made about President Joseph F. Smith at the October 1918 general conference, the last conference prior to President Smith's death: "I desire to echo the sentiments expressed of gratitude and thanksgiving to our heavenly Father that our beloved President was able to be with us at our session this morning; and I hope and pray that the exertion necessary on his part to attend may not have been so great but what he can be with us again." In conclusion, he bore testimony of prophets, saying: "I know that Joseph Smith was and is a prophet of the true and living God, that I have the abiding testimony in my heart that Brigham Young was a chosen instrument of the living God, that John Taylor, that Wilford Woodruff, that Lorenzo Snow were, and that today Joseph F. Smith is the representative of the living God, and the mouthpiece of God here upon the earth. I do not have the language at my command to express the gratitude to God for this knowledge that I possess; and time and time again my heart has been melted, my eyes have wept tears of gratitude for the knowledge that he lives and that this gospel called 'Mormonism' is in very deed the plan of life and salvation, that it is the only true gospel upon the face of the earth, that it is in very deed the gospel of the Lord Jesus Christ."

In this statement is revealed a quality of Heber's character that made him a superior leader—the quality of followership. He seemed to know instinctively that one cannot lead effectively unless he has first learned to follow. If he did not know this by instinct, he had learned it by long experience as a church and business leader. He had seen that the subordinate who is critical, disloyal, and uncooperative, who is intent on demeaning or undercutting his superior, can never command the real respect and cooperation of others when he is elevated to a position of leadership. Workers can never have confidence in a leader of this kind, for his reputation for disloyalty will follow him into the new position, creating uncertainty as to how far he can be relied upon.

The sentiments of loyalty and love Heber J. Grant expressed for his leader on this occasion were the last he expressed publicly before President Smith's eyes closed in death. Within two months, the last living link to the Prophet Joseph Smith among the General Authorities was gone. The tender exchange that passed between him and Heber before the end illustrates the durability of the prophetic bond that existed between them. "I could not and did not in my heart bring myself to feel that he was going to leave us," Heber wrote in a letter of condolence to President Smith's family, "until the afternoon of the 18th when I called and David said he wanted to see me. The President took my hand and pressed it with a power and strength that was far from what one could expect from a dying man; and he blessed me with power and the Spirit of the living God, and there was love in his eyes and a strong pressure of his hand, and with nearly every word he spoke his pressure of my hand thrilled my being, and tears of gratitude to God and love for his mouthpiece upon the earth filled my heart. His blessing was all that I could ask or expect had he been my own dear father. . . . I walked into the little front office and wept, feeling that the last words I would ever hear from his beloved lips had been spoken when he said to me 'The Lord bless you, my boy, the Lord bless you. You have a great responsibility. Always remember this is the Lord's work and not man's. The Lord is greater than any man. He knows whom He wants to lead His church and never makes any mistakes. The Lord bless you.' "

Chapter 19

The Prophetic Mantle Descends

Following the deaths of each of the first three presidents of the Church—Joseph Smith, Brigham Young, and John Taylor—a long period intervened before the First Presidency was reorganized, during which the affairs of the Church were directed by the Twelve, with the president of that quorum being the chief executive officer and the actual, though not the titular, head of the Church. This procedure was cumbersome and inefficient, especially as the Church became larger and more complex, with worldwide holdings and responsibilities. On this account, President Wilford Woodruff, once he had been ordained and sustained as the president of the Church, decreed by revelation that thereafter there should be no significant time lapse between the death of a president and the ordination of a successor. Obedient to that mandate, the Twelve convened in the Salt Lake Temple on November 23, 1918, four days after the death of President Joseph F. Smith, and there they sustained and ordained Heber J. Grant as the seventh president of The Church of Jesus Christ of Latter-day Saints.

President Grant began his administration under the most favorable circumstances. He had the unqualified support of the high circle of leadership with no schisms or controversy to interrupt the smooth flow of the work. His predecessors had laid a deep and solid foundation. The organization whose guiding reins had been placed in his hands was stronger and more fit than it had ever been. It was debt-free, thanks to the initiatives begun by President Lorenzo Snow and brought to fruition by President Joseph F. Smith; and its future solvency was assured by the way in which these leaders had inculcated the principle of tithing over the years. The new administration building had been completed, providing pleasant, well-appointed facilities in which to work. An ambitious building program was underway, including two temples, one in Hawaii and one in Canada, the first temple in this dispensation to be built beyond the jurisdiction of the United States. A burgeoning growth was being experienced in the populous areas of the Church as wards and stakes multiplied, fueled in part by conversions from the far-flung, efficient missionary system and the spirit of gathering with which the converts had been generally infused. Perhaps more significant than anything else, President Grant found himself in command of an organization comprised of able men and women whose chief object in life was to learn and to execute the will of God as directed or revealed by Him, men and women who, if called upon to do so, would gladly give all their earthly possessions, their time and talents, and their very lives, if necessary, to carry his mandates into effect. He had confidence in their will and ability to fulfill these commitments.

Thus, as the prophetic mantle descended upon him, President Grant found at his disposal all the tools necessary to fulfill the awesome responsibilities that rested upon him. The garden in which he was to toil for the remainder of his life was well-ordered and verdant, and its potential for future growth offered every inducement for diligent labor.

The vast increase in the scope of his authority and responsibility came as somewhat of a surprise to President Grant as he grasped the reins of his new office. Though he had functioned in the governing councils for thirty-six years and had watched four presidents grapple with the complex and far-flung mechanism of church government, he had never before understood precisely what it meant to have this responsibility until the mantle had descended upon him. It is one thing to counsel and advise, to support, sustain, and assist another. It is an entirely different matter, however, to have the ultimate burden of leadership. But so intensive and deep had been his training in leadership that he adjusted rapidly to the realities of his new position and began almost immediately to function with a skill and sureness that demonstrated the value of his preparation.

The most significant aspect of his new office came to the fore with the realization that he was accountable to others beyond the veil for the way in which he administered the Church. While he held in his grasp ultimate responsibility as to the conduct of Church affairs, yet in the broad, eternal sense, he was still only an agent, a messenger, a servant. He remained accountable to his principal, Jesus Christ, whom he recognized as the living head of the Church. It was a chief function of his apostolic calling to testify that He lives, the Master and Redeemer of mankind, the King of Kings and Lord of Lords, who would return to earth to assume his rightful place of direct leadership over the Church. But there were others through the veil to whom the president felt accountable also. This feeling was traceable in large part to the profound experience he had had in the Arizona desert when he had received spiritual confirmation of the divine nature of his call to the apostleship. From that experience, he learned that the system of priesthood authority and accountability that exists on the earth is but a shadow of a comparable, much more sophisticated and perfect system that exists beyond the veil. This knowledge imbued him with feelings of responsibility toward Joseph Smith and the other presidents who had preceded him. In turn, he recognized the integral role played by other prophets and patriarchs who had served from the creation of the earth.

Thus, upon commencing his prophetic duties President Grant, more than ever before, began to pray mightily that he would receive the spiritual direction through the veil to carry on the work as God would have it done were he present personally to oversee it. As President Grant began to live more completely in this way, seeking only to learn and execute the will of God, he found events evolving and combining in very unusual ways to produce surprising results.

A dramatic example of this new dimension in his life occurred less than two months after he became president, as he prepared to fill the vacancy he had left in the Twelve. As he reviewed in his mind the men he considered to be worthy and able to fill that position, he returned again and again to his lifelong friend, Richard W. Young. A retired general of the army, lawyer, successful businessman, and stake president, this distinguished man seemed to possess every qualification to fit him for high ecclesiastical leadership. Moreover, President Grant had great personal love for him, and over the years had thought to himself that, if ever he had the opportunity to do so, he would call his friend to the apostleship. This recognition, he felt sure, would be richly deserved and would be pleasing to the Lord and to Richard's grandfather, Brigham Young, to whom President Grant felt specially indebted. Following his ordination as president of the Church in November 1918, he began to reflect and to pray about filling the vacancy, discussing the matter with his counselors and others. He mulled it over all during the Christmas and New Year's holidays, and by January 7, 1919, he felt confident that Richard W. Young was the man. Receiving the support of his counselors, he wrote the name "Richard W. Young" on a slip of paper and, at the appointed hour, went to the temple for the weekly meeting of the First Presidency and the Twelve, where he intended to present Brother Young's name. Reaching the business portion of the agenda, President Grant removed the paper with the name written on it, fully intending to present him to the council for approval. But for a reason he could never fully explain, he was unable to do so; instead, he presented the name of Melvin J. Ballard, president of the Northwestern States Mission, a man with whom he had had very little personal contact.

Coming as it did in the early stages of President Grant's tenure, this experience taught him an invaluable lesson from which he was to profit throughout his administration. Reflection convinced him that the desires of Heber J. Grant had been too evident in the discussions and analyses that preceded the temple meeting on January 7. He knew that God would have ratified and approved anyone he had designated, since the power of selection lay within the scope of his prophetic authority. But he also knew that with an appointment of this importance influences beyond the veil, where vision was not clouded by the encumbrances of earth life, would dictate the selection. The experience confirmed what President Joseph F. Smith had said as he lay dying: that the Lord knows whom he wants to lead his church, and the Lord makes no mistakes. It also gave President Grant reason to ponder anew his leadership role, a role that he now saw more clearly to be one of serving as a conduit through which the mind and will of God were to be conveyed. It brought him a sense of peace to receive confirmation that he did not stand alone, but that the powers of heaven were available to assist him if he would but invoke them and rely upon them.

Knowing the background of Elder Ballard's call, it is interesting to contrast it with the circumstances surrounding Anthony W. Ivins's call as a counselor in the First Presidency.

Although Elder Ivins and President Grant were first cousins, their relationship had more of a brotherly quality about it. Fondly called "Tone" or "Tony" by his intimates, Elder Ivins was several years older than Heber, toward whom he had always assumed a somewhat protective, big-brotherly attitude. Extremely proud of him, Tony seemed to derive as much satisfaction from Heber's achievements as if they were his own. His loyalty was absolute, and Heber knew he could trust Tony with anything he possessed and in any circumstance.

These feelings were shared by many prior to Elder Ivins's call to the Council of the Twelve. Once he had become a member of that distinguished body, the feeling took root that he would one day sit as a member of the First Presidency, not alone because of his inherent and highly polished capabilities, but also because of the confidence reposed in him by the one who had the power of selection. The events immediately preceding his call to the Twelve reflect how widespread this feeling had become.

Coincidentally, the news of the death of Anthon H. Lund, the counselor in the First Presidency whom Elder Ivins replaced, reached President Grant while he was on a trip to California with his cousin. After the first day on the train, February 28, 1921, President Grant made this entry that revealed the depth of the feelings he had for Elder Ivins and foreshadowed the more intimate relationship they were to share: "Had a very pleasant day today on the Southern Pacific with Brother Ivins and Sisters McKay and Cannon. It is a long time since I have had a good long visit with my cousin Tony. I have often wished that we could so arrange our affairs that we could have taken long trips together during the years that he has been a member of the Council of the Twelve. This pleasure has come to us very very seldom."

President Lund's death on March 2 prompted the entire party to return home for the funeral. All except President Grant went directly there, and he went via Los Angeles to get Augusta, who had been vacationing in Santa Monica. In Los Angeles, he met Bishop Charles W. Nibley, who returned to Salt Lake City with him and who, en route, expressed a feeling that was widely held. In his journal President Grant wrote: "Bishop Nibley remarked that he expected me to appoint my cousin Anthony W. Ivins as my counselor, that there was no doubt in his mind that people generally would expect it, as he considered Bro. Ivins the best informed and wisest man among the apostles and that he would be the greatest help to me as a counselor." Perhaps recalling the experience he had had in the call of Elder Melvin J. Ballard, and not wanting his personal desires to dominate in the important decision to be made, he concluded: "Personally there is no man living who would please me more to have as a counselor than my own relative. However I desire to choose whoever the Lord wishes me to and certainly do not want to make a choice because of any personal preference."

Several days after returning home, President Grant broached the subject of a replacement with his remaining counselor, Charles W. Penrose: "Between the temple meeting and the funeral I had a little chat with Bro.

Penrose and I asked him if his mind had rested on anyone as his associate in the Presidency for a counselor. He said he had thought of only one man and that was Bro. Anthony W. Ivins. I told him that my mind had rested upon Bro. Ivins also and that unless the Lord indicated someone else I would undoubtedly select him as a counselor."

After following this decision-making process, President Grant received the desired confirmation, resulting in his cousin Tony being called to fill the vacancy in the First Presidency. That being decided, he turned to the important question of who would succeed Elder Ivins in the Twelve, and here we see again the same process at work. "Had a conference with Bro. Penrose," he wrote, "regarding nominating somebody to fill the vacancy in the quorum of Apostles after Bro. Ivins is made one of the Presidency. It was decided it would be wise to wait for the impression of the Spirit until April conference."

In point of fact, the inspiration President Grant sought descended upon him before the conference, for on March 17, 1921, Elder John A. Widtsoe was ordained an apostle. The apostolic summons extended to this distinguished scholar and university administrator must have aroused in President Grant a lively remembrance of the new apostle's plucky little mother, Anna Karine Gaarden Widtsoe, whom he had met in Norway during his term as European mission president; she was serving there as a missionary. The inspired call to the son of this immigrant widow, whose iron will and unbending faith had caused her to accept the gospel in faraway Trondheim despite the opposition and antagonism of friends and family, was a fitting benediction to her life of service and devotion to the Church.

But President Grant's duties were not limited to the spiritually taxing one of seeking the divine will in the selection and call of men to fill vacancies in the high councils. These sacred and comparatively rare occurrences were intertwined with a large and complex amalgam of duties that kept him fully occupied from early morning until late at night. Early morning to President Grant often meant two or three o'clock, as the insomnia that afflicted him intermittently during much of his adult life frequently aroused him then and set him at work planning his day or talking into his ever-present dictating machine. If it was not so early as to disturb the sleep of Augusta or visitors in the house, he would sing several of his favorite hymns, all the while rejoicing in the magnificent view of the towering Wasatch and Oquirrh mountains and the valley in between.

Each day's schedule was filled with a seemingly endless round of meetings and appointments—ecclesiastical, business-oriented, and ceremonial. Practically every visiting dignitary of significance desired to pay a courtesy call on the president of the Church, and usually these requests were granted, not only to accommodate the visitors, but also to extend the Church's influence among persons and organizations of power and authority. Typical of the visitors who met with President Grant during the early period of his administration were the poet Edgar A. Guest and General John J. Pershing, who was especially impressed by the stately dignity of the recently dedicated Church Administration Building. Invariably these visitors left with some memento of their visit, usually an autographed book; more importantly, they left with an elevated opinion of the leaders whose spirituality and vital energy were evident to all who entered their presence—and this confidence in its leadership was inevitably transferred to the Church.

His preoccupation with family, church, and business affairs, the volume of which constantly increased, did not alter President Grant's lifelong recreational habits. "Played volley ball from after lunch until about three P.M., having nearly an hour of pleasure," he recorded on March 9, 1921, during the time he was wrestling with the selection of a new counselor and a new member of the Twelve. "I play this game almost as a matter of duty to keep myself in proper trim physically; at the same time I thoroughly enjoy it."

During the early years of his administration, President Grant began to emerge more clearly as a powerful ambassador to the nonmembers in the community.

Infused with dual enthusiasms rooted in his religious beliefs and his penchant for salesmanship, he extended his influence far beyond the limits of the Saints. He was active in civic and community affairs, holding membership in both the Salt Lake Rotary Club and the Bonneville Knife and Fork Club. His openness and candor, his lack of guile and secretiveness, and his genuine interest in people and their welfare, regardless of color, creed, or economic status, caused everyone, member and nonmember alike, to feel a sense of kinship toward him.

Once on a trip to San Francisco to attend the launching of a naval vessel he was honored at a dinner where the toastmaster introduced him as the president of the Mormon church and as "president of the gentiles in Utah as well." The toastmaster then noted that on "his recent visit to Salt Lake all the gentiles with whom he mingled expressed in very warm terms their good will" for President Grant and their hopes for his success as president of the dominant church in Utah. In responding to this flattering introduction, President Grant revealed the sense of humor and goodwill that so much endeared him to all: "I related an amusing incident of having taken my hat off when I first went east as a young man of 26 [when] a lady in the Palmer Hotel wanted to see if I had horns. When I took off my hat I made the remark 'my hair is coming out but the horns of the Mormons do not appear until they are at least 30 and I am only 26.' She said she had heard the Mormons had horns. I assured her that they did, but that they did not grow until they were at least 30 years of age."

It has been said that each president of the Church, in turn, has provided the qualities of leadership that the exigencies of his time and place have required. This axiom most certainly applies to President Grant. Viewed in retrospect, the term of his administration bridged the gap between the early years when the word *Mormon* was a reproach, a hiss and a byword, and the later years when it assumed an aura of distinction and high respectability.

President Grant caught the crest of this wave of changed public opinion and rode it during his administration with skill and agility. He never lost an opportunity to strengthen bonds of friendship with those outside the Church. He became in deed and in name an untiring and resourceful ambassador for the Saints. His years of experience in business had opened important doors for him and for the Church in large cities throughout the United States and abroad. More than any of his predecessors, therefore, this prophet was prepared to deal with the world on its own terms. The constantly expanding influence and power of the Church and its members made them a national force to be reckoned with in religious, economic, and political matters; and as their earthly head, Heber J. Grant was generally regarded as being personally invested with the cumulative power and influence of the entire body.

But these trappings of power and influence never altered President Grant's basic character. Beneath the outward show of dominance and authority in both their spiritual and material aspects stood a man as unpretentious and humble, albeit as aggressive and determined, as the tearful boy who had shaken his fist at the ancestral home on Main Street that day long ago. However the world might regard him, whatever motives and purposes it might impute to him, he remained throughout his life the child, the fruit of his Mormon ancestry and upbringing, aiming only to learn and execute God's will and to prepare a people worthy of a celestial habitation.

Chapter 20

The Prophet as Patriarch

Frequent allusion has been made in the preceding chapters to President Grant's love of family. He often attributed to his mother major credit for anything he had accomplished in life. Although he never knew his father in mortality, he honored him and sought to emulate his impressive example. We have seen how he revered his wives, cherished his vivacious, accomplished daughters, and mourned over the premature deaths of his beloved sons. As his grandchildren and great-grandchildren came on the scene, he lavished upon each one all the love and attention that his ever-expanding duties and diminishing free time would allow. Seldom did he neglect to write or call a member of the family on the occasion of an anniversary or a special achievement or during a time of stress. Never did he fail to rush to the aid of one of the family who found himself in need, providing solace, encouragement, or dollars, as the circumstances required. Thus, all that he did in reference to his family reflected a patriarchal awareness and sensitivity of the most brilliant hue. He was a father in the best sense of the word, subverting his own desires in the interests of all, inspiring each one through his example and providing stern, though loving, discipline where it was merited. And when sickness came, he was as concerned as if he were mother instead of father, bestowing solicitous care without restraint.

This laudable quality in President Grant's makeup seemed to be both instinctive and learned. There was within him an innate sense of family, a special feeling of kinship and loyalty toward those who shared a common blood heritage. His journals are studded with frequent, kindly references to assorted relatives—brothers, sisters, uncles, aunts, cousins, nephews, and nieces—not to mention those who stood within the circle of his most intimate familial relationship—wives, children, and grandchildren. The impression created by these references and by the habitual attitude he manifested toward his family conveys a sense of loyalty and strength that could withstand any strain or pressure.

While it is true that these feelings and attitudes seemed to be inherent in him, they were given powerful impetus by the living examples he had observed from infancy and by the theology he had learned and taught through years of apprenticeship at home and abroad. The main emphasis of his life from birth was upon family. During his most impressionable, formative years, he had lived under a roof where several families had been effectively combined into one. While the father of that home was not present physically, his spiritual presence was a constant reality to young Heber, whose sensitive and faithful mother never let him forget for an instant who he was and what he might become, conditioned upon his faithfulness and obedience. And the absence of a father from his home found partial compensation in the patriarchal examples that were all about him, the prophetic influences that pervaded the society in which he grew to maturity.

Most of the homes Heber visited during his early, formative years were presided over by men imbued with a patriarchal concept. He observed it in operation as families knelt together in prayer under the direction of the father. He witnessed it as he saw sons and daughters continue to pay honor, respect, and obedience to parents even though they may have left the family hearth to create homes of their own. It was especially evident as he saw fathers, in the exercise of their priesthood, confer special blessings upon the heads of their children as they prepared to go out in the world to preach the gospel, to marry, or to advance their schooling.

Consequently, the attitudes of President Grant toward his family and his dealings with them over the years were conditioned by innate feelings and by principles he had learned through study and observation.

But his ideas about family loyalty and solidarity were not restricted in scope to those living during his lifetime. They extended backward to include those from whom he had descended and forward to those who would constitute his earthly progeny. He saw himself as the link between the past and the future, a link whose importance lay not only in the essential cohesion it provided, but also in the key role assigned to it by Mormon theology. That role, as defined by the Prophet Joseph Smith, involved becoming a "savior" to deceased family members. And to his unborn progeny, President Grant became a beacon, pointing toward heavenly goals and warning against the dangerous shoals and reefs of life.

The spiritual embodiment of this novel concept was to be found in the person of Elijah, the ancient and much-revered prophet who was taken up into heaven without tasting death. It was Elijah who, with Moses, had appeared on the Mount of Transfiguration, and who, as a resurrected being, had appeared to Joseph Smith and Oliver Cowdery in the Kirtland Temple on April 3, 1836, conferring upon them the keys of the sealing power, thereby making available the fulness of salvation to both the living and the dead. Specifically, this investiture of authority by Elijah had empowered living men to forge an eternal bond with their deceased ancestors and, as proxies, to perform essential ordinances for and in their behalf. It is in this sense that the living act as saviors, doing for departed ancestors something they are incapable of doing for themselves, even as Jesus, through his infinite atonement, did something for us that we are powerless to do alone.

The physical symbol that most dramatically impressed these concepts upon President Grant's mind was the imposing Salt Lake Temple, whose slow and tedious construction he had watched for almost thirty-seven years. There were times when visitors, and even some Latter-day Saints, doubted that this ambitious project would ever be completed. Some pointed to it in derision, others in pity, as representing the unreasonable aspirations of a misguided people who had conceived a plan far beyond their reach. But as it slowly took shape, as the

walls inched upward, as the roof and the magnificent
spires were set in place, and as the interior was plastered,
scrubbed, painted, and furnished, the structure became
a landmark and a matter of civic pride rather than the
object of negative and derogatory comments.

To President Grant and others who shared his convictions, the temple and the ordinances performed in it
became the focal point of their community and lives.
The building was the holy place, the specially dedicated
and sanctified house of the Lord, the abode to which the
Savior might come were he disposed to favor his people
with another personal visitation. Moreover, it was the
place where couples undertook their sacred and eternal
marriage vows and where worthy members received
their endowments and lovingly performed vicarious ordinances for their departed ancestors. For President
Grant and his associates in the First Presidency and the
Twelve, it was the sanctuary to which they withdrew
each week to implore the Lord for guidance in directing
the affairs of the Church and to counsel about important
matters of policy and procedure that only that body
could decide. They never entered the holy edifice without there settling upon them a sense of peace and security not to be found in the chaotic world outside. Here
they could counsel, plan, and reflect in a way that was
impossible elsewhere. Here they felt closer to the Lord
and more amenable to the promptings of his spirit. Here
they experienced a feeling of greater continuity with
those who had preceded them in the ministry and those
who would follow. And here they felt a special kinship
toward their earthly ancestors and toward those who
would, in the generations ahead, descend from them as
their earthly progeny.

The yearnings and love for his family, and the feelings of kinship for his associates in the ministry, both on
earth and beyond the veil, were to draw President Grant
to the temple again and again throughout his life. In
later years, as his family grew and multiplied, he began
to invite the adult, endowed members to be his dinner
guests one evening a week at the Hotel Utah, following
which they would all go to the temple for an evening

session. More often than not, they would perform the proxy endowment and sealing work for departed ancestors whose genealogical work had been done by researchers financed by President Grant himself. Over the years he spent large sums of money employing others to help him discharge the keen responsibility he felt toward his kindred dead, a responsibility he could not discharge personally because of the ever-increasing press of his ecclesiastical duties, but which he could and did discharge, in part, with money earned by his industry and thrift.

This interest in temple and genealogy work was given further impetus as President Grant was honored to preside at the dedication of three temples. The first of these, in Laie, Hawaii, was the first temple to be constructed outside the continental United States. In the several talks he delivered during the five dedicatory sessions, he made frequent reference to the continuity of life and personal associations that extend through the veil. Members of his family were specially mentioned, as were his predecessors in the ministry. Repeatedly he returned to the regrets he had that President Joseph F. Smith, who had dedicated the land for the building of the temple, was not permitted to participate in the temple dedication services toward which he had looked so eagerly.

Almost four years after dedicating the Hawaii Temple, President Grant dedicated a second temple that had been commenced during the administration of President Joseph F. Smith: the Alberta [Cardston] Temple. This temple, dedicated on August 26, 1923, claimed distinction as the first temple built outside the jurisdiction of the United States. Fourteen General Authorities in addition to President Grant participated in the impressive services, which included eleven separate sessions held over a four-day period. President Grant was in rare form and relished every aspect of the occasion. The enthusiastic, self-confident attitude he displayed is seen clearly in these remarks that prefaced the sermon he delivered at the conclusion of the first session: "I expect, in the course of these services, to make a few remarks at the close of each of the sessions, because there will be practically an entire change of congregation at every meeting. I shall do this, not because I have anything special on my mind to say, but because I realize from my own experience, from the days of Brigham Young until the present time, I having been intimately associated with all the leaders of the church since I was a little child, first becoming acquainted with Brigham Young when I was only six years of age, that the Latter-day Saints have reverence and a respect for the man who is chosen to stand at the head of the Church, and that therefore they would be very pleased to have me speak to them. For that reason, as well as because I would be pleased to do so myself, I shall make the closing remarks at all of these meetings that are to be held here." Then, revealing again the good humor that always endeared him to his audiences, he added, "In doing so, I shall not restrict myself at all by looking at my watch. If I happen to feel like talking long enough so that it will be difficult for some of you to get to your lunch and be back in time for the afternoon session, I shall do so. Dedications of temples come very seldom, and for that reason I am perfectly willing to detain you."

In the sacred setting of the Alberta Temple, under the special circumstances that prevailed, he was prompted to reflect upon the unusual role he played and upon some of those who had preceded him in the prophetic office. "I have attended, as a child, family prayers in the Lion House," he said, "and I have actually turned and looked when Brigham Young was praying, for it seemed to me as though the Lord must be standing there. He seemed to be talking as one man speaking to another when praying to the Lord. There are few men that I have ever listened to that seemed to me could get so close to the Lord in prayer as did Brigham Young and Erastus Snow and as does Anthony W. Ivins." He then paid this high compliment to others among his predecessors: "I have been very thankful indeed to know beyond the peradventure of a doubt through my association as one of the Apostles of the Lord Jesus Christ that John Taylor, Wilford Woodruff, Lorenzo Snow, and Joseph F. Smith had their hearts set absolutely and

unalterably upon laboring for the advancement of the
Latter-day Saints, for the spread of the gospel at home
and abroad, and to know that the supreme desire of
their lives was for the advancement and progress of the
gospel of life, and for the salvation of the Latter-day
Saints. I am thankful to know absolutely that all of the
slanders, backbiting and fault-finding of men out of the
Church, those professing to be Latter-day Saints, and
those that were our enemies, against the good men I
have named and others of our leaders, were not true, and
the hearts of these leaders were set absolutely on the welfare and the advancement of the people of God, and that
they never spared themselves in their labors for the good
of the people, that their daily thoughts, prayers, and
desires were for the advancement of the people. I do
know that those who sustained these men with their
faith and with their prayers, and with their good works,
were blessed of God, not only with an increase of faith
and love of God and a testimony of the divinity of the
Gospel work in which we are engaged, but they were
blessed in their basket, in their store, that their lands
were blessed, and that they were blessed with wisdom in
their families, to train them in the nurture and admonitions of God."

Three years after assuming the presidency, Heber J.
Grant dedicated a temple site in Mesa, Arizona. In the
heart of the fertile Salt River Valley, Mesa bore the in-
delible imprint of its Mormon origins. Coming early,
with their scriptures in one hand and their tools of
agronomy in the other, the Saints had gone about ener-
getically to plow, plant, irrigate, and cultivate the rich
soil, and to teach and convert the surrounding Indian
tribes—the Maricopa, the Papago, and the Pima—along
with anyone else who would listen to their message. So
successful and prolific had they been that in less than
half a century after arriving, they were ready to build a
holy sanctuary in their desert oasis where the highest ordinances of their religion could be practiced. And six
years after the site was dedicated, the impressive building, whose interior design and furnishings reflected an
Indian motif, was ready to be dedicated to the Lord.

Faithful members of the Church streamed into Mesa from the surrounding area to participate in the dedicatory services, which were held October 23-26, 1927. Not only did they come to rejoice in the completion of the new temple and to admire the quiet beauty of its appointments, but they came also to be uplifted and inspired by a living prophet and by the seventeen other General Authorities who accompanied him, including his first counselor, Anthony W. Ivins, and ten members of the Council of the Twelve.

Following the pattern established at Hawaii and Cardston, President Grant spoke at the conclusion of each of the ten dedicatory sessions, alternately amusing, instructing, and inspiring his listeners. The number enjoying the services was greatly enlarged through the use of the then novel device of radio, which carried the proceedings to rooms throughout the temple, to congregations in Mesa chapels, and to listeners in Utah. Reflecting upon the significance of this invention, President Grant observed: "It is very marvelous and wonderful how the gospel is being heard and proclaimed for thousands of miles in all directions over the radio. I often used to wonder how it would be possible for every ear to hear. But that wonderment has disappeared since the days of radio. I was reading one day a short time ago of a song, every note of which and every word of which was heard for nine thousand miles; and as these sounds travel in all directions at one and the same time it went nine thousand miles in all directions. . . . It is almost beyond the comprehension of mortal man to understand how anything of this kind can happen. I rejoice in this invention."

As he considered this modern innovation and the prosperous and promising conditions in which the Church then found itself, he could not help but contrast them with the furtive and melancholy circumstances under which the Manti Temple was dedicated during the night of darkness when many of the Saints were on the Underground: "At that time," he said, "the powers of darkness were raging against us and had been from the times of the laying of the capstone of the temple. At the time of the dedication of the Manti Temple the President of the Church and his counselors were in hiding and many of the leading brethren of the Church were also in exile. We met there secretly at night on the day of the anniversary of the dedication (as I remember it) four years before, of the Logan Temple; and that was the real dedication of the Manti Temple by the servant of the Lord, Wilford Woodruff. At that time we could not announce to the world that we had had that dedication, and advertise that Brother Woodruff was there, otherwise the deputy marshals might pick him up."

Though these stories, these remote allusions were inspiring and interesting, they were overshadowed by the exhortations, repeated frequently in varying forms, that enjoined his listeners to keep the commandments. Indeed, if one were to select a catch-phrase that typified the major theme underlying President Grant's public utterances, it surely would be this one.

This aspect of his character and perceptive teaching is evident from the admonitions he gave to those who attended the Mesa Temple dedication: "I know of no more remarkable thing in the Church than that a man to whom God gave revelation after revelation, to whom the Lord sent John the Baptist, and upon whose head the hands of that man who baptized the Savior were laid . . . should leave the Church. Think of a man upon whose head Peter, James, and John laid their hands, restoring the higher or Melchizedek Priesthood, a man who was made one of the apostles of the Lord Jesus Christ, who saw the Savior in the Kirtland Temple and who bore witness of this fact, who saw Moses, and Elias and Elijah, and who with the prophet received all the powers and keys of the Gospel of Christ . . . a man to whom an angel of God showed the plates from which the Book of Mormon was translated, declaring that they had been translated by the gift and power of God—yet such a man fell by the wayside. . . . What a wonderful warning to every Latter-day Saint to be faithful to remember that our duty is to keep the commandments of God."

Having illustrated that knowledge without application is powerless, he then demonstrated that eminence of position is a sham unless it is accompanied by dedication to principle: "I have borne testimony to the young people particularly, that I do not know one man or one woman of all my acquaintance from childhood to the present day who was an honest tithepayer, who attended to his family and secret prayers, who attended fast meetings and partook of the sacrament and renewed his covenants to remember God, and expressed his willingness to keep his commandments, who observed the Word of Wisdom, and was ready and willing when called upon to go and preach the gospel—I do not know one such individual who has ever lost his or her faith. But I have seen men who have reached the apostleship fail to do their duty, fail to keep the commandments of the Lord and lost their standing. . . . Men in my own day who have seen the Savior of the world and borne witness of that fact have lost their standing, and I have taken the time to examine into their records and found that they were not keeping the commandments of God."

During his administration, President Grant dedicated a temple site at Idaho Falls, Idaho, in the heart of the Snake River Valley. He had looked forward eagerly to dedicating this impressive structure, which would serve a locality he had seen emerge from a raw, underdeveloped frontier to a thriving farm community. As he watched the progress of construction, he could not help recalling the early days when he had visited the Saints on the Snake River with Wilford Woodruff and others, at a time when their main concern was breaking virgin soil, fencing the fields, and constructing irrigation facilities. To see a modern temple there, a holy edifice erected to the Lord, and to have the privilege of dedicating it was one of his fondest hopes. But fate decreed otherwise. He was to travel the same road as his predecessor, who had seen another pluck the fruit of the tree he had planted. So it was left to President George Albert Smith to dedicate the Idaho Falls Temple, only a few months after President Grant passed away.

Chapter 21

Depression and Politics

Except for the post-World War I recession, which hit its lowest point in 1921, and the chaos that followed the stock market crash in the waning months of 1929, the decade of the 1920s was the most prosperous one the United States had enjoyed. It seemed to symbolize the American genius for business and to foreshadow an era of boundless plenty with economic utopia apparently just around the corner. The engines of industry produced an ever-increasing stream of commodities to feed the appetites of a public whose material hungers never seemed to be satisfied.

The profits generated by this boom went mostly to fuel the fires of expansion and increased productivity, but enough was left over to create a whole host of the newly rich and to elevate the working class to a level of prosperity never before attained. In the wake of this new prosperity came a rapid surge toward urbanization, as hordes of farmers left the land to fill up the cities to which the controlling political and monetary power had gravitated and where they hoped to receive a bigger cut of the economic pie.

Urbanization brought with it increased freedom or license, especially for women, who for the first time were entering the job market in large numbers. This freedom spawned the age of the flapper with her bobbed hair, short, daring skirts, and alarmingly relaxed moral standards. The overcrowding brought on by urbanization also created numerous social problems, with crime, disease, poor sanitation, and immorality standing preeminent among the many that plagued cities across the land.

The Church, strong as it was and oriented as it was

toward the spiritual life, was not immune from the evils
and pressures created by these convulsive social changes.
The General Authorities watched with increasing alarm
as many Saints, contrary to counsel, left their farms to
migrate to the cities. Too many were being weaned away
from the practical virtues toward habits and modes of
thought that were self-destructive, that inculcated the
false notion that something could come from nothing,
that in economic matters one might expect to reap
where he had not sown.

Once the poison and its symptoms became evident,
President Grant and the other Brethren took prompt action to provide an antidote. They began to preach more
often and more vigorously about moral purity, prepared-
ness for missions, the values of farm life, and the need to
remain debt-free and to live within one's means.

To insure that missionaries were worthy and
technically prepared to serve, local leaders were directed
to tighten up on their training and screening procedures.
To supplement this initiative, President Grant announced at the April 1928 conference that thereafter
missionaries would be asked to serve for three months in
local wards before departing for their fields of labor
abroad.

Intensifying his campaign to promote frugality and
freedom from debt, he spoke out often to warn the Saints
against the speculative fevers that gripped the nation.
Using a forensic device he often employed, he read a
satirical poem at a general conference session in April
1926, dramatizing the folly of installment buying, which
was then coming into vogue:

> The story of Simon called Simple
>   Is one everybody has read;
> It is sweet, it is sad, and it tells of a lad
>   Who wasn't quite right in the head.
> When he sought to buy pie of the pieman,
>   Poor Simon was hopeful but rash,
> For he childishly thought that a pie could be bought
>   Without any transfer of cash.
>
> But we mustn't speak harshly of Simon,

Who was simply ahead of his time—
Today he could buy a whole carload of pie
  By merely investing a dime.
The up-to-date salesman would land him—
  Or, rather more likely, his wife—
By letting him pay a few cents right away
  And installments the rest of his life.

It's the way they sell pies and pianos,
  And paintings, potatoes and pants—
For a few dollars down, you can buy the whole town—
  As a prospect you haven't a chance.
The fact that you're broke doesn't matter,
  Your only escape is to die—
And as long as they take all the money you make,
  You might as well spend it for pie!

The persistence with which these concepts were taught had the desired effect upon many who changed their ideas and ways to conform with the standard set by the Brethren. The Saints generally began to adopt more conservative economic views and practices. But there were powerful national and international forces at work that were to override any efforts of the General Authorities to save the Saints from economic chaos. It did little good to keep their own quarters tidy and in order when the ship on which they sailed was headed into a disastrous storm. And it is clear that President Grant saw the storm long before it engulfed the nation and did what little he could do to avert it and to prepare for the shattering consequences that were to result from it.

In November 1928, almost a year before the disaster struck, at a time when the country was riding the crest of an unprecedented wave of prosperity and when unbridled optimism for the future was shared by most economic observers, President Grant expressed these troubling thoughts in his journal: "I had lunch with Orval Adams at the Utah Hotel cafeteria. He is very much alarmed over the frightful speculation going on in New York and looks for a terrible slump. He feels that if the slump comes the New York bankers will call for all their loans from the Utah Idaho Sugar Co. and other institutions and that there is danger that the credit of the Utah Idaho Sugar Company will be completely cut off. He said he thought it very unwise for the Church at this particular time to build a hotel or put any of its money in fixed assets. He feared the time would come when the church credit would have to be used, perhaps to its full extent in again saving the sugar company. I think his fears are well grounded."

These anxieties were shared by other Church leaders and ultimately were reflected in policies adopted by the Church and by the corporations it owned or controlled. New construction and expansion were stringently controlled. Where possible, indebtedness was eliminated or reduced. Investments in fixed assets or stocks were kept to a bare minimum or discontinued. Inventories were trimmed and production curtailed. These precautionary measures were accompanied by a new vigilance as the Brethren warily scrutinized every object that appeared on the economic horizon to determine what perils it might hold for them.

But there were too many things to be done, too many exciting plans that had been or were to be projected, to allow a spirit of pessimism or dejection to set in. Indeed, if anything, President Grant looked forward to, even welcomed, the approaching trials. It was his personal philosophy, born of a rigorous Mormon upbringing, that a mariner does not become skilled by always sailing on a calm sea. So, while he waited for the approaching wave of adversity to break upon the Church, he busied himself with the endless tasks of his office.

As the economic picture continued to darken, on the surface prospects for the future were painted in rosy hues. President Herbert Hoover, who had run on a platform of continuing and expanding the rich prosperity that had marked the earlier part of the decade, took office in the early part of 1929 and appeared to have the expertise to deliver on his campaign promises. Notwithstanding this, President Grant continued to have a great uneasiness. April of that year found him concerned about the condition of the domestic sugar industry that meant so much to the farmers in the intermountain area.

Having survived innumerable crises over four decades, the industry now faced a challenge of such ominous proportions as to threaten its very existence. That threat consisted of the seemingly inexhaustible supply of cheap Cuban and Philippine sugar that glutted the American market. Produced by grossly underpaid labor that received barely a tenth of the wage paid to local workers, this foreign sugar could be sold profitably at a price that was ruinous to American competitors. Confronted with this dilemma, it was only natural that influential leaders of the sugar industry fought back with the only effective tool at their disposal, the tariff, the object of which was to neutralize the competitive advantage of the foreign producers. Joining in the fight were leaders of other domestic industries that were similarly threatened by a flood of goods and commodities produced by cheap labor abroad, which literally inundated the American markets. The result was the passage of the Smoot-Hawley Act, which reaffirmed a high tariff policy and hiked customs duties on sugar and other imported commodities to the point that domestic producers could remain in business and compete. This act, co-sponsored by Senator Reed Smoot, was critized or lauded by foe or friend as the bill that either helped to aggravate the worldwide depression that had already begun at the time of its enactment, or that was the savior of many domestic industries, including the sugar industry.

Meanwhile, the initial shock waves of the approaching depression rattled through the financial community, creating the first real awareness of the fatal disorders that were soon to overwhelm it. On September 7, 1929, following a spring and summer that had seen the market climb to new highs, a reaction set in that rapidly gained momentum during six weeks of turbulent, frantic trading and that culminated on October 24 with the utter collapse of the stock market, when thirteen million shares of stock were sold and prices slid to lows that a year before would have been thought a fantasy. This tragic day, later given the somber name "Black Thursday," brought a startled America to the realization that the illness that ate at her economic vitals was a deadly

malignancy, that the remedy would be costly and pro-
longed, and that the chances of a cure would be ques-
tionable.

Black Thursday initiated a steep descent into the
mire of depression and despondency that was to slow,
then stall America's powerful economic machine. So
unexpected was the collapse and so total and devastating were its effects that many became unhinged from
reality. The number of suicides skyrocketed, especially
among the wealthy, educated classes. Others were
numbed into a kind of aimless stupor, unable to appraise
or to understand precisely what had happened.

But although the causes of the debacle were unclear,
and to a large extent have remained so, its deadening
effects soon became apparent. Companies whose ware-
houses bulged with goods, produced to satisfy the
enormous American appetite for consumer products,
found their markets drying up. Credit sources evaporated in the face of the great uncertainties the crash
had engendered. As production ground to a virtual halt,
wholesale lay-offs occurred as harried executives slashed
budgets to avoid immediate bankruptcy. The loss of
worker income emasculated the public buying power,
thereby creating even more stagnation.

As the waves of the depression, spreading outward
from the impact of the market crash, reached the hinter-
lands of the Mountain West, the effects were traumatic.
The initiatives taken by President Grant and his
brethren, their exhortations about simplicity and frugality, and the natural Mormon bent toward conser-
vatism had cushioned the initial blow. But unfortu-
nately for all, the drama that Black Thursday unveiled
was not a one-act play; it was a tragedy that was to
continue for what seemed to some to be an eternity. Day
after week after month after year it became progressively
more intense and deadening. Because the roots of the
disease lay below the surface of human understanding,
the leaders were unable to prescribe a reliable cure.
Many nostrums were tried, but they invariably failed to
bring about any significant improvement.

Thus unemployment and consequent economic decline descended upon the land, obscuring the vision of all. The nation groped uncertainly for something stable to cling to, awaiting the dawn of a better day. It was against the background of these chaotic times that the voters flocked to the political standard of a leader whose hopeful message was that the only thing the people really needed to fear was fear itself. His buoyant self-confidence, jaunty appearance, and infallible political instincts swept Franklin D. Roosevelt into office in the presidential election of 1932. With the aid of a willing Congress, he put into effect an almost bewildering array of remedial legislation that produced varying degrees of success or failure. The philosophy underlying these New Deal policies was anathema to the Mormon hierarchy. Men accustomed to the freedom and independence they had developed in building an empire in a wilderness could hardly understand, let alone embrace, the idea of a paternalistic government that planned and controlled their economic lives. Indeed, they found the idea repugnant, and this repugnance was reinforced by doctrine that enjoined the Church to stand independent of all outside institutions and forces. Thus, from the beginning of the New Deal regime, President Grant fought most of its programs. Except for the work projects, he could find little good to say about it or about those who were its chief architects. However, due to his sensitivity concerning church intervention in politics, he made few of his criticisms publicly or in print, limiting them to the privacy of his inner family, church, and business circles.

These private criticisms were not limited to the New Deal's economic policies, but extended as well to its stand on the repeal of the eighteenth amendment, the Prohibition amendment. In fact, President Grant aimed some of his most pointed and biting criticisms at this aspect of the platform on which President Roosevelt campaigned for the presidency.

It was with difficulty that the prophet refrained from entering the lists to debate the issue publicly. Had he not occupied the high church position he did, Heber J. Grant likely would have fought aggressively to thwart the efforts of the anti-Prohibition forces for repeal. He

was too much of a competitor, too convinced of the
social dangers posed by liquor, and too outspoken in his
views to have remained silent, were it not for an inner
compulsion that sealed his lips in public. For over fifty
years as an apostle, he had witnessed the gradual withdrawal of the Church from the political arena, an arena
in which it had played a dominant role in the first few
decades following the exodus. As church influence in
politics declined, there occurred a corresponding increase in the harmony between the Saints and their
gentile neighbors, a change that appealed to President
Grant's diplomatic instincts.

While the issue of Prohibition had clear moral overtones, President Grant recognized that it was so
inextricably tied up with the issues of a red-hot political
campaign that it would be difficult to draw for many the
moral distinction. It is a reasonable supposition, too,
that he foresaw that repeal was inevitable in light of the
powerful, well-financed campaign the anti-Prohibition
forces had mounted, coupled with a generally held feeling across the land that a viable liquor industry would
help solve some of the nagging problems of the
depression by creating new jobs and broadening the tax
base. He knew that because of his strongly held views on
the subject, no one could reasonably infer a change of attitude from his silence, especially as word filtered out
about the scathing statements he made in private de-
ploring what he considered to be dishonest and dema-
gogic efforts for repeal. This journal entry of July 31,
1933, provides a revealing insight into his public stance
toward Prohibition and his attitude toward the chances
of repeal: "Brother J. Wyley Sessions called and told of
his labors in connection with the allied interests against
repeal of the eighteenth amendment. I explained why I
was not willing to make a speech at Lava Hot Springs in
favor of the Drys of Idaho. I told him I hoped he would
be successful in having Idaho go dry, but acknowledged
I had doubts that success would attend his labors but I
wished him well."

Whatever the reasons, President Grant maintained
public silence on the issue, sadly watched the U.S. House

of Representatives and the Senate adopt the repealing amendment, and watched the states ratify it one by one. The whole affair was made especially poignant to him as he also watched with disbelief as Utah became the thirty-sixth and deciding state to ratify, thus providing the needed three-fourths majority for adoption.

Although President Grant had resigned himself to the likelihood of repeal, it nevertheless was a bitter pill to swallow. In it he saw the destruction of decades of painstaking work rendered in a cause about which he had the deepest feelings. He was angered by the specious arguments of the proponents who falsely contended there was more drinking and drunkenness during Prohibition than beforehand. He was also appalled that the proponents ignored the destructive aspects of alcohol.

When the end came, however, and Utah had pushed the repealing amendment over the top, he accepted the decision with good grace. "Frank Y. Taylor called and we had a long talk about Prohibition," he recorded, "both expressing sincere and heartfelt regrets that Utah voted to repeal the eighteenth amendment." In the *Church News* a few days later he observed: "I feel to have charity at the present time for the Latter-day Saints who have voted for the repeal of the Eighteenth Amendment, notwithstanding the fact that they knew very well, without my coming out and saying 'I want you to do it,' that I would have been mighty happy if they had voted the other way. . . . I lived in hopes, and I announced myself in public, that if all the other states in the union went 'wet' Utah would go 'dry.' "

With the legal barriers against liquor having been destroyed, President Grant moved promptly to enlarge and strengthen the moral barriers guarding the Saints. "But I am very grateful indeed that the repeal of the Eighteenth Amendment will not make any difference to any true Latter-day Saint," he said in a subsequent press interview. "No Latter-day Saint will patronize those things when the Lord has told us it is His will that we let them alone. If our people are going to take license to follow after the things of the world and the people of the world, and do those things that the Gospel of Jesus

Christ teaches them not to do, they are not living up to their religion. So really, the repeal of the Eighteenth Amendment will make no difference whatever to a true Latter-day Saint." (*Church News,* December 23, 1933.)

This, then, was the general theme on liquor President Grant was to stress during the remainder of his days. His clarion call to the Church was abstinence and self-control rather than prohibition. To a large extent, the Saints heeded that call and refrained from drinking despite the ready availability of liquor. But as he observed the adverse effects of free-flowing liquor, he felt impelled to speak out strongly about the blindness and venality of those who had urged and voted for repeal. He said in a general conference talk in April 1937: "I warned them against lies that were being circulated to the effect that there was more drunkenness and more use of liquor than there had been when we did not have Prohibition. Millions of dollars of money, I am sure, was expended to have the Eighteenth Amendment repealed." And eight years after the event, he returned to the subject again with this denunciation: "I tell you that no greater crime was ever committed than the repealing of the Prohibition law. Billions of dollars squandered, and poverty, and heartaches, and death and damnation to many men, have come because of liquor." (*Church News,* October 11, 1941, p. 7.)

Chapter 22

The Prophet and Education

Few men have exerted a more profound influence upon Church education than did Heber J. Grant. Deprived of advanced schooling as a young man, he was eager that coming generations be extended the educational opportunities he had missed. This desire was rooted in an acceptance of the truth taught by Joseph Smith that the glory of God is intelligence, and that knowledge gained in mortality will be a useful tool both here and hereafter.

Once Heber had been called to the Twelve and had acquired seniority and experience in that body, he began to make his influence felt in educational matters. In 1892, a decade after he was called to be an apostle, he presented a resolution at the April general conference for the appointment of a committee of five to look into a general plan for founding and endowing a church university. In furtherance of this resolution, which was approved by the conference, Willard Young, Karl G. Maeser, James E. Talmage, James Sharp, and Benjamin Cluff, Jr., were appointed to the committee. Thus were sown the seeds of a renowned center of learning, Brigham Young University.

While Heber lacked the academic background to contribute in a scholarly way, he enthusiastically offered his enormous administrative and fund-raising talents to the struggling new institution. He used his persuasive techniques to induce wealthy men to donate money or property to the cause. Two of the most liberal donors to the school in the early days were Abraham O. Smoot and uncle Jesse Knight. It was the latter who once told Heber, following an incident when he had donated twice as much as the apostle had originally requested, "The next time you ask for money, don't tell me to pray about it."

While these and other contacts Heber had with the church school system over the years were significant, he played his most historic role in church education in the year following his ordination to the presidency. That role, which lay in the direction of budgetary reform, seemed tailor-made for one who, throughout his adult life, had been accustomed to trimming the budgets of numerous and diverse businesses, eliminating all frills and nonessentials. As he analyzed expenditures, he found that the bulk of the Church's annual budget went to finance its far-flung educational system. It was obvious, therefore, that any substantial economizing would have to result from a slash in spending for the schools. Given his commitment to learning, it was not his intention or desire to downgrade or to minimize church education. Rather his aim was to perpetuate and to strengthen it while reducing expenditures. This led to a reappraisal of the Church's role and responsibility in providing secular education for its members.

The academy system, spawned in the aftermath of the Edmunds-Tucker Act, had as its goal religious instruction for Latter-day Saint students in tandem with their secular training. The leaders of that day wisely saw that the eager, inquiring minds of youth needed more disciplined and intensive training in church doctrine than could be provided by intermittent instruction in priesthood and auxiliary classes. Since government restrictions prohibited the merger of religious and secular teaching in the public schools, the Church decided to provide both kinds in its own schools, privately financed and directed. More than thirty academies, or private schools, were established by the Church between 1888 and 1891.

Shortly after Heber J. Grant assumed the presidency, he and the Brethren reconsidered the decision that had caused the Church to assume the burden of secular training. The obvious question that arose was whether religious and secular training could continue in tandem with the Church bearing the financial load only for the

former. An affirmative answer to that question necessarily entailed the construction and staffing of small
units near or adjacent to secular schools where, during
the weekdays, Latter-day Saint students could con-
veniently intermingle religious and secular instruction.

This idea gave birth to the seminary and institute
system. There had been some experimentation with
seminaries as early as 1912, when the first one was established at Granite High School in Salt Lake City.
After 1918, when Heber J. Grant became president of
the Church, the movement toward seminaries accelerated rapidly, partly because of ballooning costs that
marked the post-war period. By 1920 there were about
twenty seminaries in operation, and the rapid increase in
the number of these facilities sounded the death knell of
the academies.

Coincident with and symbolic of this change in
educational policy came a major change in organizational structure at the highest level. In 1919, President
Grant appointed Elder David O. McKay as Church
Commissioner of Education, marking the first time a
General Authority had occupied this position. Appointed as assistant commissioners at the same time were
two other members of the Council of the Twelve, Elders
Stephen L Richards and Richard R. Lyman.

Given the success that attended the abandonment of
the academies and the development of the seminary
program, it seemed inevitable that a similar metamor-
phosis would take place as to the Church's college
system. In the 1920s, besides the Brigham Young
University, the Church maintained four colleges in Utah
and one in Idaho. Beginning in 1926 the issue of divestiture of these colleges was weighed carefully by President
Grant and his associates, and by 1930 a decision was
made to turn the Utah colleges (with the exception of
the LDS College in Salt Lake City, which was closed)
over to the state, a decision that was influenced in part
by the depression, whose dark shadow had begun to steal
over the land. The divestiture was completed by 1933. In
the meantime, institutes of religion were being established adjacent to university and college campuses

throughout the intermountain area, the first one of which was established in 1926 for the LDS students attending the University of Idaho at Moscow.

These radical changes in the school structure, made under the leadership of President Grant, were to alter completely the course of church education for generations to come. The system that evolved out of them was a hybrid, in that the Church continued to provide secular training to a limited extent, as in the case of Brigham Young University and Ricks College. But these represented isolated exceptions to the general rule, the application of which insured that Latter-day Saint students would receive adequate training in church doctrines and procedures at a fraction of the cost entailed in financing a full, combined secular and ecclesiastical curriculum. These changes bore the unmistakable imprint of President Grant's influence and philosophy. He was never niggardly or stingy with his own means, or those of the Church, when the object of spending was appropriate and essential, but he insisted that all expenditures meet these strict conditions.

Through the years, President Grant maintained a keen personal interest in schools, especially Brigham Young University. He saw in it a powerful instrumentality to help fulfill the mission of the Church. "In this school," he said of BYU, "we are seeking to implant in the hearts of the young men and the young women an absolute testimony of the divinity of Jesus Christ and of the restitution again to the earth of the plan of salvation."

Having taken this view, he was insistent that the faculty not make any uncertain sounds whose effect would be to mislead or confuse the students. "We have reached a point," he wrote in a letter to Franklin S. Harris, president of the university, "where we must be perfectly clear that all those who are engaged in teaching in the university shall be sound on the fundamental questions which deal with church membership." He directed the president to "conduct a very strict examination of all teachers to see just where they stand . . . so that we can put a stop once and for all, both to the reports that appear and reappear, and to any improper teaching which may be taking place."

Anyone who bridles at the thought of imposing restraints upon academicians should recall the origins and purposes of BYU and the source of the funds that finance it. The prophetic injunction given to Karl G. Maeser, its first head, was to not teach even the multiplication tables without the Spirit of God. This admonition had special meaning for the erudite German scholar, who, following his baptism, and in answer to a fervent prayer, had enjoyed the gift of tongues as he communicated freely with Elder Franklin D. Richards, though neither of them spoke or understood the language of the other. Thus to Dr. Maeser, and to those who had appointed him, the existence of spiritual, otherworldly powers and beings was a reality that had to be reckoned with in administering the affairs of BYU and in instructing its student body. To them, the expenditure of sacred tithing funds to finance the university was justified only if, in addition to teaching essential knowledge and skills, it helped to sharpen and perfect spiritual perceptions, an end they deemed preeminent above all others. Therefore, anything that tended to blunt or to obliterate that aim was not tolerated. Nor were the Brethren overly concerned about the cries of academic suppression that their actions evoked. It was not their purpose to stifle free inquiry or debate as to any subject. Indeed, their repeated counsel was to seek and to accept truth wherever it might be found. There was never an attempt to force all Latter-day Saint students or professors to attend or to teach at BYU, nor was there opposition to the faculty and student body delving privately into any subject that interested them or leaving to go elsewhere if they elected. What they did oppose was any effort to use the university as a forum to advance unproven theories that directly, or by implication or innuendo, ran counter to fundamental doctrines of the Church.

While President Grant was anxious that BYU not be deflected from the course set by its founders, he was equally concerned that it reach its full stature as a university of international repute, and that a thirst for education be created among the Saints of an intensity that would cause them to strive for academic excellence. To this end, he called into play his great oratorical talent and his unfailing sense for motivational publicity. In an address delivered in Kansas City, he extolled the commitment the Church and its people had for education. Noting that even in territorial days Utah had one of the highest literacy rates in the nation, he said, "Utah was a territory and we had no public lands to sell to help us in education, we had forged to the front without receiving one, single, solitary dollar from the sale of public lands from the United States." His talk was later published in a private magazine, and to make sure it would be available throughout the Church, President Grant had it reprinted in the report of the April 1921 general conference. At that same conference he established an unusual precedent by inviting a nonmember, Perry G. Holden, a professor at Iowa State College and a Congregationalist by faith, to address the Saints. A year later, President Grant added strength to the precedent by inviting not one but three nonmember professors to address the April 1922 general conference: Professor Thomas Nixon Carver, political economist of Harvard University; Walter Ernest Clark, president of the University of Nevada; and Charles Lory, president of Colorado Agricultural College. The last speaker accurately voiced the philosophy of education and life held by his host: "We must build spirituality," he said. "The curve that represents the growth of spirituality is a rather flat one; the curve that represents the increase in wealth, the increase in material knowledge, is a rather steep one; and somehow, we must learn to do as you are doing; carry our religion into our day's work—not religion on one day only, but religion on seven days, and every hour of the twenty-four."

By these and other means, President Grant glamorized the role of education in the eyes of the Latter-day Saints. It was his aim that they become the best-educated and most productive people on earth and, beyond the veil, that they become perfect as God is perfect.

As to Brigham Young University, he held the view that
it would become the greatest institution of higher learning in the world.

Chapter 23

The Advancing Years

As President Grant advanced in years, each birthday became an event of major significance. The tributes that poured in on these occasions expressed the love and respect both members and nonmembers had for him and for the vigor and enthusiasm with which he discharged his prophetic duties. To those who may have sought counsel about how to carry one's age with dignity and grace as he did, he had a stock answer, aptly expressed in this simple verse he quoted on his seventy-fifth birthday:

> *Age is a quality of mind.*
> *If your dreams you've left behind,*
> *If hope is cold,*
> *If you no longer look ahead,*
> *If your ambition's fires are dead,*
> *Then you are old.*
>
> *But if from life you take the best,*
> *And if in life you keep the zest,*
> *If love you hold,*
> *No matter how the years go by,*
> *No matter how the birthdays fly—*
> *You are not old.*

These lines were delivered with a zestful exuberance that left no doubt that the reciter, though advanced in years, was youthful in his aims and perspectives. While there lay behind him an impressive train of achievements and good deeds, wrought during a long life of dedicated service, there also stretched ahead a road whose vistas and byways he was anxious to explore. And he forged ahead along this road with all the eager expectancy of a youth who had not yet savored the thrill and challenge of the journey.

As his birthdays accumulated, there seemed to be a disposition on the part of his associates and family to make each succeeding one an event that outshone all the others in creative magnificence. Every means that human ingenuity could devise to demonstrate love and admiration was employed on these occasions. Perhaps the zenith of these annual outpourings was reached on his eighty-second birthday, when, according to the normal standards of mortality, it was realized that he might depart this life at any time. As the date, November 22, 1938, approached, his friends and loved ones, both in and out of the Church, put the finishing touches on a birthday celebration that stands distinct from all the others he enjoyed.

The festivities began on Tuesday, his natal day, when the Brigham Young University band played a concert for him in the Church Administration Building. Later that day the jaunty 82-year-old leader was feted at a birthday dinner in the nearby Lion House, where eighty of his direct descendants—children, grand-children, and great-grandchildren—had assembled to pay their respects. As he watched the dramatic skits that depicted various incidents in his life and listened to the music, he was caught up in a reverie of nostalgic reflection. The days when he had visited in this home as an obscure widow's son, and had heard its owner, Brigham Young, pray to God with such sincerity and fervency, seemed so remote and distant. And yet, in another aspect, it seemed only yesterday that he had been a young man about town, filled with business and political ambitions, diligently courting Emily Wells, and anxious for the day when he would enjoy the status of a ruling patriarch in the midst of a numerous progeny. As he now surveyed the scene before him and saw in it a partial fulfillment of his most cherished hope, he knew there lay ahead a more distant and exciting prospect, when these eighty descendants would become a mul-titude as numerous as the sands on the seashore, a mul-titude that would regard him in the same reverential light in which he looked upon Father Abraham.

The following day, the celebration shifted from the comparatively quiet and secluded confines of the Lion House to the LaFayette Ballroom of the Hotel Utah, where over five hundred church, professional, business, and political leaders had assembled to pay homage to President Grant at an anniversary banquet. Symbolically, the general chairman of the event was John F. Fitzpatrick, head of the Salt Lake *Tribune,* the local paper that, in President Grant's earlier years, had been so unrestrained in its criticism of the Church and its leaders. An editorial appearing in the paper, reporting on the banquet, eloquently reveals the dramatic change in the climate of Mormon-gentile relations that had occurred during the life of one man: "There was something more than individual tribute in this bond of friendship. In all of Utah history there is no signal of unity more poignant with peaceful understanding than this one. To attain such a goal is the work of generations devoted to all that is good in civilization. At this testimonial dinner tendered President Grant, honoring his eighty-second birthday, this spirit was manifest. . . . To be the medium for such an expression was pleasing to the venerable church leader, loved and admired by all his associates without regard to religious ties."

Lending emphasis to the ecumenical flavor of this signal affair was the presence of Salt Lake City's non-Mormon mayor, John M. Wallace, and the Most Reverend Duane G. Hunt, bishop of the Salt Lake Diocese of the Catholic Church.

As a token of esteem and a symbol of President Grant's philanthropies and his unflagging support of Utah industry, he was given a chest of Utah copper made by Utah craftsmen and filled to the brim with one thousand silver dollars. A plate attached to the chest contained the engraved inscription: "Presented with love and esteem to President Heber J. Grant on his birthday anniversary by a group of friends and associates."

The terse journal entry President Grant made of this event conveys the depth of the gratitude he felt for the honor thus bestowed upon him: "I was overwhelmed with the kind compliments that were paid to me, and appreciate very much indeed what was said. In my talk I remarked that there were few men that had the privilege of hearing their funeral sermon before they passed on." And hinting at the unsettling effect this extravagant display of affection had had upon him, he concluded: "I forgot to even thank them for the thousand dollars in my speech."

The remembrance of this singular evening shone bright in President Grant's memory during the remainder of his life. It seemed to represent a kind of accolade for the untold effort he had expended over the years in the interest of friendly relations with his non-Mormon neighbors. It also stood out as a reflection of the feelings of brotherly love he had entertained toward all, member and nonmember alike, from the beginning of his apostolic ministry.

But while President Grant enjoyed and appreciated these manifestations of public acclaim, they were secondary to the feelings generated by his familial associations. He was first and foremost a family man; and as he grew older, as his progeny multiplied and increased in stature and influence, nothing gave him more satisfaction than to have them close about where he could enjoy vicariously the excitement, the challenge, and the trauma of each rising generation.

In his family associations, President Grant demonstrated the inexhaustible and indivisible quality of love. To show his love meant to lavish all he had upon the one who, for the moment, was the object of his affection. But such a manifestation neither diminished the supply of his love nor hinted at any favoritism toward a recipient or any rejection of others not present. Invariably, he greeted his daughters and other close family members with a fatherly kiss. Invariably, each member of the rapidly growing Grant clan could expect a birthday greeting from him, together with a gift of money. Invariably he and his wife came forward with special financial aid to assist family members who were confronted with unusual or unexpected expenses: the birth of a new baby, an illness, a mission, schooling, or the purchase of a new home. And their largess was often extended to those who, though not within the immediate family circle, were bound to them by ties of affinity or brotherhood. A typical illustration of their liberality to those outside the family occurred with Whitney and Alice Colton Smith, a struggling student couple to whom the Grants gave money to defray the hospital and medical costs of a pregnancy. The gift, made so graciously by "Aunt Gusta" as not to make the couple feel themselves to be the objects of charity, was offered on the premise that the Grants liked to help all their grandchildren in this way, and they regarded the Smiths as their "grandchildren."

The examples of President Grant's liberality are legion, and those that have come to light doubtless represent only the tip of the iceberg, for he was not one to make a public show of his liberalities. This testimonial from his secretary and friend Joseph Anderson, who knew him as well as any man, is revealing: "President Grant was the most liberal and generous man with his personal means that I have ever known. . . . In fact, I doubt if any have excelled him in this respect. . . . He was a man who thoroughly enjoyed making money, but not for the purpose of accumulating it. His only desire was to have money that he might do good with it. On various occasions he would come to me and ask how much money was in his bank account. Knowing the purpose for which he wished the money, I hesitated at times to give it to him without reminding him of certain expenditures he would have to meet in the near future. Invariably he would ask me to draw a check for the amount he desired, perhaps for $1,000 or $1,500, telling me to make the check in favor of some widow whose name he would give, explaining that he wished to pay off the mortgage on her home. I recall on one occasion before the Salt Lake Theatre was torn down, and at a time when the theatre was not making money, President Grant bought some theatre stock from the daughters of one of his deceased friends, giving them for the stock far more than the market price. A few years later when the theatre was sold, the return to the stockholders was in excess of the amount that he had to pay these women for their stock. He gave them his check to make up the difference in the price even though the transaction making the purchase had been consummated several years previously."

Somehow, President Grant seemed not to notice that he was already a decade beyond the three score and ten years normally allotted to man. Over the protestations of his family and associates, and in the face of dire predictions by his doctors, he continued to lead the vigorous life of a man half his age. The single-minded dedication with which he pursued his exercise regimens and the apparent bloom of health that customarily adorned his person seemed at times to convince those close to him that he was as young as he acted and that their concerns and admonitions about his physical welfare were unfounded. But deep within his physical being, shielded from the eyes of all, lurked an anomaly that, when subjected to intense pressures, erupted into a paralytic stroke that would impair his mobility, reduce his vital energies, and raise his frustration level to a height theretofore unknown.

President Grant had no warning of the awful occurrence that was to rob him of the earthly gift, his health, that he prized more highly than almost any other. The circumstances of this fateful incident were no different from those surrounding the many other instances when he had gone to Southern California for a little winter sun and a change of pace. As he left Salt Lake City on January 26, 1940, the eighty-three-year-old prophet looked forward eagerly to a few weeks in the idyllic surroundings of Southern California, where, while carrying on a normal work routine, he expected to enjoy the diversion of golf that he pursued now with increasing delight.

With him on the train were Augusta, Mary, and his almost constant companion, Joseph Anderson. He used the travel time to catch up on some of the correspondence that burdened his desk in an ever-increasing volume.

Soon after arriving in Los Angeles, President Grant

and Preston Richards made business contacts with Arch W. Anderson, Harry Chandler, publisher of the Los Angeles *Times*, and Herbert D. Ivey, each of whom was given a copy of the biography *Joseph Smith, An American Prophet*, written by John Henry Evans. It took little deliberation for the Church president to accept Mr. Ivey's invitation to lunch at his country club, following which they played nine holes of golf. In the evening, President Grant and his party dined at the home of Preston D. Richards. It was quite unlike President Grant to acknowledge in his journal, "The day has been a rather strenuous one." This grudging concession, from the man who appeared to some to be indestructible, contained only a vague hint of the tragedy that was to befall him in just a few days as his aging body rebelled against the exhausting pace at which it was driven.

Unheedful of the silent warning he had received to slow down, he was off and running early the next morning, Sunday, on a trip to San Diego, where at noon he attended and spoke at the dedication of a monument honoring the Mormon Battalion, and in the evening spoke to an audience of six hundred assembled at one of the branch chapels. In recording the events of the day, he expressed gratitude for the "good liberty" he had enjoyed in talking, but noted in closing, "I am quite tired tonight."

During the next three days in San Diego, President Grant intermixed business with speeches and golf. Monday, following a morning of writing in his journal and dictating, he addressed the Hammer Club at the U.S. Grant Hotel, where he discussed the sugar situation and government tax policies. Afternoon found him on the links with his friend Marley Golden. Of the game he noted, with some disconsolance, "I did not win a single hole." But the next day things picked up when in a foursome he shot a 45, "the best game for a long time I have played." A partial explanation of his improved performance may be found in the fact that he "practiced fifty cents worth of balls" before the round commenced.

The round of golf he played in San Diego on Wednesday, January 31, 1940, was his last. Had he

known that, it is doubtful he would have altered one
aspect of it, except he may have wished he had shot a little better. But it was a beautiful day, spent in the open
with men whom he loved and in whom he had confidence, his friend Joseph Anderson and Brothers
Cheney and Crandall of the district presidency.

On his return to Los Angeles Thursday afternoon,
President Grant found the city locked in one of those
drizzling, soaking rains for which the area is noted, effectively scotching any plans for golf during the remainder
of the week. Settling down into the mission home there,
he busied himself as usual. "I dictated several letters today, one to Ada Dwyer and another to Brother Sterling
D. Wheelwright. I sent some books to Wallace John-
son—'Stories of the L.D.S. Hymns,' 'Treasures I Would
Share,' and 'Joseph Smith, An American Prophet.' "
Saturday was more of the same: "I dictated a letter today to my daughter Lutie, one to Preston Richards
about the book 'Children of God' and thanked him for
the account he had prepared regarding H. D. Ivey's
hobby. I wrote to President Clark answering his telegram; wrote to Fred W. Shibley and sent him a copy of
the Improvement Era. Wrote Richard L. Evans, telling
him to send the Era to Mr. Shibley. Wrote to E. W.
Wilson's widow, sending a letter of sympathy."

It was in this way that President Grant filled up the
hours when, presumably, he was on a vacation break.
And all the while, he had in mind the Inglewood Stake
conference that he was to attend the coming weekend.
As the time for the Saturday evening priesthood session
approached, however, he became aware of a nervous
tension that he could hardly describe or diagnose, but
that he knew was unlike anything he had ever experienced before. The extent to which he was troubled is
shown by the fact that he did not attend the priesthood
session Saturday evening merely because Elder George
Albert Smith phoned to say it was not necessary to do so.
Under ordinary circumstances, nothing could have
deterred him from attending a meeting where he was expected and to which he had agreed to go. The compulsion that drove him was a deep sense of duty coupled

with the realization that the prophetic mantle he wore drew many people to meetings they would not otherwise attend, and that disappointment at his absence could produce feelings of frustration or negativism. So the agreeable, nonresistant way in which he acceded to the mere suggestion of Elder Smith that he not attend the priesthood meeting is perhaps the clearest indication that all was not well with him.

President Grant spent a restless night Saturday, and Sunday's dawn, which he greeted listlessly after hours of nervous insomnia, found him no stronger and in no better spirits than the night before. Although he doubted he had the vigor and stamina to carry it off, he prepared for a full day of three major meetings, the first at ten o'clock at the Inglewood Stake Center. Feeling as he did, it is possible he would have refrained from attending had he been encouraged not to go as he had been the night before. But as no such suggestion was forthcoming, he went forward with his preparations for the day, outwardly wearing a facade of good health, but inwardly knowing that something was radically wrong with his physical system.

Promptly at 9:30 A.M. President W. Aird MacDonald of the California Mission drove President Grant and Joseph Anderson to the Inglewood Stake Center for the morning session of the conference. As the car pulled into the parking lot, President Grant felt a surge of dizziness that increased in intensity as he began to step from the car. The vertigo caused him to lose his balance and he stumbled to the ground. Helped to his feet, he found, as he expressed thanks for the assistance, that his tongue was thick and his speech quite indistinct. Shrugging off any suggestion that he not attend the meeting, now that he had come this far, he insisted on going into the building and taking his place on the stand, which he was able to do with an arm to lean on to avoid falling. But he did not feel up to speaking and sat mute throughout the meeting, occasionally feeling aftershocks of the vertigo. However, a brief nap during the noon hour seemed to revive him, and at the afternoon session he spoke for almost forty minutes with his usual vigor and forcefulness.

Those who heard President Grant on this occasion would not realize until later that they had heard the prophet speak for the last time in the manner to which the Church had become accustomed during the fifty-eight years he had served as an apostle. Never again would he lift his voice from a pulpit in the free-flowing, extemporaneous style that had become his trademark. From that point to the end of his earthly ministry, his talks would be read for him, or, if he spoke, he would do so in a more measured, deliberate way.

Despite his apparent recovery from the dizziness that had afflicted him in the morning, and his effective talk at the afternoon session of the conference, President Grant was persuaded not to attend the evening meeting. Instead, he retired early at the mission home, but not before being examined by a doctor, who incorrectly diagnosed his problem as uremic poisoning, and not before receiving the president of the Hollywood Stake and two associates to discuss the possibility of holding a special Latter-day Saint celebration in Southern California on the anniversary of Pioneer Day. As his last official act before being stricken he asked these brethren to write up their plans and send them to him in Salt Lake City.

The next morning, Monday, as President Grant attempted to get out of bed, he suffered another attack of vertigo, stronger than the one on Sunday, and fell. He called for his daughter Mary, who in turn summoned a doctor. The paralysis of his left side and his impaired speech now made diagnosis easy and certain; he had suffered a stroke. Admitted to St. Vincent's Hospital in Los Angeles, he began a six-week ordeal of medical treatment, therapy, and convalescence. This depressing, and in some respects frightful, interlude was ushered in with the following terse journal entry on February 7, the last until April 27 when President Grant was prepared to resume his duties on a severely limited basis: "Spent the day at the hospital. Brother Anderson called at noon, and at my suggestion he wrote six letters to those who had sent flowers to me at the hospital, thanking them for their remembrances. He brought them up this evening, and I signed them, and he took the train for home. He leaves at my suggestion and that of President McKay."

Chapter 24

The Final Challenge

During the seemingly endless days of President Grant's convalescence in Los Angeles, he oscillated between troubled, nauseous wakefulness and fitful sleep. The paralysis of his left side and the inability to speak distinctly made him almost wholly dependent upon others, a disability difficult to be borne by one who had always prided himself on his independence and self-reliance. Added to these crushing physical and emotional burdens was the vague, nagging concern about the neglect of his duties. He was aware of the inevitable drift in the administrative affairs of the Church that would occur while he was unwell. This awareness did not imply any lack of ability in his counselors or the Twelve nor any lack of confidence in them. It was merely a recognition of the preeminent role the president plays in the administrative affairs of the Church, a role clearly defined in church doctrine and practice and one whose prerogatives no one would presume to exercise except in the rare and unlikely case of the president's total incapacity.

He did take comfort in the strength, the ability, and the complete loyalty of his counselors, who kept him briefed about church affairs and sought his direction from time to time on matters that did not lie within the scope of their delegated responsibilities.

As April drew to a close, it was decided that his condition had improved to the point that he could return home. His son-in-law, Robert L. Judd, had gone to Los Angeles to accompany him; on the morning of their departure, they went to the office of Dr. Ruddock, who had been the chief of the corps of doctors who had attended President Grant, for a final checkup and parting instructions. "They saw my heart, lungs and other inside organs and made comments," the patient noted clinically. Then came the bombshell, as the doctor defined what came to be the charter governing President Grant's personal activities during the balance of his life: "He wound up by saying that there were three things I must do. One was, I must take it easy, as any energetic work like I had been in the habit of doing would undoubtedly knock me out; that I must reduce a little the amount of food that I have been in the habit of eating and that under no circumstances must I take any heavy physical exercise." Becoming more specific as to the last restriction, President Grant wrote with regret, "He doubted that I should ever try to play golf again."

The difficulty with which one changes habit patterns becomes more pronounced with age. President Grant brought to this formidable task the same iron determination with which he had confronted other adversities throughout life. The point at which he first waged the new warfare was at the level of his emotions. For a man of his vigor and activity, his zestful enjoyment of athletics, and his aggressive style, suddenly to find himself fettered by a crippling injury and restricted in his work regimen to a few hours a day was a devastating blow.

The first natural reaction of one so habituated to conflict and challenge was to confront the problem head-on with an eye to solving it. Up until now, President Grant could hardly recall a significant problem or difficulty he had not overcome in time. When, therefore, the initial shock wave of this shattering blow had subsided, he began to marshal his forces for the climb up still another Everest. If he was to be restricted in the vigorous exercises he had enjoyed all of his life, then he would replace them with more moderate exercise. While he could not walk extensively or play golf or volleyball, he could give his weakened left side isometric exercises, which he did by carrying a hard rubber ball in his left hand and squeezing it intermittently during the day. While from the beginning he was aware of the serious nature of his illness and of the possibility that he would never recover from it, yet he nourished the vague hope that he might conquer this problem as he had so many others in the past, and toward this end, he pursued isometrics with the same intensity and dedication as he had earlier pursued his penmanship and his musical and athletic goals.

But it was a discouraging business, and it was frustrating. It was not unlike the experience he had had in Japan when nothing seemed to yield to his constant and persistent efforts. And his frustration occasionally found expression in an unaccustomed irascibility and impatience. It irked him that he could not do all the things he used to do, and at times he seemed to take it as a personal affront, a reflection on his manhood, when someone offered unsought-for aid in rising from a chair or going up or down steps.

In time, however, and by gradual degrees, President Grant came to accept the fact that his disability was a condition with which he would have to cope the rest of his days. That acceptance represented the watershed point in the emotional battle he waged following his paralytic stroke. Thereafter, he became resigned to his fate and commenced to perform his daily tasks within the severe limits of his physical impairment.

In this resignation is to be found one of the most significant achievements in a life filled with achievement. It represented an acknowledgment of the limitations imposed by man's mortality and a recognition of the truth that victory or success is not necessarily equated with winning, but rather with the quality of one's performance in difficult and constantly changing circumstances.

With this altered focus, and having to a large extent resolved the problem of his emotions, President Grant turned to the second phase of the new warfare—how best to utilize his time and talents within the structure of the new life-style his disability had imposed.

The heart of his day under the new regimen was the two-hour block of time allotted for his administrative duties as head of the Church and as a director of several Church-owned or controlled corporations. Of necessity, he made broad delegations of authority to his subordinates, and he did it without hesitancy or compunction.

He had always been a good and effective delegator, so the procedure he used at this critical time was merely an extension of a tried and tested administrative tool he had used effectively throughout his ecclesiastical and business career. In the short time he was able to devote each day to this important work, he was able to give the necessary overall direction, keeping a firm hand on the general policies and decisions of the Church while turning over to his counselors and others the responsibility for handling the multitudinous and ever-growing details of administration.

Once he was back on the job and was available to attend key meetings and to make important decisions of policy, the administrative work of the Church ran without any real impediment. Although he had been slowed down physically and was severely restricted in the number of hours he could work each day, he continued to be strong in his mental perceptions and in his ability to make sound judgments. On this account, he had no real concern about the operation of the Church, for he had the reins of leadership firmly in his grasp and was in a position to give the emphasis and the direction he thought necessary. What did concern him, though, was how to fill up his days with activities that were meaningful and enjoyable and yet not overly strenuous.

There were, of course, reading and dictating, which he could do without great exertion and which he did do extensively. But a steady diet of these, day after day, weighed heavily upon him. What he needed was a diversion, something to take the place of his athletics and to provide variety and enjoyment to his daily routine. He found this in the automobile rides he had enjoyed so much in earlier years, viewing the scenery and reveling in the company of friends and loved ones. He added an important dimension to this activity, using it as a means of promoting family solidarity and love and of bringing happiness and excitement to many outside the family circle. He never took these daily rambles alone; always accompanying him was a chauffeur, usually Cannon Lund, a son of his former counselor Anthon H. Lund. Augusta ordinarily went along, when her household and other domestic duties would permit. Rounding out the entourage would be two or three members of his family—daughters, sons-in-law, or grandchildren. As the months wore on, it was found that the members of the family, except Augusta, were able to go less and less frequently because of their complicated schedules of work, housekeeping, and school. Since riding was almost a daily affair with him, and because his gregarious nature craved companionship, he began to reach out beyond the family and to invite assorted friends and neighbors to accompany him. It is difficult to imagine the thrill and excitement generated in a widow or an invalid, or for that matter in anyone who knew Heber J. Grant, to be invited to go along on one of his daily rides. To be in the presence of a prophet of God for an hour or two under such choice and intimate circumstances was an opportunity that faithful members of the Church would wait a lifetime to enjoy. The memory of such a special occasion would endure with the participants as long as life lasted, and in most instances would be preserved as family lore through journal entries or frequent retelling in family gatherings. And it was not unusual during these daily forays for President Grant to stop at the hospital or at the home of someone who was ill to extend his love and best wishes.

During these daily outings into the countryside to view the canyons, the peaks, and the valleys of the Wasatch and the Oquirrh mountains, President Grant not only indulged his yen for companionship and conversation, but also satisfied a deep-seated hunger for the natural beauties of the mountain country he called home. The sight of an unusual, picturesque scene aroused in him a joyous, almost poetic feeling that often was reflected in his journal entries. Of an outing on March 15, 1941, he wrote: "In the afternoon we had a ride with Brother and Sister B. S. Hinckley and Sister May Anderson. Nearly all of our rides for the past week have been up Emigration Canyon, over Little Mountain, down into Parleys and home. The view as you go down the canyon to get into Parleys is very fine. I love the mountains when they are covered with white snow.

On nearly all of our trips we have had the pleasure of seeing a few deer. One day we counted 81. The government rangers feed them about half way down the mountain. I have never had the pleasure of being present at one of the feedings, but on one occasion a dozen or more ran in front of our car and we stopped and I think it was eight or ten feet on the other side of the road, and to see them spring to the top of the bank was very interesting. They went up just like they were on rubber balls."

But these outings did more than satisfy President Grant's need for recreation and cement good relationships with his family and associates. They also helped create the kind of matrix within which he did his most effective work. Away from the pressing demands of the office routine, and stimulated by the conversation of the able people who accompanied him and by the grandeur of the mountains, he saw things and understood things that might otherwise have escaped his notice. Lending emphasis to this idea is the fact that the journal entry just quoted also contained this significant sentence: "During the day I had quite a long talk with Brother Clark and Brother David O. McKay regarding calling some men to help the Quorum of the Twelve."

In this entry we see the genesis of a formal action taken at the April general conference in 1941 when five Assistants to the Twelve were called and sustained. That action represented the most far-reaching organizational initiative taken by President Grant during his ministry. Indeed, there are few changes in the basic structure of the Church that have occurred since the days of the Prophet Joseph Smith that equal or exceed this one in importance, unless it be the formation of the First Quorum of the Seventy, which occurred thirty-five years later, during the administration of President Spencer W. Kimball. And this later act traces its origin to what took place in 1941, since the Assistants to the Twelve comprised the bulk of those called into the First Quorum of the Seventy at the time this body was activated by President Kimball.

President Grant looked forward with anticipation to the general conference to be held in April 1941. Although still severely restricted in his activities, he basically felt good and was able to carry on his duties effectively. He was anxious to mingle again with the brethren and sisters from throughout the Church who would throng to Salt Lake City with their enthusiasms and excitements that always charged the conference atmosphere with an electric feeling. That feeling was heightened on this occasion by the knowledge that a new member of the Twelve likely would be sustained, since Elder Reed Smoot of that quorum had passed away quietly at St. Petersburg, Florida, on February 9. And there was added excitement created by the appointments of Marion G. Romney, Thomas E. McKay, Clifford E. Young, Alma Sonne, and Nicholas G. Smith as the first Assistants to the Twelve. The excitement arose from a realization that the Church stood on the threshold of important changes.

The prophet appeared vigorous and strong as the conference opened on April 4, 1941. In his keynote address, he expressed regret that so many young men were at war and prayed they would carry the missionary spirit with them; admonished the leaders to teach by example; and recounted some of his early spiritual experiences, including the enlightenment that had come to him in the Arizona desert almost sixty years before. What moved the audience more than anything else, however, was the positive and fervent testimony he bore: "I have been happy during the twenty-two years that it has fallen my lot to stand at the head of this Church. I have felt the inspiration of the Living God directing me in my labors. From the day that I chose a comparative stranger to be one of the Apostles, instead of my lifelong and dearest living friend, I have known as I know that I live, that I am entitled to the light and the inspiration and the guidance of God in directing His work here upon the earth; and I know, as I know that I live, that it is God's work, and that Jesus Christ is the Son of the Living God, the Redeemer of the world and that He came to this earth with a divine mission to die upon the cross as the Redeemer of mankind, atoning for the sins of the world."

The high spiritual tone set by this keynote seemed to pervade all the conference sessions and reached its crescendo on Sunday, April 6, when the General Authorities were sustained. At that time, in addition to sustaining the five new Assistants to the Twelve, the conference also sustained a new apostle in the person of Elder Harold B. Lee, a dynamic man of forty-three who had proven himself as a leader of uncommon administrative skill and high spirituality. In his acceptance talk, Elder Lee commented on President Grant's keynote address: "One could not have listened to the soul-stirring testimony of President Grant, in bearing testimony as to his feelings when he was called to the apostleship, or his experiences in calling others to similar positions, without realizing that he has been close to his Heavenly Father in this experience."

Although President Grant was exhilarated by the conference and was built up spiritually, he was physically exhausted. When the conference came to an end, he was convinced as never before that time was running out on him. These feelings were reinforced by the stern lectures delivered by his doctor about overdoing and about living within the limits of his physical capabilities. He hardly paid even lip service to this counsel at the opening of the October 1941 general conference. "The doctor gave me only twenty minutes," he began, "but I have concluded to take a lot more than twenty minutes." By way of justification, he added: "By not speaking loud I do not believe it will hurt me."

Then followed the most detailed and exact description available of the physical effects President Grant's stroke had had upon him. His words provide an important insight into the mental and spiritual struggles through which he passed as, by degrees, he reached an accommodation with his fate: "I have been asked for a year and a half, in fact a little longer than that, 'How do you feel?' I have said, 'Better than yesterday,' and I believe it is true, but the improvement has been limited, and I am not yet in good health. . . . I am very, very happy to be here this morning, grateful beyond my power of expression for the blessings of the Lord, when I realize that I could not move my left arm at all, nor my left leg; that I could not possibly touch my chin with my fingers; that one of my eyes was crooked; and that my mouth was twisted. I feel very happy that I look quite natural." The statement that followed revealed the oscillating view President Grant took of his illness and the resulting carelessness or diligence with which he heeded the doctor's mandate. "I thought I was better than I am, and the doctor had allowed me two hours a day. I spent four hours and twenty minutes one day, and I felt so fine that after dinner I went down to the doctor's office to insist on having four hours a day, only to be sent home and sent to bed. He discovered that my blood pressure had gone out of sight, and so I have not tried to fool him since."

President Grant was to be permitted to raise his voice only once again at a general conference of the Church, in April 1942. In the interim, the country had been plunged into the holocaust of war following the December 7, 1941, attack upon Pearl Harbor. A comprehensive message from the First Presidency, read at the conference by President J. Reuben Clark, Jr., dwelled at length upon the war and its consequences and admonished the Latter-day Saints in the armed forces to live the high standards of their religion.

The keynote address delivered by President Grant followed closely the pattern of the one he had given six months earlier. He began with an allusion to his physical ailment, the effects of which, he said, would make it necessary for him to speak more quietly than usual. He shared with his audience the procedure he had followed in preparing to deliver the last sermon of his illustrious career: "Last night I had a very good night's sleep and slept until five o'clock this morning. I got up and decided to dictate a sermon for this occasion. I dictated two cylinders and then decided not to give you anything I had said, but to come here and trust to the Lord to speak as I was led. I desire more than I have language to tell that what I say may be for your good and that I shall have the benefit of your faith and prayers." Then followed a powerful sermon, delivered extempor-

aneously, that demonstrated his effectiveness as an ora-
tor and a preacher of righteousness. In the first place, it
was interesting. It was filled with personal experiences
and anecdotes that riveted the attention of his audience
on what was being said. But they were not the vacuous,
banal kind of stories we sometimes hear in our public
meetings. They were stories that related to his ministry
as an apostle and that illustrated the character and the
source of strength of the men who had preceded him as
presidents of the Church. Of them he testified, "I know
as I know that I live that they were inspired, wonderful
men, that they had no ambition of any kind or description but to lead the Latter-day Saints in the paths of
righteousness, to set examples worthy of imitation in all
respects. They were in very deed men of God."

After having thus lauded his predecessors and having
borne testimony of the rectitude of their lives and the
selflessness of their ministries, it was entirely appropriate
that in his concluding remarks he added his own personal witness of the divinity of the work: "I can only
hope that the people of the world may realize the fact
that we are in very deed the Church of Jesus Christ and
not the church of any man, and that there is no ambition in our hearts for personal power or prestige in the
world. All that we desire is the salvation of mankind."
Then the venerable prophet spoke the last words he was
to utter from the pulpit he had occupied for sixty years,
words that so accurately typify the life and character of
one of the most persistent workers and strugglers the
Church has produced: "I never forget one little statement . . . in the . . . Doctrine and Covenants: 'And if it so
be that you should labor all your days in crying repentance unto this people, and bring, save it be one soul
unto me, how great shall be your joy with him in the
kingdom of my father!' God bless you all, amen."

Chapter 25

The End Approaches

With those words of benediction, the powerful voice was stilled from its public utterances. The church had heard the great preacher for the last time. Never again would the walls of the Tabernacle reverberate with the words and tones of the voice that had thrilled and motivated the Saints for six decades, and made them alternately laugh and cry, had taken them into the valley or to the mountaintop, depending on whether the call was to repentance or to high achievements. Nor would they ever again hear that voice admonish, cajole, and entreat them to shun tobacco and alcohol, to patronize home industries, and to work—strive and work.

But President Grant had retreated into silence, not oblivion. He still had several years left, still had important work to do. He continued to labor behind the scenes within the limits of his disabilities, attending council and board meetings and overseeing the work of the Brethren.

As the October 1943 general conference approached, he faced the challenge of selecting two new members of the Council of the Twelve, necessitated by the passing of Sylvester Q. Cannon, who died May 29, 1943, and Rudger Clawson, the president of the Twelve, who died on June 21, 1943. Through revelation he selected two vigorous and able young stake presidents whose names evoked fond memories among those in the Church acquainted with its early history. Spencer W. Kimball, a descendant of Heber C. Kimball, and Ezra Taft Benson, a descendant of the early apostle of the same name, were sustained at the conference and were ordained by President Grant on October 7, 1943.

Within a few weeks after they were closed with the
ordination of Elders Kimball and Benson, the ranks of
the Twelve were shaken by the excommunication of one
of their number, Elder Richard R. Lyman. The trauma
of Elder Lyman's excommunication was minimized to
an extent by the deep spiritual qualities and the achievements of the man called to replace him in the Twelve.
Elder Mark E. Petersen, general manager of the *Deseret
News*, noted for his precision in writing and speaking,
was sustained to fill the vacancy at the general
conference in April 1944. As was true with the other
General Authorities called through his prophetic inspiration, President Grant's influence was to be extended into
the decades ahead through the ministry of this able and
dedicated apostle.

The competitive fires that had burned so brightly
during President Grant's eighty-eight years of hectic,
joyous, and fruitful living began to subside and flicker
out in the latter part of 1944. The aged prophet now
found it to be an almost herculean task merely to arise in
the morning. The debilitating effect of his stroke had
hampered his movements, and while his mind remained
sound and alert, the concentrated effort required to
perform the everyday tasks of moving about and taking
care of his physical needs usurped time that had previously been devoted to his ecclesiastical and business
affairs. The inevitable result was a steady withdrawal
from most of the activities that had been his lifeblood. It
was during this period that he suspended his habit of
making daily journal entries. In place of these appear
lists of the correspondence he signed each day, correspondence prepared at his direction by the clerical
staff.

At the dawn of spring in 1945, there appeared unmistakable signs of President Grant's approaching
demise, typified by a sharp decline in his work at the
office. He continued to go there now and then, but the
occasions were progressively less frequent.

On the surface, there seemed to be an incongruity
between the budding spring that lay all around and the
inevitable death that now was near at hand. Yet within

President Grant were the seeds of still another birth, seeds that were manifested by the quiet and expectant attitude that characterized his last days.

The end came peacefully in the late afternoon of May 14, 1945. It was not unexpected, nor was it greeted with the signs of anguish and despair that sometimes accompany the death of a public figure. Of course, there were the unavoidable feelings of sadness by his family and associates at the loss of his companionship. But these feelings were tempered by the conviction that the separation was only temporary, and by the knowledge that the great man would be laid to rest with no regrets or recriminations.

The eulogies at the funeral focused upon President Grant's family, his ministry, and the personal qualities that had set him apart. The fruits of his strong will and rugged persistence were counted by those who spoke, not only in the unusual achievements of his life, but also in the fires of aspiration and ambition he had lighted in countless others who had undertaken things they would have been reluctant to attempt without the encouragement of his example.

Friends and admirers from around the world, including many nonmembers, gathered in Salt Lake to pay their final respects. As the funeral cortege moved slowly east on South Temple, past Wells corner, past the Lion House and the Beehive House, thousands stood silently with their heads bared in honor of this native son, the child of a lonely widow, who had risen from obscurity to a position of such eminence. Had Brigham Young and Heber C. Kimball stood among the mourners, or had they been present in some other-worldly form, they might well have whispered to each other that this son of their friend and associate, Jedediah M. Grant, had indeed fulfilled the prediction Brigham had made at Jedediah's funeral.

As the cortege reached Third East, the deceased prophet received the ultimate accolade from the gentile community when the bells of the Catholic Cathedral of the Madeleine rang out their mournful condolences. And the nurses in training at the Catholic-owned Holy

Cross Hospital stood at respectful attention as the hearse carrying the remains of the Mormon prophet passed by.

The cemetery commanded a sweeping view of the desert metropolis that had grown apace with the man whose mortal remains were now to be interred. Both had seen their good days and their bad. Both had emerged from the pinched scarcity of the pioneer era into the luxury of the twentieth century. And both had been beneficiaries of the great law of particles, the law that conditions growth upon the regular and unceasing increments of power, influence, and capacity. But while the inanimate city owed its creation, its development, and its continued existence to the efforts and intelligence of men, President Heber J. Grant traced his origins to a spiritual world beyond, and his phenomenal growth and development to the personal diligence and persistence, steellike in their aspect, with which he had pursued every undertaking of his life.

Index

disincorporated, 74-78; Christ is head of, 77; is reincorporated, 78-79; educational system of, 202-8

Church Security Plan, 1. *See also* Welfare program

Claflin, John, 97

Clark, J. Reuben, Jr., 227

Clark, Walter Ernest, 207

Cleveland, Grover, 75, 78

Clawson, Hiram B., 60-61, 83

Clawson, Rudger, 229

Clayton, Nephi, 27

Clayton, William, 47

Cluff, Benjamin, Jr., 202

Colleges, 204-8

Consensus, principle of, 127

Converts: in Japan, 123-24, 129-30; in England, 129-30, 140

Council of the Twelve, Heber is called to, 44-48

Cowdery, Oliver, 184, 190

Cowley, Matthias F., 150

Dances, Heber attends, 29-30

Death of Heber J. Grant, 231

Debt: Heber is freed from, 112-14; tithing relieves Church of, 111-12; Saints warned against, 193-94

Dedication :of Logan Temple, 62, 73; of Japan for proselyting, 116-19; of Alberta Temple, 173, 186-87; of Hawaii Temple, 173, 186; of Arizona Temple at Mesa, 188-89; of Manti Temple, 189-90; of Idaho Falls temple site, 191

Democratic party, 100

Depression, 1-2, 196-98

Devil. *See* Satan

Diphtheria, Heber's children contract, 83-84

Dole, evils of, 3

Doremus, Abraham, 20-21

Dupont Powder Company, 27

Economic panic of 1891, 89, 94

Economic policy: of Church, 1-3; tithing instituted as, 111-12; home manufacturing is, 158-62; stringency is, 193-96

Economic speculation, 192-95

Edmunds Act, 44-45, 61

Edmunds-Tucker Act, 68-78

Education, 202-8

Eighteenth Amendment, 157, 198-201

Elijah, 184

Endowments, 185-86

England, Heber purchases mission home in, 136-37

Ensign, Horace S., 114, 118, 123, 131-32

Escheatment: of Church properties, 74-78; process of, reversed, 78-79

European Mission, 134, 135

Evans, Mary Wells, 165

Faith of modern prophets, 5-6

Family activities, Heber's, 164-65, 182-86

Farrell, George L., 161

Federal government appoints territorial officials, 100

Finances: of Church, relieved by tithing, 111-12; of Heber, before mission to Japan, 112-14; use of dollar in world of, 160-61; of Church, concerning education, 203-5

Fitzpatrick, John F., 211

Free agency, 158-59

Funeral: of Emily Grant, 148-49; of Heber J. Grant, 231-32

Genealogy, 184-86

Gibbons, Andrew S., 51

Gibbs, George F., 38-39, 47

Golden, Marley, 215

Golf, 164, 215-16, 220

Gowans, Hugh S., 46